The
Princeton
Review

GRADUATE SCHOOL
COMPANION

Peter Diffley

Random House, Inc.
New York
www.PrincetonReview.com

The Princeton Review, Inc.
2315 Broadway
New York, NY 10024
E-mail: bookeditor@review.com

ISBN 978-0-375-76574-2

Publisher: Robert Franek
Editors: Spencer Foxworth, Lisa Marie Rovito, Adam O. Davis
Designer and Production Manager: Scott Harris
Production Editor: Christine LaRubio

Printed in the United States of America.

9 8 7 6 5 4 3

ACKNOWLEDGMENTS

I want to acknowledge the patience and support of my family, who said that they would kill me if I didn't. I also wish to thank Professor Franklin Sogandares-Bernal for his help in getting me into graduate school in the first place.

—Peter Diffley

TABLE OF CONTENTS

CHAPTER I
Introduction

In the Middle Ages, if you wanted to be a silversmith or a baker, you became part of a craft guild. You apprenticed under the tutelage of a master for up to seven years before becoming a journeyman. As a journeyman, you could only become your own master if you passed exams and produced a beautiful piece of work. To become and remain the master of your own shop—a craftsman—you needed the necessary administrative and social skills to do so.

Graduate schools operate much like medieval craft guilds. As a graduate student, you work with a faculty member who points out the big questions, demonstrates research methods, helps analyze the data you collect, and who teaches how to present your results. Instead of mastering a craft, you learn how to do research. You take exams and the masterpiece is your dissertation. Now as much as then, a master researcher needs to develop personal and social skills that cannot be taught in class. Yet, as opposed to then, women are full participants in this academic guild.

As a researcher, you've been given the Herculean task of adding to the sum total of knowledge in the world—nothing less—certainly a difficult ride. But judging from the 40,000 PhDs granted every year, it won't be impossible.

But what about the significant number of PhDs who aren't academic, government, or private-sector researchers? Over 80 percent of the academic jobs aren't even in research universities but in colleges where teaching undergraduates is the primary mission. In this case, what benefit was there in learning how to do research? Plenty. Research skills are important for developing lectures, being a book publisher, or managing budgets and people. It's advanced training in problem-solving and communication.

If earning a PhD is all about learning how to do research, then where do you learn how to teach? Isn't that important? Sure it is. But it's only one of the many skills a professor must develop that are invisible to undergraduate students. Essential skills in pedagogy, grant and fellowship writing, oral presentations, journal manuscript composition, mentoring, and academic citizenship are usually developed informally and with experience. You may have a workshop here or a short course there, but most of it is learned hands-on. (If you're surprised that these important non-research factors are not being taught more methodically in graduate school, you're not alone. Many groups—like the Sloan Foundation—are currently exploring the shortcomings in graduate education. Perhaps beneficial changes will have already occurred on your campus when you arrive.)

Aren't there courses to take in graduate school and grades to worry about? Yes, but this isn't undergraduate school where breadth was encouraged and much of what you learned wasn't required for the next semester's course load. Courses in graduate school are concentrated—chosen to provide a knowledge base for your present and future research. This information will be important for the rest of your professional life. And the professors expect an A-grade effort. Since the minimal acceptable grade point average is 3.0 in most graduate schools, a B- or C does not mean average. These grades mean unsatisfactory.

This all sounds so arduous; what's the carrot at the end of this stick? Professors tend to retire later (because they love their jobs) and live longer. This clearly suggests that the academic life can be more rewarding and less stressful than survival in the private sector. Some might say that tenure—"guaranteed job security"—is the reason. Tenure is nice, but it's neither guaranteed employment (just ask someone whose department has been eliminated), nor does it contribute to job satisfaction. Many PhD's work in the private sector where tenure is unlikely. Some might say money is the reason for an enjoyable life in academe. Indeed, people with doctorates tend to make more money (averaging approximately $100,000 annual salary for PhD-holders in 1999) than those with a master's or baccalaureate degree. But for the hours, the energy, and the imagination that a PhD must put in to be a successful researcher/scholar, the pay is meager. Professional degrees are much more lucrative.

Personally, I think a career in research is attractive because every facet of the job is intellectually stimulating. You're exploring ideas and concepts and trying to find something new, surrounded by books and equipment, and your coworkers are also searching for new ideas and eager to talk about them; shop-talk takes on an intellectual tone. And there is something pure about the pursuit and dissemination of knowledge as a career.

Researchers have more independence than most workers. Searching for questions and the means to answer them are jobs that don't lend themselves to boss-induced deadlines or 9-to-5 lifestyles. Just like a farmer, you'll be judged on what you produce—not how busy you appeared to be.

No matter how important your discovery, if you don't report your findings, they'll have zero impact upon society. Researchers have to be teachers. Academe provides ample opportunity for teaching, but even a hermit-poet or an R&D scientist deep in a laboratory of a pharmaceutical company has to communicate her discoveries in a coherent and compelling way. And teaching, especially if some of the ideas presented are yours, can be a heady experience. Getting people as excited about your discipline as you are is very rewarding.

Finally, a career in research engenders respect. People understand that you're searching for ideas that may benefit society. They appreciate the role of the teacher and are awed by intellectual activity. In other words, you probably won't be rich or famous, but your family will be proud.

No matter how much experience you received in undergraduate school or on the job, graduate school will be a novel experience. It'll be easy for you to get unintentionally blindsided and short-changed. This book was written to help you understand what to expect in graduate school and what is expected of you. If you follow this roadmap, you'll have the credentials upon graduation to get—and succeed in—the career of your choice.

CHAPTER II

How to Find the Best Program for You

You need to know what subdiscipline excites you the most before you even apply to graduate school. Identifying a major field—political science, for example—isn't enough. You must determine if international relations, comparative politics, American politics, public policy, or political theory is what you want to spend the rest of your professional life studying. All fields have subdisciplines, and if you don't know which one is best for you yet, start reading. If you want to go into the humanities or social sciences, pick up a copy of *The Real Guide to Grad School* (by the editors of now-extinct *LinguaFranca*) or the *Complete Book of Graduate Programs in the Arts and Sciences*, published by The Princeton Review.

If you're currently an undergraduate, you could take a graduate-level course in one or more of the subdisciplines. You could simply get the syllabus and read assigned readings without taking the course. You could knock on professors' doors and ask what research is going on in the field and for the titles of important books to read. The more your research interests are defined, the easier it's to find a compatible graduate school. Maybe you'll discover not only a fascinating line of research, but a graduate advisor as well.

If you're no longer a student, you could sign up for advanced courses as a non-degree student. Call or e-mail faculty members that you had as an undergraduate and ask their advice on what to study. Go to a university library to peruse the professional journals. Go to the local library and read nonfiction by academic authors in fields that interest you.

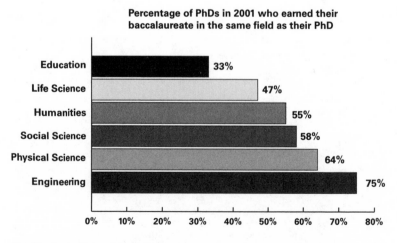

Percentage of PhDs in 2001 who earned their baccalaureate in the same field as their PhD

Field	Percentage
Education	33%
Life Science	47%
Humanities	55%
Social Science	58%
Physical Science	64%
Engineering	75%

What if your interests have changed since college? Chances are they have. According to the *Survey of Earned Doctorates* published by the National Science Foundation, many successful graduate students actually received their baccalaureate degree in a different field than their doctorate.

Switching fields will require work before you apply to graduate school. You'll have to convince the graduate admissions committee that you understand the basic concepts of the discipline. To do this, you must take—and excel in—the introductory course and one or two advanced courses in your subdiscipline. A letter of recommendation from these courses' professors will also help. You may have to do well in required courses outside the major; for example, biologists must also take organic chemistry. You'll have to do well in the GRE subject examination, if such a test is required. Earning a master's degree in a second-tier institution before you apply to a top-ranked PhD program is one of the best ways to establish your competence in your new field of choice.

In undergraduate or professional school, your goal is to get into the best institution that will accept you and that you or your parents can afford. The goal in graduate school is to pick an individual faculty advisor who will train you and be instrumental in finding you a career. There are some pretty lame professors in the best-ranked schools and vice versa. How do you find the good ones?

Your most obvious and accessible sources of information are **faculty members** who've been teaching you undergraduate courses in your major. Get more than one opinion; it's an important decision.

Rankings might help you get started with a ready-made list. The National Research Council (NRC) ranks at the departmental-level and occasionally at the subdisciplinary level in huge fields like biology. The rankings only come out every ten years but reputations don't change that much. *U.S. News & World Report* also publishes rankings at the subdisciplinary level. But rankings won't tell you who is working at these schools or what research they are doing. So how do you find out what research is being done where and by whom?

Departments use several guides to self-describe their programs, list their faculty, and describe their research. If someone's research seems interesting, look up what the researcher has published. In humanities and social science, check out books and journals. For scientists, engineers, and social scientists, look up journal articles. If you find someone who is doing what you want to do, write him or her and ask if they might have the time to be your advisor. Send a transcript (if it's good) and a resume. If they say "no," then take them at their word and scratch them from the list. If their response is non-committal, that's a good sign. When you submit an application for admission, send them a copy. If you can get a faculty member on your side, he or she may be an important voice when the graduate admissions committee meets.

Maybe you can't identify a single faculty member. Don't feel left out. Most incoming graduate students can only point to a vague research area. In that case, choose a school with several professors in your subdiscipline and then align yourself with a compatible mentor after you have been there for awhile. (More about that later.)

What about going to graduate school in the same place that you earned your baccalaureate? You know the professors; maybe you even did a little undergraduate research with them. This is probably not a good idea. You'll be amazed at how much more you learn in a new environment. First, because everything is new, you're more alert. Second, you realize that different researchers have different ideas and approaches to problems. Third, getting a job is all about networking. If you only know one small group of faculty, you'll be limited. Finally, job search committees know that exposure to different educational environments is valuable.

One final bit of advice about choosing the best graduate program for you: Visit their campuses. If you've been accepted into one or more programs, ask if there is a recruiting visit planned or if funds are available for you to travel to campus alone. If there is no organized event, go anyway and ask the director of graduate studies for an appointment well in advance of your arrival. Ask the director to meet with faculty working in your area of interest, and if if he or she would arrange for you to meet some graduate students working on projects that interest you. Plan to spend a couple of days looking around. Trust your feelings. Is the place cold and intimidating? Are the students hardworking but content? Do the faculty members appear to be interested in having you around?

HOW TO GET IN

Be a full-time student. It takes less time to earn the degree and you'll stand a better chance of financial aid.

Be a PhD candidate if that is your ultimate goal. For most disciplines, the master's degree is not a prerequisite for your application to the PhD.

Mark "yes" for financial aid. When an institution's application asks if you wish to be considered for financial aid, by all means, say yes. This won't penalize your application.

Study for the Graduate Record Examination. The computer-based test requires a strategy that is different from the SAT multiple-choice questions. Practice builds confidence.

Study for the GRE subject test if one is required. Reread the texts that you used in the introductory course and reacquaint yourself with knowledge and skills that you haven't used in several years.

Provide a list of academic accomplishments to the professors you've asked to write letters of recommendation. Talk to these people face to face so that they will know who you are.

Research the faculty's interests before you apply. If you want to do research on something that has no local experts, it doesn't matter how good your other credentials may be. Your application will be rejected.

Edit your personal statement and writing sample(s) thoroughly and have someone also edit it, too.

CHAPTER III

Paying For It

Paying For It

Post-graduate school is expensive no matter how you look at it; attending an in-state public institution can cost anywhere from $5,000 to $15,000 when tuition, fees, supplies, and cost of living expenses are totaled. If you go out-of-state or to a private school, that cost can go up anywhere from $15,000 to $30,000 per year. While pursuers of a law, medical, or professional master's degree can more easily accept the loan payments they'll eventually make as a business expense, your PhD will probably take longer to obtain and the financial payoff—a salary in academia—will likely start out less substantive than that of a physician or a lawyer. This doesn't mean you should mortgage the rest of your life to follow your dreams, but to right a lopsided cost-benefit ratio, you need to reduce the expenses associated with going to graduate school. The best way to do that is to find someone else to pay your tuition and provide you with a stipend and money to do your research. According to the National Center for Education Statistics (NCES), in the 2003–2004 academic year nearly three-fourths (73 percent) of full-time graduate and professional degree students received some form of financial aid totaling an average of $15,100 each. Here's how and where they got it.

University Aid

The most lucrative source of financial aid is the institution you'll attend as a graduate student. The more they want you, the more of their resources they'll be willing to offer you. Here are some of the types of offers that you may receive; a few dollars may be just for showing up, a few you may have to work for, and a few you may have to pay back.

Tuition Scholarships and Waivers

In the 2003–2004 academic year, 39 percent of full-time master's and professional students received about $5,750 in scholarships each, versus nearly 55 percent of doctoral students, who received an average scholarship of $10,200. You do not have to pay back scholarship money, and most of the time you don't have to work for it either. If the scholarship has no service requirement, it is not considered taxable income. Therefore, it should not appear on W-2 or 1099 forms, and you do not have to report it on your annual 1040. You do not have to report it when applying for loans or state aid. Obviously, however, you can't claim the tuition bill covered by the scholarship as an educational expense, either. Occasionally, some bureaucrat will try to add your scholarship as income. If that happens, you should then demand that the tuition bill be added as an expense. Then the two wash, and everyone is happy. If work is required for your tuition scholarship or waiver, the money may be considered taxable income. Be sure that you have in writing what work— if any—you need to do for scholarship money.

Generally, tuition scholarships are Monopoly money, good for internal transactions only. In other words, if you get a $15,000 scholarship but decide to take only $10,000 worth of courses, you cannot collect $5,000 to pay the rent (even if it's campus housing).

Sometimes, state schools find it easier not to bill someone than to find scholarship money because state legislatures are very tight with tax dollars—hence the invention of tuition waivers. You are simply not billed for the courses taken, or the additional out-of-state tuition charge may be waived. Sometimes partial tuition scholarships are called fellowships. You receive a cash award that is promptly subtracted from your tuition bill. There probably will be no money left over to pay the electric bill.

Stipends

There are two major ways that you earn a student stipend: By teaching for a department or by doing research for a faculty member. The percentage of students who receive stipends and the amount paid to each will vary depending on intended degree and field, enrollment status (full- or part-time), and years of enrollment. A small number of students may get a stipend just for showing up (i.e., recipients of fellowships).

Graduate/Teaching Assistants (GA/TA)

In return for nine months of career-related work, you will be paid a stipend to cover your living and otherwise uncovered educational expenses. A stipend may be associated with a title: full-time graduate assistant, half-time teaching assistant, etc. The title will vary; the important things to know are how many hours you are supposed to work and for how many dollars per semester.

The career-related work associated with the stipend should add luster to your curriculum vitae. Less experienced teaching assistants will supervise course laboratories, grade examinations, give guest lectures in class, run tutorials, or lead discussion sections. More senior graduate assistants may actually design their own courses and give all of the lectures.

How do you get a teaching assistantship? You answer "yes" to the question on your application that reads, "Do you wish to be considered for financial aid?" If the department has the money, it will offer assistantships to its best applicants.

Research Assistantships

Research assistants get a stipend for doing research for a faculty member. The amount of the funding will vary depending upon the discipline. The source of your stipend as a research assistant may be a government grant or the university coffers. But it's all legal tender. Grants require frequent renewal to keep the money flowing, so this route may appear risky. But university RA money is not guaranteed, either.

Generally, in social sciences and humanities, you will be helping faculty members with their research. The more you pay attention, get involved, and ask questions, the more you will learn about the research process. The methods that you learn will come in handy when you approach your own dissertation.

In science and engineering, on the other hand, your dissertation research will most often contribute data to the overall research goals of your graduate advisor. In other words, you will be paid as a research assistant to do your own dissertation. The downside is that you may find yourself on a data assembly line where it will be difficult to get involved with the planning and publication ends of the research. In order to avoid becoming a lab technician instead of a researcher, you will need to assert yourself and get involved with the generation of ideas, the planning of experiments, and the writing of grant proposals and journal articles.

Sounds good! Where do I sign up? In general, the faculty members who get the research grants hand out research assistantships. Therefore, if the faculty member happens to be your graduate advisor, you will be first in line. Even if your advisor doesn't have any research dollars, another faculty member may. Sometimes, researchers have extra work or special needs (e.g., translations, Web work, statistical analysis, etc.). Such piecework will probably not support you completely, but it will be a nice career-enhancing supplement to your income.

A stipend is supposed to allow students the time to devote their full attention to their studies instead of having to flip burgers to pay the rent. If, however, you are married with children and trying to get a master's in art history in downtown Boston, survival on a stipend alone is unlikely. You will need to know the cost of living within the school's locale for you and your dependents. If there is a gap between stipend and fiscal reality, ask the director of graduate studies what students do to make ends meet and how many hours a week they need to do it.

You also need to know how many academic years you are guaranteed a stipend, assuming satisfactory academic progress. Of course, your next question should be: What is the average time it takes students in your discipline to earn a degree? There may be a gap in funding between the two, and you need to ask the director of graduate studies how students support themselves after the assistantship runs out.

Stipends are taxable income (federal, state, county, and city), and if you are classified as an employee, you may also lose part of your paycheck to that guy FICA. It is important to know how much of your earnings will disappear before you get your paycheck.

You may be expected to pay school fees, supplies, and books out of your stipend, as well as tuition. Don't forget medical insurance and health center fees along with parking, technology, and general student activity fees. Then there are the normal living expenses of room, board, and transportation. There won't be much left over for entertainment, but hey, you're an imaginative person; think of cheap, fun things to do in the limited time that you have to yourself.

Fellowships

A fellowship is an honor. Every academic department, however, will have a different definition of what a fellowship is, so it's important that you don't make assumptions. How many years does this fellowship last? What happens after it expires? Is the stipend for 12 months or 9? Is a full tuition scholarship included? Does the tuition scholarship include summer courses? What fees and benefits, especially health insurance and on-campus parking, are covered? What work do you have to perform for the fellowship and for how long? Does a research allowance come with the fellowship? A research allowance that can be used to purchase equipment (e.g., a computer) and books or travel to professional meetings is an increasingly popular recruiting perk. It pays for many hidden professional development costs, but it is not considered income so Uncle Sam does not get a chunk of it. The research allowance is not a common feature for most university fellowships, but it may be available with certain federal fellowships (like the NSF Graduate Fellowships, Javits Fellowships, and others).

The best fellowships will last for three to five years and include a 12-month stipend. There should be more stipend money and less work than what is required of a TA, but don't be surprised if TAs, especially on unionized campuses, get more benefits, health insurance, parking, special book rates, and office space than fellows. Subtract their benefits from your fellowship stipend to determine if they get the better deal.

On the one hand, fellowships provide unobstructed time for study and research that will help you get good grades and reduce your time to degree. On the other hand, Barbara Lovitts, author of *Leaving the Ivory Tower: The Causes and Consequences of Departure from Doctoral Study*, warns that multiyear, service-free fellowships can be a recipe for disaster. Fellows can find it difficult to socially integrate themselves into the departmental culture without the work-related contact with faculty and fellow students. Furthermore, when you prepare lectures or laboratories, you learn the subject at a much deeper level than if you were sitting on the other side of the lectern taking the notes. The final argument against service-free fellowships is that a graduate with no teaching experience is at a disadvantage when applying for a faculty position. The faculty search committee will wonder about your pedagogical skills. And even if they hire you, you will arrive on campus with no lectures or laboratories already prepared. For one 50-minute lecture, it can take five hours of research to produce three to five pages of double-spaced information. And a new assistant professor is expected to come up with three lectures a week for 14 weeks for one to three different courses!

It's possible for you to mitigate the downsides associated with multiyear fellowships. First, find out if and when there is a teaching requirement. If there is none, then you might volunteer your services to the director of graduate studies. Teaching a semester of a course that you know you will teach as an assistant professor is a good deal. Teaching different courses each semester also broadens your experience. It'll be an easy sell, since directors of graduate studies always need help. What's really nice about a fellowship is that you are in a position to set the scope, and limits, of your volunteer service.

So how do you get in line for this free university fellowship money? Unlike fellowships awarded by foundations or the government, there usually is no separate application. The department will nominate you based on your application to graduate studies. Don't assume anything, though, and ask the director of graduate studies if there is anything you need to do to apply for a university fellowship.

Money for Research

So you manage to get a tuition scholarship and even a stipend that will cover your tuition and living expenses for the year. What more do you possibly need? How about the cost of research? For most experimentalists (scientists, psychologists, and engineers, for example), your project will probably be possible to complete using solely the supplies and equipment already in the lab of your graduate advisor. Most students in the humanities cover their research costs with a library card, but what if you need a piece of equipment or supplies for experiments not available in your department? In these cases, you end up doing the same thing that a faculty member does when confronted with the same questions: You look for an interested party to help fund your research. More than likely, funding will come from an off-campus foundation or government agency, but you should not overlook less competitive opportunities at your school. Ask your graduate advisor, your director of graduate studies, and the campus research office what local research grant opportunities exist.

NON-UNIVERSITY AID

Extramural Fellowships

Extramural fellowships—that is, awards that don't come from faculty research grants or university coffers—are funding sources for which you apply directly independent of the school. Some of the largest extramural fellowships come from the government; some of the most prestigious come from private foundations. Some support you for several years, while still others last for just long enough for you to get started with your field research or your dissertation. A few fellowships even support a year of travel between college and graduate school.

At the very least, extramural fellowships usually supply a healthy stipend and a partial- or full-tuition scholarship, and, since you're being supported by an institution or organization outside of the university, you probably won't have to teach or do research for a faculty member. But don't assume anything; some fellowships will have an academic requirement to teach courses at some point during your graduate career, and as I stated before teaching and research assistantships have definite advantages. With an extramural fellowship, however, because you are bringing in your own stipend and at least some tuition, you're in a much better position to negotiate with departments than you would be receiving only university aid.

Negotiate what? First, you can discuss what courses you want to teach, how many times, and when. Second, you get to pick the faculty that you want to assist with research. Third, even a four-year fellowship will not cover your entire stay as a graduate student. Remember that the average time-to-degree for a PhD is about six years, even if all goes well. So you need to find out how much the department will guarantee you when the fellowship runs out. Finally, you need to negotiate the institutional allowance that may accompany the fellowship. Universities will oftentimes put that money toward your tuition. But if everyone else in the department is being covered by departmental scholarships or waivers, you should ask if your educational allowance could be set aside to cover your other expenses, such as fees, health insurance, course books, school supplies, research equipment, or professional travel. This untaxed benefit will definitely put you into the highest of graduate student income brackets, which will almost approach the poverty level for a family of four. Sometimes departments will buy your ideas concerning the educational allowance, sometimes the fellowship sponsor defines exactly what the money is to be spent for, and sometimes the university has a different view on how the money should be spent. It's in your best interest to ask, and it will be an interesting point to consider when negotiating with more than one department concerning their offers of admission.

Tips on Writing Grant and Fellowship Applications

Fellowships that fund the early part of your graduate career generally rely more on your undergraduate record and GRE scores than on an elaborate research plan. This section deals mostly with dissertation grants and fellowships. You can apply for these only after you have a dissertation topic in hand.

Writing grant or fellowship applications is an integral part of any researcher's career, so even if you don't need that much money for research, early experience in the practice could prove crucial to your professional needs in the future. Additionally, it tells future faculty search committees that your research ideas are marketable. And success is self-perpetuating; the mere fact that you were funded once will make you more competitive for the next fellowship or grant.

It is important to remember that a grant or a fellowship application is a sales document. You are selling your credentials and your ideas to a selection committee whose members have to read far more applications than there are awards to hand out. If you cannot quickly convey a research question in a clear, forceful, and enthusiastic manner, it's unlikely that the committee members will be persuaded by you or your idea. As a graduate student, the task of developing a dissertation grant application is even more difficult because the time between knowing what you want to do and graduation is so short.

It's important that you plan a year or two ahead. Many research fellowship applications are written a year before the funding kicks in. The research idea has to be developed; the methodology learned; researchers who can help you contacted; and the potential sources of funding identified at least 14 months before you actually get the money to do the work.

Once you are ready to sit down and write the proposal, your goal should be to state clearly what the research question is and why the answer is important. This argument should be both compelling and concise; the case should be made in the first page (preferably the first paragraph) of the proposal. Later you have to prove that you are a person qualified to do this research and that the plan and methods you will use are valid and feasible.

Many sponsors will define the length and format of the proposal. Do not deviate from the directions. If there are no directions, I suggest you begin with enough background to understand the research question followed quickly by a clear and succinct statement of purpose. Follow up with a section on the significance of your research; don't make the mistake of assuming that everyone will intuitively understand its significance. The second half of the proposal should contain preliminary results from pilot studies or short field trips (if there are any) and the methods that you propose to use to answer the research question. The more specific you can be concerning methodology without becoming tediously technical, the better: Rather than saying that you will be doing archival research in Paris, tell the reviewers which archives, which important documents you discovered in a previous field trip, the method for gaining access to the archives, and the courses you have taken to assist you in the translation of these documents. Listing every single document is technically tedious. Also, instead of saying that you will be taking courses at the university, tell the reviewers which courses, who will be teaching those courses, and who has invited you to participate in the classes. Giving course numbers and times is overkill. Finally, make sure that your project is manageable within the time frame of the grant or fellowship.

With regard to writing style, always keep in mind that reviewers have a stack of proposals in front of them and not much time to stop and wonder what the hell they just read; keep most of your sentences short and direct, choose active over passive voice, and avoid jargon. Jargon is disciplinary shorthand and is useful for those in the subdiscipline. Award committees, however, may be interdisciplinary in nature and unfamiliar with your language. Use positive language such as "will" and "can" instead of "may" or "might." The former verbs convey confidence.

With regard to appearance, remember that a well-conceived layout will emphasize your important points. White space and boldface are important organizers. Don't cram more information into the narrative by reducing the margins or decreasing the font size. Use spelling and grammar checkers and be neat. Put the proposal down for a week and then proofread it. Get your advisor and other members of the dissertation committee to read the proposal. They will tell you whether your objective is clearly stated and the research plan is logically arranged. Ask researchers from outside the field. They will circle undefined terms and jargon and tell you if you made a compelling case for doing the project.

Just remember that a reviewer will not appreciate your idea if it is presented poorly. The assumption is that the quality of the proposal will mirror the quality of the research and the final product. You don't want to spend another year in graduate school revising the application.

Can you submit the same idea to more than one funding agency? Absolutely! Once the first proposal is written, it is a much smaller project to adapt it to fit a different format. What is unethical is accepting two awards to accomplish the same project without first discussing the matter with both funding agencies. If neither agency is fully funding the project, you have a case to ask for both. Maybe the two agencies will negotiate with each other to see who will pay. It's a nice problem to have, but don't get sneaky and greedy or you will end up ruining your reputation.

Employer-Financed Opportunities

On-the-job training is the best way for part-time students to get support for going to graduate school. It is also the best deal for students who are anchored to a specific geographical area for personal reasons. The National Center for Education Statistics (NCES) reported that 21 percent of graduate students received on average $3,000 in support from their employers in the 2003–2004 academic year. Employers, however, are not altruistic in their support. They will expect the advanced degree to enhance your performance and/or make you eligible for a different job within the company. They may also expect you to stay on for a number of years after you get the degree. Be sure that you understand all aspects of the contract between you and your employer before you sign on.

The military has several educational opportunities for active duty personnel, even rare money for degrees in law and the health professions. For instance, the U.S. Air Force has the Funded Legal Education Program (FLEP), which provides $6,000 in tuition and maintains your base pay. See Jaguaf.hq.af.mil for more information. The Air Force health professions scholarship is even more lucrative, paying full tuition, books, and fees and offering a stipend. Call 800-531-5800. The U.S. Army has advanced training for active duty personnel in occupational therapy, physical therapy, pharmacology, clinical psychology, and dietetics as well as a physician's assistant program. If the base educational benefits officer can't help you, call the local recruiter, or call 800-USA-ARMY. Active duty personnel of all services may also try for the health professions scholarships listed in the next section. Of course, the Montgomery GI Bill helps keep the wolves at bay when you head off for graduate school.

Another government agency, the Peace Corps, offers fellowships to its returning volunteers. The Peace Corps Fellows/USA graduate fellowship program provides funding to earn certification, master's degrees, or doctorates in a wide variety of disciplines, including education. Visit PeaceCorps.gov/gradschool for more information. Americorps programs (VISTA, Americorps National Civilian Community Corps) provide a $4,725 educational allowance for its volunteers as well. Visit Americorps.org or call 800-942-2677.

The university is probably the employer that will give you the widest latitude in selection of disciplines with the lowest level of commitment on your part. Many schools have tuition scholarships or waivers for a few credits per semester. It may take you awhile to get the degree, but the time of transit between job and school will be eliminated, and the price will be right. Just remember that there are often two tracks, nondegree- and degree-seeking. You must be admitted to the department as a graduate student in order to put the credits toward your degree, and you may not be able to transfer in credits that you earned in a nondegree status.

Assessing Multiple Offers and Negotiating

If you receive multiple aid offers from different graduate programs that include a stipend and tuition scholarship, there are objective and subjective ways to help you make a decision.

The objective criteria include the net worth of the offer and the reputation of the department. You need to subtract the student fees (e.g., health center, student activity, technology) and medical insurance costs that you are expected to pay. Then you should determine whether you are classified as a student or as an employee. If you are considered an employee, FICA taxes will be irretrievably withheld, union dues may be charged, and your tuition scholarship may be considered as taxable income. Next, determine how much summer stipend money is available and the percentage of full-time students who are funded in the summer. Finally, go to the library to determine what the cost of living index is for the school's geographical area. Once you have all of these data points, you will know the net worth of the financial package in the first year.

At this point you ought to ask how many years of support are guaranteed, assuming satisfactory academic progress, and the time-to-degree in your discipline for full-time students. This will tell you how much the degree will cost over time and how much you will have to take out of savings or loans to make ends meet. If the net stipends are within $1,000 of each other, there is no financial reason for choosing one department over another.

More important than the money is the reputation of the department that you are considering. A highly regarded department will have faculty doing cutting-edge research. You are more likely to pick an advisor who is well placed in the field to help you get a job upon graduation. You will also be in a more highly selected peer group that will both challenge you and help you succeed. If you have already hooked up with a highly regarded faculty researcher, then the overall reputation of the department and school is not as important.

The most important consideration is subjective, and to appraise it, you will have to visit the departments that show interest in you. Many schools have recruiting weekends and will even pay for your trip. Whether it is an official paid trip or an unofficial visit, you ought to go to the department, talk to the director of graduate studies, meet faculty who are doing research that interests you, and interview graduate students in the department. Finally, check out the resources you'll use in your research. Remember that departments are evaluating you at the same time, so be appropriately impressed and appreciative. Expect big departments and big schools to be more impersonal and urban campuses to be grittier.

On your way home from these visits, grade the students, the faculty, and the facilities and list what turned you on and off. Compare your experiences at one school to those at the other schools you're considering. At the end of the process, pick the school with which you feel the most comfortable, a place that is challenging without being intimidating and has people whom you can work with and for. As Barbara Lovitts explains, attrition happens not because you washed out academically but because you did not fit into the culture.

EDUCATIONAL LOANS

If your expenses exceed the amount of free money that you receive, then you may need to take out a loan. Hundreds of lenders nationwide now offer educational loans, including those guaranteed by the federal government. Government-sponsored loans were originally called "Guaranteed Student Loans." Almost any student (U.S. citizen or permanent resident) enrolling in college could pretty much count on securing one (barring previous bad credit history). At the same time, the lender (usually a bank, credit union, or other financial organization), assuming it provided some level of due diligence in carrying out its responsibilities, would likewise be assured repayment by the government, even if the borrower defaulted. This program was created by the Higher Education Act of 1965 and has seen tremendous growth and remarkable success over its long history. Literally millions of students have received billions of dollars, and by far the vast majority of them become more successful and more productive members of society and have also repaid their obligations in full. This is especially impressive when one considers that borrowers are typically very young and without any established credit, have no assurance of completing their education and securing employment, often change their original plans, and incur the obligation with no creditworthy co-signer required.

While many changes have taken place in this federal student loan program since its creation in 1965, the basic partnership between government and private resources has remained and continues to be the single largest student aid resource. One of the most significant revisions to the program, however, is worthy of note. Students have historically been required to demonstrate in some manner their need for the loan. The 1992 Reauthorization of the 1965 Higher Education Act made the loan program available to any student, regardless of family resources, by revising eligibility criteria. Except for a relatively brief period since the program's establishment, only students falling under certain income levels, or later only those "demonstrating financial need according to a federal formula," had been eligible to secure the funds. The major change in the 1992 legislation provided for an "unsubsidized" student loan to any otherwise eligible student. Unsubsidized borrowers enjoy most of the provisions of the student loan program, such as low interest rates (which would be capped regardless of the cost of money), deferred payment of principal, long-term repayment options, and government guarantees. However, the most significant distinction between those receiving "unsubsidized" versus "subsidized" loans is that unsubsidized borrowers do not have the support of interest subsidies paid on their behalf to the lender while they are enrolled as students and during other periods of deferment or grace. Instead, unsubsidized loans accrue interest during periods of enrollment that the borrower has to repay.

The Application and Delivery Process

Applying for educational loans has become easier than ever through advances in technology and because of competitive dynamics within the student loan industry to simplify and standardize the entire process. What had once required the completion of many forms and a lengthy processing cycle has now become an online, almost instantaneous review and approval process with electronic communication of data among lenders, schools, and agencies. The delivery process most often concludes with electronic disbursement of funds to the student's school account. Students can typically view the status and progress of their application on the lender's or school's website, use an electronic signature to complete their promissory note, get an up-to-date reading on their borrowing, and receive online customized counseling regarding their rights and responsibilities as borrowers. Eventually, once in repayment, borrowers can also have electronic payments made to their loans directly from their employer's payroll system or through their own checking account. Efficiencies, standardized processes, and many other enhancements have created a relatively simple and seamless application and delivery process, and at least the appearance of a much less daunting overall set of steps and procedures. While this new efficiency is impressive and has resulted in a fairly painless process, borrowers should never lose sight of the fact that they are taking on a very major and serious obligation that will eventually require repayment and usually impact their lives for many years after they complete their degrees.

Stafford FFELP Loans vs. Ford Direct Loans

The bank-based education loan program has become known as the Federal Family Education Loan Program (FFELP) and now provides for both student loans (Stafford) and parent loans (PLUS Loans) for dependent students. The student loan program itself came under some serious attack in the early 1990s because of growing defaults, lack of standardization among lenders and state guarantor agencies (which had come to serve as intermediaries for the federal government), complexity and confusion, and excessive cost of administration. A major change in the program, again in the 1992 amendments, intended to address all of these problems by eliminating the "middlemen," primarily lenders and guarantors, and by applying the efficiencies that modern technology could provide. Institutions were offered a choice to remain with the bank-based program, also referred to as the Stafford FFELP Loan, or to move to a new "Ford Direct Loan" way of doing business. (Stafford and Ford are the last names of former members of the U.S. Congress who played leadership roles in authorizing federal student assistance.) Since that time, and as a result of this reform movement, significant enhancements and improvements have been made in the bank-based Stafford FFELP program, while the new Direct Loan program continues to provide schools with another option. Approximately 70 percent of institutions currently participate in the Stafford FFELP bank-based program, with the remaining 30 percent administering the Ford Direct Loan. In a few institutions where both programs are administered, some part of the institution (e.g., undergraduates) may be directed to one program and others (e.g., professional students) to the other program.

The FAFSA

For either program, the borrower submits a federal application known as the Free Application for Federal Student Aid (FAFSA). The application is available on the Web (www.fafsa.ed.gov), and applicants are encouraged to apply online, as the likelihood of making mistakes is reduced. You will need to indicate the name and federal identification code of the institution(s) to which the FAFSA data is to be sent. Codes may be found on the federal student aid website at StudentAid.ed.gov or by calling 800-433-3243 (800-4-FED-AID). An acknowledgment called the Student Aid Report (SAR) is sent to the student filing the FAFSA, which provides an index called the "Expected Family Contribution" based on a formula (the federal methodology) used to determine federal aid eligibility. Institutions will advise you of your eligibility and whether they participate in the Direct Loan or in the Stafford FFELP bank-based program. If it is the bank-based program, you will typically be advised to select a lender from a list of one or more "preferred" lenders recommended by the school because of the school's positive evaluation of the products and services these lenders provide. Regardless of whether it is the Direct Loan or Stafford FFELP bank-based program, no further application is required, and you are asked to review and sign a promissory note. By law, the basic terms and conditions for both programs are virtually the same. Disbursements are made directly to your account at the school at the beginning of each term. Further details on current provisions are outlined below and can also be viewed on many institutional and participating lender websites, also referenced in the back of this book. Because provisions are subject to periodic change, check directly with lenders and schools for the most current terms. The calculation of an Expected Family Contribution is the result of a federal formula applied to the data submitted annually on the FAFSA. This Expected Family Contribution, or EFC, is then sub-tracted, along with any student financial aid, from the institution's cost of atten-dance. Other student financial assistance would generally include scholarships, fellowships, and grants from any and all resources, including other educational loans. Any remaining need would effectively become your eligibility, that year, for additional aid through student loan programs.

Because costs, family circumstances, and funding levels and eligibility criteria of programs are likely to change from year to year, a new application for financial aid, especially government and privately funded student loans, is required annually. The FAFSA can be submitted at any point after January 1 prior to the school year for which the funds are being requested. Students should keep a copy of their previous year's FAFSA to help them with the following year's application. The renewal FAFSA process has become as easy as ever, as the government offers an online "Renewal FAFSA," which requires the updating of only certain data elements.

It is very important to understand that institutions using the FAFSA may request additional information along with the FAFSA. If a school does, it should be so noted in its published procedures for determining financial aid eligibility and awards. While deadlines for government loan programs are relatively less restrictive, students should understand that institutional funds are limited and often distributed on a first-come, first-serve basis to those who meet the published deadline. When institutional funds are gone, they're gone. As a general rule of thumb, file no later than March unless the institution's deadline is earlier.

Student Loan Eligibility

The major government loan opportunities are provided to eligible U.S. citizens or per-manent residents through either the Direct Loan or the Stafford FFELP bank-based programs. Current loan limitations allow graduate and professional students to bor-row up to $18,500 annually from these programs. Certain conditions and limits may impact each borrower's annual amount.

Another very important point needs to be made regarding "subsidy" benefits. Based upon your annual eligibility, which begins with the submission of the FAFSA, you may, during periods of academic enrollment on at least a half-time basis, have the interest on your loan amount up to $8,500 paid (i.e., subsidized) by the federal gov-ernment. If you are not eligible for any part of this subsidy because of the results of the FAFSA or other factors, including the receipt of other forms of student financial assistance, you may still secure the $8,500 but without the subsidy. Again, this means that the interest on the loan will be accruing at the going rate and may be paid quarterly or, as is more often done, deferred until repayment begins, usually six months after you leave school.

All of the interest on these loans, as well as that for future years' loans, will be added by most lenders (capitalized) all at once when the borrower enters repayment. The wise borrower should inquire specifically about the capitalization of interest prior to selecting a lender, to be sure such capitalization will occur only all at once and only upon the beginning of repayment.

All eligible borrowers may also request an additional $10,000 annually through this government program but will not be provided any interest subsidy, regardless of their eligibility for the subsidy on the first $8,500 of borrowing. This kind of loan is referred to as an "unsubsidized" loan. Both the initial $8,500 (subsidized or unsubsidized) and the $10,000 unsubsidized loan can be combined so that the student may borrow up to $18,500 annually to a maximum of $138,500 ($65,500 subsidized and $73,000 unsubsidized). This aggregate limit includes any money borrowed as an undergraduate. Students in health-related fields may borrow an extra $20,000. As will be noted with many aspects of this program, all of these current provisions are subject to change, and interested students are advised to secure more current information directly from lenders and institutions at the time of application.

Other Financing Options

Because most government loan programs have annual as well as aggregate borrowing limits, many students, especially those enrolled in professional programs, require additional financing beyond the current annual government limit of $18,500. These options are plentiful but should be pursued only if there are no other alternatives and the additional funds are absolutely needed. In considering private loan options, you should understand that loan consolidation options when repayment begins are currently restricted only to government loans. Many providers of private student loans do offer a "bundled billing" provision for those borrowers whose government loans and private loans were provided by the same lender. You should check carefully regarding this possibility by reviewing the information published by the lender, as well as by institutions participating in the Stafford FFELP program. Indeed, many institutions have developed and negotiated special arrangements with certain lenders, which include a "bundled bill" option. Of the many considerations that graduate borrowing entails, this is one of the most important and should be carefully researched prior to selecting a private lender.

Unlike most government loans, private loans do not have annual limits other than one that is restricted by the amount of the school's published annual cost of attendance, less any other student aid, including other student loans, which you may be receiving. In other words, you can't privately borrow more than the difference between what the school costs and how much aid—whether it be loans, fellowships, grants, or some combination of these—you're already receiving. Because there is no government subsidy or guarantee, private loans are also usually more expensive in terms of interest rates. They're also not typically protected by interest caps. You should carefully consider the long-term risk posed by interest rates, which will typically change quarterly throughout the time the loan is outstanding, including through the repayment years, and which will be adjusted as the cost of money changes. This is one very significant difference between the government program and private loans.

A number of lenders also provide private educational loans customized to certain professions, such as law, business, and medicine. In addition to accommodating the special needs that these students may have during formal periods of enrollment, these loans may also offer assistance to those students preparing to take exams for accreditation or licensing, as well as for those involved in financing expenses related to residencies and even relocation.

Personal Financing Options

In addition to government and private student loan programs, other forms of financing may be possible for certain students, especially those who have accumulated some assets. Such possibilities for borrowing could include financing through equity in property, or from life insurance policies, or even from certain retirement programs. Even though most students are not in such a position when they are considering graduate or professional school, for those who are so fortunate, the good news is that such borrowers would be repaying themselves with interest. Moreover, the interest in at least some of these scenarios could offer limited favorable tax considerations, effectively reducing the net cost of such financing. For those individuals who may find themselves with such alternate financing options, seeking professional advice from qualified tax consultants is recommended.

Repayment

Selection of a repayment plan for student loans, if such an option presents itself, should be done with careful consideration. Certainly of prime importance is the ultimate cost of the loan. In most cases, the longer the length of repayment, the greater the ultimate cost of the loan. For example, if you were to take out $20,000 in Stafford loans and had to pay them off at the maximum variable interest rate of 8.25 percent in 10 years, you would make monthly payments of about $244, for a total cost of $29,236. If you were to pay off the same amount of loans at the same rate in five years instead, you'd have to make monthly payments of about $405, but the total cost would end up being $24,308. That's five grand you would save.

In making arrangements for the repayment of government loans, lenders are required to offer borrowers various options. While more years to repay usually results in lower monthly payments, the additional years in delaying the final payment on the loan create additional financing cost to the borrower. In most cases, the early years of repayment typically find former full-time students faced with a number of expenses related to starting up their careers and their lives as truly self-supporting individuals. These early costs can result in difficult choices. Too often the individual rushes into long-term solutions for spreading out loan repayments in order to meet monthly obligations, where in many cases a little control and frugality in lifestyle decisions in the first few years of being on one's own could more properly—and with far less expense—address the budget concerns without any serious impact. With patience and restraint, standard loan repayments can be absorbed and eventually become less of a burden as each year goes by, thus allowing the individual's lifestyle and quality of life to gradually improve. Nonetheless, current government provisions (always subject to change) do offer some significant measures of relief for borrowers whose total government student loan obligations are too excessive to shoulder in full at the start of repayment.

Loan Consolidation

The consolidation of student loans has become a very attractive option in recent years. Current legislation allows the eligible borrower to secure a long-term fixed interest rate based upon a rate driven by the cost of money at the time—specifically (in repayment), the 91-day T-bill rate plus 2.3 percent. Eligible borrowers may currently lock in reduced rates on a permanent basis throughout repayment by arranging a federal government consolidation loan. The government changes the variable rate (it can go up or down) every summer (see below), and with rates currently at their lowest levels ever, consolidation is becoming a popular step to take. General information on student loan consolidation can be obtained from any participating FFELP lender or by contacting the U.S. Department of Education at 800-557-7392 or by visiting LoanConsolidation.ed.gov.

CHAPTER IV

What to Expect When You Get There

ASSIMILATION INTO ACADEMIC CULTURE

Who will be your peers in graduate school? The National Center for Educational Statistics (NCES) has compiled statistics to answer this question.

Most likely, your peers will be their early 30s. Half of them will be married and a quarter will have children. About two-thirds will be attending a public university as full-time students. Many of them will have been working in the "real-world" before deciding to go back to school. The number of women and U.S. citizens in your peer group will vary considerably according to discipline.

If you get into graduate school, this means that you excelled in the classroom. A combination of verbal, writing, and analytical skills, along with imagination, natural curiosity, and motivation put you at the head of the class. By your senior year in college, you knew the ropes. But in graduate school, the entire class is composed of students equally as good, or even better than you. Furthermore, it's just like your first year in college. You don't know the name of the faculty member at the lectern. You don't know the students sitting next to you—but clearly, some of them have been here for awhile and know what is going on. You don't even know where your next class is.

It's finally dawning on you: Graduate school is very different from your undergraduate years. The bar is set higher in your classes. You may find yourself in the new role of educator as a teaching assistant. And what's all this about oral comprehensive exams and dissertation research that you keep hearing about?

This new environment can be intimidating, but don't let it be. Remember, you survived your first year of high school and your first year of college. Graduate school has got to be easier. Why? Because you're older and you have proof (your acceptance letter to graduate school) that you are academically successful.

Building a Network

Early in your first year, you will have opportunities to meet the other members of the incoming classes. There will be orientation activities, both professional and social. Don't be a wallflower. You and your classmates will all have similar academic interests, goals, experiences with teaching, individual faculty members, and coursework. Find out where your classmates went to undergraduate school, which subdiscipline they are interested in, and what research area or graduate advisor they're thinking about. It's okay to talk shop.

Characteristics of PhD candidates

Age	34
Female	50%
U.S. citizen	76%
Married	55%
With dependents	25%
African American	6%
Asian American	19%
Native American	1%
Hispanic or Latino	5%
Going to a public university	63%
Full-time student	69%
Started right after BA/BS	25%
Waited over 7 years after BA/BS	35%

from a 1999 NCES study

In experimental sciences and engineering, you may get involved with lab rotations or brown-bag seminars to acquaint you with ongoing research. Sometimes graduate students in the social sciences and humanities gather in the library stacks of interest. Talk to more advanced students about what they are doing and how much financial and intellectual support their graduate advisors provide.

Of course, there's always the classroom. You'll meet fellow graduate students at all stages of their careers in the classroom. On more enlightened campuses, you may even have an office that you'll share with other students.

If you're a teaching assistant (TA) for sections of a huge undergraduate introductory courses, you'll have meetings to discuss next week's work. There's time for small talk before and after the session. Don't come late and leave early. If you have a service-free fellowship, this opportunity for socialization (and professional development) will not be available.

As an undergraduate, you may have steered clear of professors outside the classroom. After all, they always seemed so busy, so distant, so authoritative. Besides, what on earth do you have in common? Such an attitude towards the faculty in graduate school is lethal—it's time to consider them as senior colleagues (not to be confused with a "buddy"). Without appearing too familiar (be respectful) or obsequious (no sucking-up), talk to the professors after class or research seminar about your questions concerning their lectures. At social gatherings, ask them about their research or what's good and bad about academic life. As a graduate student, you do have something in common with your professors—a love for a particular research topic—and you understand this topic better than you did as an undergraduate.

It's essential to get to know your professors—some of them will have the equipment and techniques you'll need in your research, some of them may be on your dissertation committee, and one of them will become your graduate advisor. At least three of them will be evaluating your worth in their letters of recommendation after graduation. They should know who they are writing about.

Of all faculty, your graduate advisor is the most important influence. If you already know who you want to work with upon arrival, meet with him. Ask about course selection and which reference materials you should read to familiarize yourself with the general research topic. Talk about the current research the advisor and his other students are engaged in.

Most of you won't have an advisor in mind upon arrival at graduate school. Spend the first semester or two evaluating faculty during seminars, in class, and during laboratory rotations. Ask advanced graduate students what they think. Being called a "really nice guy" is wonderful accolade, but the more important attributes of a mentor are the amount of personal and critical interest she takes in her students' research and how successful her students are in landing jobs upon graduation.

It is also important to extend your professional network beyond your university. Once you pick a research topic, you'll quickly discover the big players in the field because you'll be reading their journal articles, reviews, and books on the subject.

You'll also hear them at professional meetings. Try to meet these experts. If you have developed any depth to your understanding of the research topic, you'll have plenty of questions to open the conversation with. Talk to your advisor about adding this person to your dissertation committee. Just make sure that you know more than the expert about your dissertation topic than he does.

A Word about Teamwork...

Most dissertation research is a lone-wolf experience; you're attempting to carve out a particular intellectual niche. You want to become the local expert on a particular topic. However, early in your graduate career, you may have an opportunity to work with faculty and other students in their research projects. Don't hesitate to get involved. Not only will you learn how to do research by watching others, you'll be developing an important talent: teamwork. This experience comes in handy, especially if you decide to look for non-academic employment upon graduation. The private sector looks for evidence of cooperation and often complains that doctoral education seldom provides the opportunity to develop such talents. If you can't find a research team to join, think about a position in graduate student government or on a university committee.

One warning: Don't be exploited. If you have done a significant amount of the work or provided a critical element to a research project, ask to be a coauthor. To be acknowledged in the publication is a fall-back position. Second warning: Don't let university committee work consume all your time. Remember, influencing important administrative decisions is nice, but your dissertation is your only ticket out of graduate school.

A Note for International Students

If English isn't your native tongue, be prepared for a strenuous first year. In many departments, you'll be taking several advanced courses, given a teaching assignment, expected to find a research advisor and then, in your spare time, adapt to a complex and fast-paced American culture. Take solace in the fact that most of your American peers probably don't know your native tongue and would have just as much of a problem getting a PhD in your country.

Here are a few survival hints:

1. Once you decide where you'll go to graduate school, develop a local network. Find out who else from your country is attending the university and how to contact them. Perhaps your new American school has a club that will help you develop a network of students from your country. The school will have an international office that can help. The local network will help you with basic questions, such as: What should I bring? How do I get from the airport to the school? What temporary living quarters are available until I can find a place to live? What do I need to do to get a place on campus during the academic year? What do I need to do to get my kids into school? Once you get onto campus, the network will help you with questions concerning health care, permanent housing, transportation, and other basics of setting up.

2. Take advantage of every function that the university has to offer. If campus housing is available, grab it. Usually, it's close to campus, furnished, relatively inexpensive, and full of folks like you. Take advantage of all of the orientation activities. Take English as Second Language (ESL) conversational, reading, and writing courses. Accept a campus host family. Immerse yourself into your new culture.

3. Don't speak your mother tongue at home or among friends. Keep speaking and listening in English until you don't have to translate words in your mind. Keep at it until you start to dream in English!

4. Please realize that the American curriculum and expectations are different from what you may have experienced. Class attendance is mandatory. Exams given during the semester are important for your grade (it isn't just the final exam that matters). If you don't follow this advice, your grade point average (GPA) will suffer, you may lose funding, or—worst of all—you may be asked to leave the program.

5. You're expected to "respectfully disagree" with classmates, professors, or your mentor when you have an alternative idea. Just make sure that you have the facts to back you up. You are also expected to take initiative in your dissertation research project, all the way from generating the research question to writing up the results.

6. Don't say you understand something that your advisor is telling you when you really don't. It is less embarrassing to admit that you don't understand than to do something potentially dangerous.

7. Don't travel outside of the U.S. until you thoroughly check your visa status. Too many students are going home for semester break and not getting back for a year. Go to your campus International Student Office for advice.

8. Writing will take a long time because your advisor will be editing your work several times. Don't be embarrassed; American students are given the same treatment. Start writing presentations, publications, and your dissertation early, and give each section to your advisor as you finish it.

9. If at all possible, finish the dissertation before you go home. Otherwise, you'll lose the daily advice, resources, and time necessary to finish.

A Note for Female Graduate Students

In some fields, women quit school before earning their degree at higher rates than do male students. Female students are as qualified as males, and they work just as hard and effectively. Some researchers say that the disparity in attrition is due to a lack of female peer support and faculty. Other research concludes that women are the child bearers and primary child caretakers, responsibilities that leave less time for studies and research. And still other researchers claim that wives most often drop everything to move when their husbands get a new job, rather than the other way around.

Two tendencies cited in *The Women's Guide to Navigating the PhD in Engineering and Science* appear sex-specific. First, men tend to externalize criticism (it's someone else's fault or "no problem") while women internalize it ("it's my fault"). Giving criticism is what graduate advisors do, and many times, it isn't couched in soothing, positive language. Nevertheless, your advisor doesn't want you to feel badly; she just wants you to understand a problem and then fix it.

Second, many women seek affirmation for the work they do. More than likely, a male advisor won't provide it. Therefore, women need to find a support group that can provide encouragement, serve as a sounding board, and help address other important personal questions. If your advisor, research group, or department can't provide this support, find it outside of the department. Some valuable websites:

Society for Women Engineers:	www. swe.org
Association for Women in Science:	www.awis.org
Association for Women in Computing:	www.awc-hq.org

A Note for Someone Unique in Their Department

You may be a female in mechanical engineering, an international student in English Literature, a male in nursing, a single person in a class of young married students, or a student of color in any field. You look around at your fellow graduate students and faculty and find yourself in the minority. If that doesn't bother you, read no further. If you feel anxious and a bit isolated, it's time to find where people like you hang out on campus.

University offices and student organizations can probably help you find places to relax and blend. If you're an international student and your native tongue is taught at your school, go to that department and find out what's happening there, or take the ESL course and meet the other international students in the class. But don't forget the folks in your department. Start small. Get to know your DGS (Director of Graduate Studies). Pick your graduate advisor quickly so you can get to know her and the other students working with your advisor. Get to know the other students in class, in the coffee room, in the hall. These friends and acquaintances will be the nexus of your professional network.

A Final (and Somewhat Ominous) Note for Everyone

In her book *Leaving the Ivory Tower*, Barbara Lovitts claims that many graduate students leave their programs because they never get socially and intellectually integrated into their departmental culture. Feeling out of the loop is not a morale-booster. Being out of the loop means that you're missing out on important contacts and information. Build a network.

COURSEWORK

The bulk of your coursework will occur within the first three years of graduate studies. Before you pick a dissertation advisor, you'll discuss course selections with your Director of Graduate Studies. Perhaps you'll have a set curriculum in the first year, maybe you'll have choices. If you have choices, remember that the purpose for taking these courses are first, to provide information for passing the qualifier or comprehensive examinations; second, to provide a basis for your dissertation research; and third, to introduce you to the faculty and your classmates. In other words, if you want to take a course on the history of photography, you'd better be an art history graduate student.

Even without a set curriculum, you may have required courses outside the department. Language courses are common in the humanities, statistics in life and social sciences, courses in pedagogy for teaching, and English as a Second Language. If the skill that you will learn in the course makes no sense for your particular research project, talk to the DGS. You may have to take the course anyway, but more likely than not, the DGS will have a good reason for you to learn the material. You don't have to shine nearly as brightly in these courses as those close to your research area (unless you want this lecturer and his expertise on your dissertation committee).

What about undergraduate courses? Check with the DGS first to determine if these courses will count towards your graduate degree or if your tuition scholarship covers these courses.

Even after comprehensive examinations, you may find courses that are important to your research. You might also want to sit in on classes that you are likely to teach as a brand-new assistant professor. However, don't overdo it. Your ticket out is a dissertation, not another course grade on your transcript.

The differences between graduate and undergraduate courses are manifold: You'll take only three or four courses per term, and they'll be concentrated in your discipline. You'll have small classes. You'll also be expected to participate in class and do better than B-grade work. It would be wise if you developed a personal/intellectual relationship with your teacher. It will also be wise to develop respectful relationships with your classmates. Habits to avoid: personal attacks and hogging the stage. Habits to develop: Preparing for class by doing the reading assignments and homework, thinking about the material, deriving ideas, and generating questions. Don't be afraid to express yourself even in a hostile environment. If one of your ideas gets cornered by an unexpectedly strong opposing view, admit it. You don't lose the argument (or face) by saying, "That was an interesting point, although I'm not sure that I agree with you. Let me give it some thought before I respond."

In seminar courses, you probably will have to prepare at least one lecture. Note how long it takes to develop the topic—and how much more you had to know than what you ultimately presented. Identify talking points and thought-provoking questions to stimulate discussion. Practice the talk until you don't have to read it. Prepare the necessary handouts, overhead slides, or power-point slides. Then multiply the time it took for one lecture 40 times—that's how long it takes to develop a single three-credit course. For additional resources on what to expect in graduate school, see Appendix E: References.

TEACHING

What to Expect

Most of you won't be assigned to teach a class on your own the first semester in school. In fact, most of you, especially in science and engineering, may never teach a course by yourself during your entire graduate training. Those of you in the humanities, math, or the social sciences in public universities may be asked to teach the first semester that you arrive.

To prepare yourself as a teacher, enlightened universities will have short courses on pedagogical techniques. Departments, concerned about undergraduate teaching, will start you off in introductory courses as a teaching assistant. You may assist in a class laboratory, run discussion groups or problem sessions outside of lecture, and grade exams. You should attend the lectures to better help students with their questions. Besides, relearning basic concepts will come in handy during the qualifier examinations. Another good reason to attend class is that you can sit back and critically analyze what works and what doesn't work when a professor delivers a lecture. If you are really new and nervous, you could attend an earlier scheduled lab or discussion section in order to see how more experienced graduate students deal with the exercise and the undergraduates.

At some point, especially in the humanities, you may be assigned to teach your own course. You will likely be assigned to classes that the faculty don't want to teach—for instance, an introduction to a modern language or writing comprehension. Do not cop an attitude. Do not consider this a demeaning assignment. Freshman pay tuition too, and they deserve your best effort. Besides, they may be grading your performance in a teacher/course evaluation at the end of the semester, and the faculty will find out how well you did. Furthermore, if your goal is to land a faculty position in a liberal arts college, this is the experience that search committees are looking for. They don't have graduate students. Instead, they use assistant professors to teach these survey courses.

If you are in a department that normally doesn't have graduate students teaching their own courses and you want a career on the faculty, there are a few ways to get experience. First, ask your advisor if you can deliver a guest lecture on a topic that you already know well. After the lecture, ask for an evaluation of your performance. Keep asking for more guest lectures. Second, find out how firm the policy is that keeps graduate students from teaching a course. Maybe it's just because no one asked. Be sure to have your advisor on your side for this venture. The advisor will know how much time it takes to develop a course and may think that you should be working on your dissertation research instead. Your advisor will also know if teaching experience is something that faculty search committees in your discipline care about. If you still have the itch to teach, try to convince your mentor that this experience will help you develop a firmer grasp of the subject matter as well as make you competitive for a job in a demanding academic job market. Third, if the obstacles to teaching in your home institution are impenetrable, then look for adjunct or visiting positions in the local area. Many community colleges, branch campuses of state universities, and liberal arts colleges have temporary vacancies that you can fill for a semester.

With an eye to your future plunge into the job market, try to vary your teaching assignments every semester. If you must stay involved in the same course, try to get assigned to a different professor. You can compare course outlines and presentation styles. Use force, if necessary, to get assigned to courses that you will likely teach upon graduation. Faculty search committees will look favorably upon such teaching experience.

Preparation

Whether you are assisting in a laboratory associated with a science survey course or offering a lecture course to upperclassmen, obey the Boy Scout motto, "Be prepared." If you wait until the night before the class to think about the lecture, your students will quickly realize it. Your disorganization and fumbling will give you away.

For laboratories, read the exercise to see if it makes sense. Learn the underlying concepts that drive the procedure. Perform the procedure until you have mastered it. Make sure you know how to properly use the equipment. On the day of the lab, make sure the reagents and supplies are there in sufficient quantity and that the equipment works. You may be able to present a short talk at the beginning of lab to introduce the exercise. This is your chance to practice writing and presenting a lecture so don't blow it off, but don't get carried away with long presentations either. After all, the function of the lab is to get the students *doing* things.

The purpose of the discussion, review, or problem sessions is to let the students ask questions, discuss the lectures, and get a personal experience that cannot be generated in a large lecture hall. You will not have to prepare a 50-minute lecture, but you will need to know the material well. This may require going to the lectures and doing the assigned readings, because you should be able to anticipate the questions and find out the answers well before class.

One of most difficult aspects of the discussion or problem-solving class is turning your monologue into a class dialogue. Generally, the students sitting up front will join in early and often. The trick is getting the back of the class engaged. One useful strategy is breaking the class into groups of three or four and then posing a question that lends itself to several answers. Let the groups talk for five minutes, and then have a spokesperson present the consensus solution to the problem. You can ask other groups for alternate answers. If the same students are still the only ones talking, pick your own spokesperson when you arrange the groups or stick all of the leaders in one group.

Whether you are preparing a single seminar talk or a semester of lectures, start preparing early. You need to become so familiar with the material that you will be comfortable and confident in your delivery. Determine the central points that you wish to convey and then determine what the audience will need to know in order to understand that central point. Let the path to the central point be straight and relatively short. Highlight each step (so the audience will know where they have been) and shine a bright light on the central point (so that the audience will know that they have arrived). Don't try to pack in more than three major points per lecture.

Do not assume that your audience knows the important words that you are using in the lecture. Define your terms, especially disciplinary jargon. Jargon reduces complex concepts into single words or phrases. It is a quick way to converse with those also steeped in the discipline. But if you're overusing jargon to an audience of sophomores, you'll find their frustrated glances quickly turning into glazed expressions.

Allow time for the audience to reflect on your lecture and to ask questions. You might consider shutting up every 15 to 20 minutes to get some audience participation. Ask if there are any questions or ask one of your own., but keep control of time or you'll never get onto the next topic.

Avoid tangents. We've all been bored or frustrated into comas by teachers who consistently wander around verbally until it becomes impossible to figure out their original point. Irrelevant anecdotes and distractions don't cover up a lack of preparation or organization, two major grading points in the teacher-course evaluation.

Presentation

While being organized and anticipating questions are hallmarks of good preparation, the most important attributes of presentation are enthusiasm and confidence. If you aren't excited about the topic, how can you expect your class to be? If you don't get off on bringing a class step-by-step to an epiphany, you're missing the biggest reward of teaching. No, not everyone in the class will get it, but most will appreciate your enthusiasm—just don't go overboard.

The same goes for confidence. You want to convey to the class that you know what you're talking about, but don't come off as aloof or arrogant. Remember, the students in your class know less than you do or they would be in a higher-level class. Never put someone down who can't answer your question or who asks an irrelevant question. And for everyone's sake, do not try to B.S. an answer to a question that one of your students lobs at you. It only fortifies your image as seer by saying, "Good question! I'll research the answer and get back to you." Make good on the promise the very next lecture, in front of the whole class. Sometimes it's a good tactic to lead the class to a question that no one knows the answer to—yet. It opens the door of research to them and demonstrates that your field isn't composed of static and rote facts.

Demeanor

To many students, you'll be the most intimate contact with academe during their undergraduate years. Especially in large lecture sections, professors appear distant and unapproachable. Therefore, it is important to learn your students' names in the smaller group setting of a laboratory or discussion session. Talk to the students one on one, but keep it professional. You can talk about big campus social or sports activities, but that should be about as far you want to stray from course material.

Don't concentrate on a few favorite students. It becomes an issue of fairness with the other members of the class. Deal with individual bad student behavior promptly and firmly. The old adage "praise in public and reprimand in private" is useful. Your students cannot be your drinking buddies, because you may have to tell one of them to pay attention or another that her performance in the last quiz rated a D.

For these reasons, you may want to distinguish yourself from your students in class in dress and speech. You are not one of them, and you might as well set the tone early.

Tests, Papers, and Grades

You can and should demand much from your students as long as they feel that you are being reasonable and fair. Being fair means treating everyone with the same respect during discussions, when you correct their papers and tests, and when you assign grades. Being fair means treating everyone the same.

Being reasonable means not expecting your students to know the materials as well as you do even after one of your most brilliant lectures. They need to know the core concepts that you are trying to teach and the necessary facts that lead to and support the concept, but they shouldn't be expected to know extraneous details. Don't expect the students to know what is important and what is not. As a teacher, it's up to you to define the concept well and highlight the supporting data both in the lecture or lab and in review sessions. Being reasonable means understanding that you are teaching only one of five subjects in a typical undergraduate schedule. Keep this in mind when you assign reading and writing assignments.

Two Rules for Graders

1.   Give the class every chance to succeed.

   - Have review sessions a couple of days before the test. It can be a simple question-and-answer period; you could point out important facts and concepts.

   - Give three to four exams during the semester and allow the students to drop the lowest grade. Exclude the final from this deal or you may only be talking to yourself for the last fourth of the course.

   - Expect students to use what they learn over the course of the semester, but don't make the final a detail-rich comprehensive examination.

   - Give extra credit take-home exercises that are due on the day of the test. The exercises should help the students understand the material better. They may be "thought" type questions that would be difficult to do during a one-hour exam. In order to foster teamwork, tell the students that they can discuss possible solutions to the problems but that they have to answer the question in their own way.

   - With large classes (over 50), give objective tests, grade on a curve, and tell the students what the score means grade-wise. With small classes, give subjective tests, score one question on each test at a time (which maintains consistency), and provide percentile scores that easily translates into a grade (i.e., a

75 percent means that the student has mastered three-quarters of the material and has earned a C).

- If more than 75 percent of the students missed a particular question, it was a bad question. Admit it, don't count it, and tell the class your decision.

- Grade quickly (within a week) and go over the answers to the test or your expectations for the paper.

2. Resist giving individual students a break just because they asked—unless you're willing to give all your students the same break, although they kept quiet.

- This goes for turning in papers late, taking tests early or late, and extra credit assignments.

- This goes for re-grading tests and papers. Tell students that they can argue for an enhanced score on a particular question but that you reserve the right to re-grade the entire test to eliminate breaks that students may have been given elsewhere.

- A student's desperate desire to go to medical or law school isn't sufficient reason to give them a higher grade. If it helps, tell this type of student that you're not a judge who can reverse decisions but merely a scribe who's recording what the student earned. If the student demonstrated mastery of only 75 percent of the material as gauged by the test, then their grade is a C.

In summary, if you are organized and know the material, if you appear enthusiastic and confident when you deliver the lecture, if you are reasonable in what you expect the students to learn, and if you treat the students fairly, you need not fear teacher-course evaluations at the end of the term.

For additional references for teaching, be sure to check out Appendix E: References.

COMPREHENSIVE EXAMINATIONS

The comprehensive examination is exactly what it sounds like—the ultimate final exam. Oftentimes, the exam consists of a written portion—broad, essay-type questions—and an oral portion, for which several faculty members ask everything from broad questions about the field to specific questions about your research topic.

While these tests are important, don't obsess for years over them. After taking two to three years of graduate courses, teaching undergraduates, and studying by yourself for four to six months, you still won't know everything anyway. Get the test over with before you start to forget the stuff you just learned. While these tests appear excruciating, don't procrastinate when it comes to taking them. They won't be less unpleasant a year later. Get them over with, and get on with your life.

Every department will have its own ideas about comprehensive examinations. You need to know what to study for, so do some research. Every field is vast and full of details. Are you supposed to know everything superficially? A selected number of topics surrounding your research interests in depth? Will you need to construct a reading list? If so, will the questions require opinion and comparative analysis among the authors or just the facts? Do you pick a selection of subdisciplines to master or will the questions be directed towards your dissertation research? Will you have to present and defend your dissertation proposal during the oral examination?

In other words, your goal is to get some boundaries around what you have to study. To do this, choose your dissertation committee wisely and then ask every player what you should expect.

Departments may have a different set of rules and expectations for the written versus the oral exam. Most often, the written test is a series of field exams that deal with particular subdisciplines. Often, you have few choices as to which fields you wish to be tested in or when the tests will be offered. Many times, the written tests are written and graded by departmentally assigned and anonymous faculty members. In this case, ask your director of graduate studies what to expect.

You'll probably find much more information concerning the oral examination. You and your graduate advisor pick the faculty members who will be on your committee based on their compatibility and expertise. Often, you'll be presenting your dissertation proposal during the oral examination, and the questions will tend to focus on the interface between your committee members' expertise and your research interests.

Once the committee is assembled, talk to fellow graduate students in your subdiscipline who have already successfully jumped this hurdle. Ask them how they prepared for the exams and how long they took to prepare, how broad or how specific the questions were, and about the differences between the oral and written exam questions.

Talk to your graduate advisor. Ask him/her about the nature of the exam and what the faculty expectations are and to provide an example or two of the written and oral questions that you would be expected to know. This will tell you the degree of specificity that you will need to study. Ask your advisor what he/she thinks the other members of the panel will concentrate on.

Talk to the faculty members who are on your dissertation committee. Ask them what you can expect and what they expect. It might help if you took their most recently taught advanced course.

Just remember: Probing people for their expectations and for examples of questions isn't immoral; it isn't cheating. However, browbeating students and faculty members into telling you exactly what questions will be asked is just stupid, obnoxious, and unlikely to yield any useful information.

Preparing for the Written Examinations

If you have done well in setting the boundaries around what you need to know, then you'll have a finite and manageable amount of information to digest. Enroll, audit, or better yet, be a TA in the introductory course for a particular subdiscipline (e.g., biochemistry, Byzantine history). Read the assigned introductory text carefully. Move to the library and read recent annual reviews. Take notes. Study. Anticipate questions and write down the answers. Get a study group together and trade questions. Take time out to think about all of this material you are absorbing. What are the central concepts? What are the links between the concepts? What counter-arguments strike you as feasible?

Most importantly, what questions remain unanswered? What approaches have not been taken to analyze the material? Which concepts appear to contradict each other? These questions may become your dissertation or a future research topic.

Preparing for the Oral Examination

The advantage to this test over the written exam is that you'll know the questioners, because you've asked them to stand on your committee. You should have talked to each of them about their expectations for the examination, which helps to define what you need to study. The disadvantage is that you have to think on your feet and use your tongue instead of a pen to answer the questions. If you can, have mock-orals with fellow graduate students in your subdiscipline. Trade questions.

One sure way to limit the questions is to have your dissertation proposal in the minds of the committee. Your advisor should have already agreed that your dissertation topic is viable. If so, send it around to the other committee members before the exam. Perhaps you can make a short presentation about your preliminary research and intended work at the beginning of the exam in order to prime the question pump. This will be playing to your strength, since you should be the person in the room who has thought about and knows the most about your topic. If a faculty member blindsides you with a question or observation concerning your research, thank her for the valuable advice, and mean it. Better to be warned before you embark on the project than at your dissertation defense.

Remember, one question tends to lead to another related question, and eventually, your inquisitor will take you to the limit of your knowledge. It is important to confess your ignorance immediately instead of fumbling around. The inquisitor may give you hints, but if they don't help, just say you will have to think about the question and get back to them later. Eventually, she will move on.

Remember, too, that once the question is thrown your way, you have the floor. The more complete the answer, the less time there is to ask a follow-up question. Just don't overdo the ploy of taking the very long way around to answer a question.

Finally, confidence is key to passing the oral examination. You need to have a firm grasp on the history, concepts, techniques, and recent advances in your subdiscipline. This confidence should not be shaken by not knowing an answer to one particular question. This confidence can only be gained by working your hardest to understand your field since enrolling in graduate school.

Personal Assessment

You need to get your nose off the grindstone at the end of every semester, find a quiet place, and ask yourself if going to graduate school is worth it.

Pick a time when you are *not* temporarily depressed or elated about something that just happened and ask the big question. Do you still want a career in teaching or research? Assuming that you have said "yes" up to and through the comprehensive examinations, you'll also need to determine if you want an academic career or a research position in the private sector or the government.

After observing the faculty up close and personal, do you still want to be a professor? You realize that it's not the nine-month, relaxed, paid-just-for thinking kind of job that folks on the outside erroneously believe. Even if academe retains its luster, are the more advanced students in your department getting jobs in academe? If so, what credentials did they bring to the job market and do you have the motivation, time, and ability to match them? How "sexy" was their dissertation topic? How much research did they present and publish? What teaching experiences did they have?

Do you like teaching? Are you chronically depressed over the 10 percent who remain clueless or ecstatic over the 10 percent who seem to get it? Are you spending so much time trying to teach that other aspects of your professional and personal life suffer? Is teaching not getting easier with experience?

Do you like doing research? Do the positive results far outweigh the failed experiments or archive searches? Can you measure forward progress or just count the number of blind alleys? When you wake up, do you really look forward to getting to the lab or to the library? Do you enjoy solving the problems that invariably arise? Do you love talking shop with others at the university? Does your mate appreciate your enthusiasm and dedication?

Are you happy with your fellow graduate students and faculty both in professional and social settings? Are faculty members positively reinforcing your existence or are you getting B– grades and bored looks? Do you become angry and argumentative when people challenge a point you are making? Do you think you're the only cool one in a herd of nerds?

If you have been miserable for the last couple of self-evaluation periods, it may be time to get out. Identify the problems and talk to a couple of friends, your director of graduate studies, and advisor to see if the issues can be resolved. If not, find another career. You have nothing to prove. You have earned a perfectly respectful baccalaureate degree. As a graduate student, you were caught in a training program for a job that no longer appeals to you. Perhaps you will have accumulated enough credits to earn a master's degree. Ask your director of graduate studies what more is needed. Get to the university career center and start looking for alternatives.

If you love research but despise teaching, look into non-academic research careers after you earn the PhD. The government and the private sector both need trained researchers. It is important that you decide that a non-academic research career is what you want as early as your third year in graduate school because you need to gain the experiences and skills that are prized by non-academic employers. Summer (or longer) internships are often the way you can get your foot in the door. In other words, the non-academic track is not a fallback position if academic jobs are unavailable. You must be prepared to enter the non-academic researcher market.

If you love teaching and dread research, you will be happy to note that most of academic jobs are in colleges that do not consider research an essential ingredient for tenure. It *is* important to engage undergraduates in their research and do some of your own at a leisurely pace, but research funding and multiple publications won't be required.

If you love teaching *and* research, you belong in a research university. Among the greater than 4,000 institutions of higher learning in the United States, fewer than 300 produce over ten doctorates per year. The complete list of research-extensive and research-intensive universities is listed by the Carnegie Foundation at their website (CarnegieFoundation.org/classification). Be sure to look at this list before you apply for an academic job. Most departments at research universities will expect you to conduct research and publish the results. If your research requires funding for equipment, supplies, technical help, research assistants, time off from teaching, or travel, your department will expect you to write and receive research grants or fellowships.

Simultaneously, you'll teach graduate or undergraduate courses. The teaching load will be less than demanded by a department with no graduate program, but that time is taken up by eager graduate students who want you to be their advisor.

You will have service requirements too, including committee membership (e.g., departmental, college, and dissertation committees) and the occasional administrative post. It gets easier after tenure, but the job is still extremely demanding.

RESEARCH

Getting Early Research Experience

A PhD is a research degree, yet you are unlikely ever to take a course in how to do it. That is because the training takes longer than a semester, it is a hands-on learning experience, and it is very culture-specific. In other words, learning how to do research involves a lot of one-on-one interaction between a faculty member and a graduate student.

How can you get started even before committing to a particular advisor? In enlightened science, social science, and engineering departments, first-year students rotate through a few laboratories. Don't be a wallflower. If you aren't assigned to a team, ask the faculty member, graduate students, postdoctoral fellows, and technicians what research question they are addressing and how they plan to get that answer. Then pick the projects of interest and ask if you can watch and then perform various procedures. After watching and taking notes, try the procedure yourself. The first several times that you attempt the technique, you will fail to get any data. Persevere until you master the method. Keep a notebook of recipes and techniques. Do the background reading to familiarize yourself with the research area. Ask questions and make an impression as someone who is interested—but don't get underfoot. During experiments, there will be time to ask the graduate students if they enjoy working for a particular faculty member. There will be time to ask the postdocs about the job market. There will be time to shop-talk with the faculty member. Ask him where the research funding is coming from. Then when it's time to rotate, treat the next lab experience with the same intensity. When you are reasonably sure who you want to work with, ask the faculty member if he/she has an opening. Have a second choice if your first choice cannot take you in.

In less structured environments, you may have to schedule appointments to discuss a particular faculty member's research. This means that you have already read his recent publications and talked to his graduate students about compatibility issues and funding. Once you decide which faculty member you are most interested in working with, ask if there is a project that you can work on with him/her.

If you are in the humanities, you may get encouraging comments about a paper you wrote in class. Do not ignore this opportunity. Ask the professor to help you re-work the document to a publishable article. Find out where you need to do more research and which journal it might be sent to. Correct the work and go back to the professor. It may take several frustrating trips, but in the end, you'll have an idea of how research is conducted and how it is presented. Furthermore, you will have developed a professional relationship with a faculty member.

Picking an Advisor

What comes first, picking your dissertation research topic or picking your advisor? Unlike the chicken-and-the-egg question, the answer is...a little of both. You should have applied to the department because there was at least one faculty member who was doing research in the same general area that you are interested in. If you want to study immunology and there is only one faculty member who teaches and does research on immunology, then the choice is obvious. It doesn't matter how bad the guy's breath is. You have only two other choices: go somewhere else or get interested in something else. That is why campus visits are so important before you commit.

If there is more than one faculty member doing research in the area of your interest, then you can shop around. Here are the questions that you need answered before you make the decision.

Will this faculty member's recommendation help when you're looking for a job?

Frankly, this is the most important question, because getting the degree is only a short-term goal. You find out the answer to this important question by asking: Is she funded (not so important for humanities and some social science subdisciplines)? How many recent publications or awards have her name on them? How have recent graduates under her tutelage fared in the job market?

Can this advisor support you?

This is an important question for experimental scientists and engineers. Departmental support ends within a year or two of entry and the advisor is supposed to fund you as a research assistant. Support includes stipend, tuition, professional travel, necessary equipment, and money to buy research supplies. You and your education are not cheap.

How much direction do you need in the dissertation?

You can easily find out from his graduate students how involved in your project this mentor is. Some of the hands-on advisors will not only point out the question you should pursue, but they will outline the chapters of your dissertation. On the other hand, the sink-or-swim advisors expect you to present the idea, and two years later, you need to show up with the results. (Most faculty advisors are somewhere in between.)

How much discipline do you need to complete the project?

Do you need someone who demands weekly results, or can you follow a rigorous, self-imposed schedule? Everyone hates a nag, but if you can't get something done without significant prodding, pick a nagging mentor. Otherwise you'll become one of those graduate students still "trying" to finish in their fifteenth year.

How does the advisor criticize her graduate students?

No matter how nice the advisor is, she must criticize your work. It goes with the job. She may pick apart your research plan or the relevancy of your research question, your results and conclusions, the way you express yourself, the way you write, even the way you dress. It's the method of criticism that may drive you to get defensive or passive-aggressive. Neither of these negative responses will get you a PhD of any value. Find out, in class or in conversation with the advisor's students, how demanding or caustic she is.

Will this advisor be around when you graduate?

If the advisor is an assistant professor, he'll probably be undergoing the tenure process while you are a graduate student. What are the chances of success? If the professor does have tenure but is really old or sickly, what are the chances of retirement or worse? If the mentor gets famous, will he be lured away somewhere else? Nothing delays your degree more than your mentor leaving. But aren't these the imponderable questions? Perhaps, but there are signs. Is your potential advisor funded? Productive? Unhappy with his place of employment? Unhealthy? Hey, you're supposed to be a researcher with a keen sense of observation. Use this capacity in choosing the most important contact in your professional future.

Picking a Dissertation Topic

Conducting research is not merely following recipes or reading lots of books and reporting on them. You have to synthesize a novel idea or question from all of your reading and experiences. Then you have to make a plan that develops and bolsters the idea or answers the question. The idea or question cannot be trivial because no one will be interested in your work. Neither can it be so centrally important that you will be competing against several other (more senior) minds who will probably scoop you. Nor can it be a question that experts have been pondering for years ("What is the true meaning of life?" "What is the cure for cancer?"). There's a reason these questions remain unanswered, and it's unlikely that, as a third-year graduate student, you'll have the experience necessary to deal with them. Finally, your procedure for developing the idea or answering the question cannot take so long or be so involved that it takes over two to three years to develop, master, and complete.

One important function of the faculty and especially your advisor is to point the way to an appropriate dissertation topic. Do not expect them to give you the topic, though. Perhaps you should start by finding out what research areas your advisor knows well. A medieval historian will not be particularly helpful if you want to study cowhands. Ask your advisor for some good reference texts to help you understand her field better. Read, synthesize, and discover interesting holes in our knowledge. Go back to the advisor and tell her your discoveries. Some of your ideas will be trivial, some will have already been exhaustively addressed, but a few might be potentially interesting. Go back to the library and delve further into the topic. Read the most recent literature.

Sometimes, you can provide a perspective that your advisor hasn't considered by looking for questions at the interface of two disciplines. There are many examples of interdisciplinary ideas that have evolved into established programs, such as history of science, genomics and computational biology, bioengineering, global studies, environmental studies. Questions abound at the interface of two disciplines because most of the established researchers in each field weren't trained in the other. You, on the other hand, are just starting out and can tailor your training to include both. Furthermore, you can tailor your dissertation committee to include both.

There are problems with interdisciplinary projects, however. It is hard work to master the terms, concepts, language (jargon), and methods in more than one field. Sometimes, your interdisciplinary idea falls between the missions of potential sponsors and you won't find funding for your project. Your finished work may be treated with suspicion since it falls in between two fields and the recognized authorities in the parent disciplines don't understand it or its importance. Finally, if your training and research are not well-grounded in both fields, you'll be marketable neither as a teacher nor a researcher. Still, for the hardworking and intrepid graduate student, there is no quicker way to establish yourself as the local authority than to pick one of many interdisciplinary questions for a dissertation topic. Just make sure that your teaching and coursework ground you in one or both of the parent disciplines.

Your dissertation topic should be attractive to funding agencies and faculty search committees. Your advisor should help you there and so will attendance at professional meetings. What are the topics discussed at the standing-room-only plenary sessions? Other clues come from fellowship program themes, requests for proposals, recent proceedings, current journal articles, and recent book awards. It will take as long to answer a trivial question as it does to answer one that is important so you might as well get it right from the beginning.

If possible, it would be great to shape your dissertation question in such a manner that either "yes or no" are interesting and publishable answers. For instance, if you set as your dissertation project the development of a vaccine for the common cold, you may be in deep trouble. Without the cure, you don't have a dissertation and you won't get a degree. If, however, you ask if three different methods of vaccine preparation vary in effectiveness against certain strains of rhinovirus, then any answer you get is interesting and potentially important.

Finally and most importantly, you must be absolutely fascinated by (and not just interested in) your dissertation topic. If you aren't, you'll lack the energy and enthusiasm to complete the arduous task.

Picking a Committee

This should fall into place once you pick a topic and an advisor. If you have an interdisciplinary topic, you'll need a second expert (your advisor being the first). If you need to learn methods and use equipment that your advisor doesn't have, pick a faculty member for your committee who does. Did you impress a faculty member in class? Ask him. To extend your network beyond campus, you might ask a faculty member in a school close by (especially if that school is better than yours). Check with the graduate school rules on outside committee members before you ask. Most importantly, ask your advisor about your choice before you invite someone on your committee. You definitely do not want to have someone who detests your advisor.

Preparing the Proposal

Ask your advisor what her expectations are for the proposal. Should you prepare a thorough review of the relevant literature? While this might take a lot of time to develop, it will force you to read, digest, and explain the known published world of your research topic. You will be able to detect significant differences in opinion and areas of general agreement. You will also learn who the players are. If there hasn't been a recent historical monograph on the subject, it might be publishable.

Whether you start with a long review of the literature or not, the purpose of the proposal is to define what you want to do and how you plan to do it. It will also tell your committee why the project is worth doing. By defining the purpose, demonstrating its importance and discussing the research plan, you have all of the ingredients necessary to write a research proposal to get some money to do the work (see the following page). All you need is a shortlist of likely sponsors who might be interested in funding the topic. This is especially important if your project is costly and your advisor doesn't have much research money. Your committee will be impressed that you thought of the financial considerations of your project and that you are making plans to deal with the money issue. Finally, a good proposal sets boundaries around your project. All research leads off in many directions and for long distances. You want to make it clear to the committee exactly what you plan to do in order to collect the degree and move on.

It would be beneficial if you have evidence that your idea might work or that you have at least mastered the methods necessary to conduct the research. Preliminary results come from a few experiments that you conducted or short field trips that you took. For mastery of things like methods, equipment, languages, computer programs, and development of survey instruments, you need to point out your preliminary results, formal coursework taken, and other experiences. For instance, if your project involves interviewing politicians in Chile about democracy, then you better show the committee that you know (1) Spanish, (2) how to construct a survey, and (3) how to statistically analyze the data.

If you can't point to experience, tell your committee how you'll gain that experience through activities like coursework, workshops, or visits to other laboratories.

If organizing your proposal leaves you at a loss, keep in mind the following points:

Specific Goals and Significance

Explain what you want to do and why it is important. This should take one to three full pages.

Background

This is the literature review. The length should vary according to your advisor's expectations.

Preliminary Results

As described in the above paragraph. This should take fewer than eight pages.

Research Plan

How do you plan to accomplish the project? The research plan should be the longest part of the proposal (unless you are required to do a very long literature review). What experiments will you conduct, who will you interview, what archives will you visit, how many steps are there to the end of data collection? You might want to discuss different approaches that you will take if the original path is blocked or mention the methods that you have already mastered. In other words, how will you collect the information that will form the basis of your dissertation? Once you define the methods, you need to tell the committee how you will treat the data. What statistical analysis is best? Which theoretical lens will you use to interpret the poetry?

Once you explain your plan, tell the committee the methods and other skills you've already learned. You might even include a timeline and discuss possible problems that might arise (and how you will correct them if they occur).

Remember, your goal in writing this proposal is to show your committee that you have an interesting idea and the capability and enthusiasm to develop it. In other words, like a research proposal, it's a sales document. Also remember that committee members outside your subdiscipline won't understand your jargon. If you must use jargon, define it.

Leave Time for Revisions

Once you've finished your first draft, give it to your advisor in plenty of time—at least a month in advance—so that she can help you revise the proposal. Give your committee time—a week or two—to assess the revised proposal. Expect them to criticize your project; that's why they're there. They might propose different ways to achieving your goal. They may demand a more precise purpose or plan. They may want more work. Don't get defensive. Write down their comments, discuss them with your advisor to determine their validity, revise your proposal (even if you pass), and meet with individual committee members to show how you addressed their concerns. You do not want to hear "That's ridiculous and I told you so three years ago" from a voting committee member at your dissertation defense.

Dissertation Funding

Well before the ink is dry on your proposal, you should think about funding. Travel, supplies, and equipment cost money, and so does time. If you want to devote full attention to the field-research phase or to the writing stage of the dissertation, you'll need a stipend that has no service requirement (like a fellowship or grant instead of a teaching assistantship). Most commonly in science and engineering departments, you need look no further for research funds than your advisor. In many universities, the department or the graduate school may also have research funding. Ask your advisor, your DGS, and someone in the college or graduate school for possible funding sources for your research.

You will need to start working towards getting the research/fellowship dollars about 18 months before you actually need it. The first six months, you'll be developing your idea, looking for sponsors, and writing your proposal. The next 9 to 12 months, you'll be waiting to learn if your proposal was accepted and, if so, waiting for the funding period to start.

Even if you can get local funding for your project, it's better to land a grant or fellowship from an agency outside of the university. This award adds a significant line to your curriculum vitae and tells faculty search committees that your research ideas are so good that outside organizations are willing to pay you to develop them.

Doing the Work

Every project presents different routes to completion, but here are rules common to all research:

Get started now.

The longer you delay after your dissertation proposal's approval, the cooler your ardor becomes. If you're waiting for funding, do the preparatory work, read books, and master methods. Don't use teaching as an excuse for not doing research. A professor is supposed to teach, do research, supervise students, and attend committee meetings. Get used to the pace now.

Do some work nearly every day.

It's amazing how a little bit everyday adds up to a big accomplishment. Furthermore, a research trail that has gone cold through neglect is a difficult scent to pick up again. Do not, however, become a frustrated workaholic. You'll need time off. Take it as a reward after one chunk of the project is completed or take it when you are banging your head against a problem for far too long. If your advisor is one of those hands-on types, tell her why you'll be missing and for how long (three to seven days ought to do it).

Expect failures.

Lots of them.

You're on the edge of discovery, and many of your approaches will fall short or give answers that you didn't expect. Learn when to try again (and again) and when to abandon that approach to begin another. Much of research is problem-solving your own problems. You will need to know the difference between a technical failure and a real, no-kidding negative result. This is especially difficult if you knew in your heart that the answer would be something else. Accept reality and determine what "no" really means to your project. Usually it changes the direction of the work—it doesn't stop it.

Stay open to unexpected findings.

In 1928, Alexander Flemming was spreading petri plates with bacteria in preparation for an experiment. He let them sit for a couple of days to allow the bacterial "lawn" to grow, but when he returned to run the experiment, he discovered that his plates had become contaminated with fungus colonies. Most of us would have thrown the plates away and started again. Flemming, however, observed a clear ring around the fungus, suggesting it was secreting *something* that killed the bacteria surrounding the colony. If Fleming had done what most of us would have done, he wouldn't have discovered penicillin. Such discoveries require an open and prepared mind.

If your data doesn't seem to be conforming to your hypothesis and it keeps happening the same unexpected way, it isn't time to change your methodology. It's time to reevaluate your hypothesis. Since most graduate students base their research projects on conventional wisdom, if you come up with something different, you've come up with something big.

Know when you're done.

With research, you'll quickly discover that when you answer one question, three more pop up. Remember the boundaries you set in your dissertation proposal and find a natural but definite end to your *dissertation* research. You'll have plenty of time to pursue those other questions when you land a research position.

Presentations and Publications

What's the point of doing all of that dissertation work without telling someone about it? Sure, your advisor and your committee will know what you did, but there is a much wider audience out there—and some of them are hiring! Do not wait until delivering your dissertation to the graduate school to tout your results. Start presenting your preliminary data or small pieces of the finished product as it gets done. Many disciplines hold regional meetings that encourage graduate student participation. These meetings are close by, small, relatively inexpensive, and low-key. You'll get to know a good number of faculty members and students in an informal environment. Once you become comfortable at regional meetings, crack the annual national meetings. In order to be heard there, you may have to get your poster approved or be invited to speak in a session. It can get lonely at these big meetings, so keep an eye out for the folks you met at the regional meetings. Remember, these presentations become lines in your curriculum vitae and evidence that you are a productive researcher.

Preparing Your Poster

The most important thing to remember when you are making a poster is that you will have to transport it to the meeting. You can do your tables, figures, and text on standard paper and dry-mount them on mounting board that has been cut to fit in your bag. Or you may have a printing capability on campus to produce a paper poster that can be rolled up and transported in a tube. Other important aspects of a successful poster session:

- Organize the poster into three columns. Readers will scan from left to right and top to bottom (just like reading a newspaper).

- Keep the text short and crisp. Use a large font so that readers can read from two or three feet away. Remember, you'll be standing by your poster to guide the visitors through; you don't need to write *everything* down, although you should accentuate the purpose of the study and the results. De-accentuate your methods. Don't provide much (or any) background or discussion of the results.

- Keep copies of an abstract of your work nearby to hand visitors. Make sure your name, department, and school are on the abstract.

- Have a plan to verbally describe your work (while pointing to the poster) in less than four minutes if someone asks you what the poster is all about. Practice the talk with peers and your advisor before you go to the meeting.

Preparing a 10- to 20-Minute Talk

A 10-minute talk is about three typewritten pages of text and no more than ten 35mm slides or overheads (slides, for the most part, should depict your data in tables and figures). You might start with a purpose statement and end with a slide summarizing your conclusions. If you're savvy with presentation software like PowerPoint or AppleWorks, use it, but don't let the bells and whistles overshadow your data and results, and to be on the safe side— PowerPoint has difficulty crossing hardware platforms—bring your presentation on your own laptop and your own LCD projector connector cables. Get to the room well before the session begins to ensure everything works—and always bring hard-copy overheads as a low-tech backup.

One last bit of advice: Practice, practice, practice. First by yourself, then again in front of your lab partners, advisor, and anybody else you can sweet-talk into watching. Have your practice audience ask questions and comment after your presentation, make sure your presentation falls within the acceptable time limit, and give yourself enough time to make necessary changes. This advice also goes for presentations before your dissertation committee, your dissertation defense—and especially job talks.

Preparing an Article

For the most part, posters and presentations aren't published information; therefore, you can use preliminary data and speculate a bit more than you might in a published work (just don't give your audience an obvious opportunity to embarrass you). But an article published in a referred journal is your contribution to the collective knowledge base. People will read it, reference it, and use it to support their own ideas. Your reputation rests on these written words. Your introduction can be your interpretation and your conclusion can postulate upon the future, but your data *must* be based on sound methodology and your results must flow directly from your data.

To get published, form is almost as important as content. Since form is discipline-specific, ask your advisor for help. Read recent issues of journals that may potentially publish your work. Follow their submission instructions exactly and make sure that your manuscript follows the same format as the journal's previously published articles. Pass the manuscript by your advisor and someone else before submitting it.

It'll take weeks to months before hearing back from the journal, so get on with your research. Eventually, your work will return "accepted" (rare), "provisionally accepted pending revision" (very often), or "declined" (all too often). Read the journal's reviews. If your work was rejected or not outright accepted, you might immediately conclude that the reviewers don't know how to read. Don't take a rejection personally. The journal's reviewers probably don't even know who you are; they're not motivated to humiliate you. If your article is rejected, show your advisor the reviews and ask if the work is (a) correctable and (b) publishable in another journal. Given the green light, get busy fixing it. This might be difficult if you've moved to your next stage of research, but make the time. Subsequent publications depend upon a sound initial publication.

It's always better to present and publish as you go, instead of waiting until after your dissertation; it's extraordinarily difficult to return to a project after leaving your host institution. Not only will you give up access to the necessary resources after leaving, it's better to have some of your work "in press" instead of "in prep" once you hit the job market. Publishing research can be intimidating, but don't let that stop you. Job search committees in and out of academe look for research productivity, and an article or two on your CV addresses that question. Besides, don't you want to show off your hard work?

Writing the Dissertation

If you did the literature review for the dissertation proposal and have been presenting and publishing your work along the way, it'll be easier to write your dissertation than having to start from scratch. With your advisor and committee, discuss how to construct your dissertation—but once you know how to attack the project, get started. Even if you have to teach all day, reserve time every night for writing. Follow the writing tips in Appendix A to get you started and keep you going.

Make no mistake—writing the dissertation is an important task, and not only because it's your ticket out of graduate school. Your dissertation greatly informs your committee's opinions of your research potential, and they'll express these opinions in letters of recommendation. The research will appear in your journal articles, monographs, or even as a full-length book. The subject matter in your dissertation will deeply interest search committees in academe, and the techniques you used will be of deep importance to people hiring in the private sector.

Nevertheless, don't obsess over your dissertation. It's not the culmination of your career in research; it's only the beginning. You can't tie up every loose end in your research, because research does not operate that way. Answers to questions only propagate more questions. You'll never read everything on your research subject, nor will you be able to capture every nuance to a problem. Finally, your dissertation doesn't guarantee you a dream job. Other elements on your resume and curriculum vitae are important for starting a career, and you must attend to them as well.

Once you're reasonably sure you've finished a chapter, bring it to your advisor for her comments. Come back at weekly intervals to see how her review is going. While you're waiting, get on with another chapter. Once your advisor is ready, sit down and discuss her comments. Don't become defensive or snippy. Work with her advice. If she doesn't understand what you wrote in paragraph three, it's unlikely anyone else will either. If she criticizes your style, comply with her suggestions. Professional writing is exact, both in grammar and vocabulary. Being stylistically adventurous won't go over well with your committee.

Defending the Dissertation

After all the work, writing, revisions, and final okay from your advisor, you're set to defend your dissertation. Give copies to every member of your committee. Notify the department that you're ready to defend, and the department will notify the graduate school and deal with other bureaucratic details. Someone will have to coordinate the meeting site and time; someone will have to make the public announcement. Find out if that someone is you or your advisor, and stay on top of these details. Your dissertation defense usually starts with your 20- to 55-minute talk on the dissertation, stressing the goal of the project, its importance, and what you did to achieve your goal. Sometimes the talk is public and many people in the department show up. Expect questions. This exercise is great practice for future job talks.

After your talk, the committee will excuse the audience and begin to question you in earnest. This will not be like your oral examinations, because the questions will deal with your dissertation and not the world of your subdiscipline. The defense will be easier too, because you should know more about the subject of your dissertation than anyone else in the room, including your advisor. Rarely does one fail their dissertation defense. Even more rare is the committee member who, during the defense, discovers a fatal flaw in the dissertation. If you've been showing your work to the members over time and provided the final copy in plenty of time for them to read and comment (be sure to ask before the meeting), you shouldn't be blindsided. If a committee member appears to come up with a damning counter-argument, tell her she's raised an interesting point—and move on. Once the pressure's off, sit down with your advisor to determine the validity of the committee member's argument. If you can resolve it by experimentation, run the experiments and include them in your revised dissertation. If her comment amounts to a mere difference of opinion, you may want to add it to your dissertation (along with reasons why you think it's bogus).

Plan on your dissertation not leaving the defense unscathed. You may have to run some extra experiments, maybe change the graphics, or work on the text. Just get it done and don't worry about missing a graduation deadline. Generally, these come about three times a year; you're bound to be done by one of them. In other words, don't send out invitations and rent a gown until your dissertation clears graduate school and your name appears on the commencement list.

RESEARCH ETHICS

Data Collection and Analysis

Data for social scientists, engineers, and experimental scientists are the building blocks to a dissertation. Other hands in other laboratories must be able to reproduce this data for it to be valid.

Don't fake data.

This is a stupid, desperate act that's bound to fail. Because others will repeat your work, they'll discover your false results sooner or later.

Once there was a young postdoctoral fellow working at a major research institute with a famous clinical immunologist. One day, the postdoc claimed that, after one experiment, he could (after some treatment) transplant the skin from a black mouse to a white mouse, even though the two mouse strains had mismatched tissue antigens. His boss pressured him to repeat the experiment, but the transplants were rejected. Rather than admitting the first experiment was a fluke, the postdoc took to using a black magic marker to color patches on white mice in order to fake a successful transplant. Needless to say, he eventually got caught, damaging the research careers of both the postdoc and the scientist.

Several morals to this story: Don't get excited about the findings of a single experiment. Do it again and again to see if the results are repeatable before telling folks of your finding. Don't succumb to pressure to produce data that you cannot get legitimately. Of course, in biology and the social sciences, experimental conditions are more complex and less controlled than in physical science or engineering. If you run a critical test that works two or three times consistently, wait a week, use new reagents and animals, and run the test again.

Don't fudge data.

Research is often messy, especially when you work with living organisms. You might like the same exact result every time, but that's unlikely to happen because of hidden variables. Try to eliminate all known variables, get a large sample size, and then use statistics to determine if there are true differences between your control and experimental groups. But for statistics to tell the truth, you cannot be throwing out data that doesn't conform to what you expected.

Don't steal others' ideas or data.

Rest assured that everyone active in your subdiscipline will read your work and will know when you are using their material without referencing them. Give your fellow researchers credit where credit is due, but don't credit them for more than that. For instance, someone may have guessed that something was going on in the discussion section of a journal article. But if you run the experiments that prove his hypothesis, you get credit for the finding. (Just remember to mention the other researcher in your introduction for posing the idea).

Writing

Any high-school student knows it's unethical to copy published or unpublished work without attribution. When you're writing your dissertation, it's actually advantageous to reference many works in your publications—this demonstrates your exhaustive literature review. Furthermore, the reviewers of your manuscript will probably be looking for references to their previously published work, and woe unto you if you haven't considered what they had to say. Two other rules:

Don't hide opposing points of view.

If others have already disagreed with your findings in advance (i.e., they published a counter-proof), don't run from the controversy. Maybe you're both correct under certain circumstances. Maybe your methodology is more sensitive. If the difference in your findings is clear but inexplicable, then say that your data does not support their findings or theories.

Don't embellish the truth.

You may be tempted in your manuscript, grant application, or curriculum vitae to say "in press" instead of "in preparation" or "under consideration." You might be tempted to adjust a finding or two to provide overwhelming support to your hypothesis. Don't do it. Research is always presented on the honor system: If you're found to be flakey, sloppy, or dishonest, find yourself another career.

Money

While tampering with data or stealing other people's ideas may destroy your career, fooling around with research funding may send you to jail. Live by two major rules:

Don't double dip.

You can apply to many agencies to get your research idea funded; you may even receive awards for your effort. You may *not*, however, collect the money twice to do the same project. For example, you apply for a Fulbright and a university travel grant to do field research in Germany for a year. You may not claim the transportation costs for the trip twice. What if the funding doesn't cover the cost of the entire project? This isn't a case of double-dipping, so long as you've made all the sponsors aware of how you're sorting the expenses. If you were to receive both a university dissertation year fellowship and an NSF dissertation improvement grant, for example, tell the university and NSF you've received both awards and would like to use the fellowship stipend for living expenses and the NSF grant to travel to buy a database and attend a workshop on its use.

Don't spend research money on non-research items.

If you're not using the expense item directly for the project for which you received funding, don't charge it to your supply, equipment, and travel budget. A professional journal subscription in your field is okay; a subscription to *Travel & Leisure* probably isn't. Buying an airline ticket to a professional meeting in your field is okay. Putting your spouse's ticket on your travel budget isn't. There are gray areas. If a single or a double room in the convention hotel costs the same, then your spouse can stay for free. (If they aren't the same, you can still claim the cost of a single.) It boils down to common sense and bending over backwards to avoid the appearances of wrongdoing.

DEALING WITH ACADEMIC BUREAUCRACY

In academic circles, ignorance of the law offers no excuse: You are solely responsible for knowing the policies and rules that you must live by. And that's only fair, since you'll be the one most affected by breaking the rules.

The graduate bulletin and your departmental guide are your rule books. Read them and sort the sections you'll need in chronological order. When is the qualifier exam? When must you pick your graduate advisor? When are oral examinations and dissertation proposals due? What do you have to do to maintain funding? When do you ask for teaching assignments? When you do you have to plan for the summer? What does "satisfactory academic progress" mean? What are the various deadlines for graduation? Compose a timetable and then put the bulletin and guide away in a safe place. Rules may change while you are a student, but you have a case for being grandfathered in if the old rule serves you better.

Don't expect to be prompted by your advisor. He may not even know much about the constantly shifting departmental and graduate school deadlines and policies. The DGS may be very busy and not prone to holding your hand at every crossing. The interpreter and facilitator of academic policy is most often the departmental secretary. If you mistakenly treat her like an inferior, you will lose a vast source of institutional history and a helpful ally. Respect breeds respect, so treat the secretary as a VIP. If, however, you find her *consistently and intolerably* incompetent or imperious, then make the director of graduate studies your new, best bureaucratic friend. Don't start the relationship with the DGS, however, by trashing the secretary, or you run the risk of being labeled a high-maintenance whiner. If the DGS tells you to take up the matter with the secretary, tell him or her (in an unemotional manner) that you have tried that already without success.

WHEN THINGS GO WRONG

Peer Relationships

By the time you reach graduate school, you'll have had over 20 years' worth making and breaking relationships. This book won't change your personality. However, now that you are entering the new realm of graduate training in a new place and few acquaintances, it might be a good time to evaluate and reinvent yourself. Draw up a list of what is good and what is bad about you (a spouse or your immediate family will be all too happy to help you with that). Concentrate on eliminating the negative and accentuating the positive. After a year and no notable relapses to the old you, you can consider yourself a new person. But remember, your goal is not to make everyone your close personal friend. It is to develop cordial, mutually respectful professional relationships. Some of these professional relationships will naturally turn to personal bonds.

Family Relationships

Please remember that while you're trying to cope with this whole new environment of graduate school, your family is trying to cope with the changes in you. Your hours at work will change. Your income will change. Your interests and friends will change. You will change. You may not even notice the evolution, but the family that you live with will. You'll use them at the beginning as a stable life preserver in this sea of change. Once you get comfortable in the new environment, you must become that life preserver for your spouse and kids so that they don't feel obsolete and left behind. You will have to pull your head out of your books on a regular basis to do this.

Most universities have a counseling center associated with the student health facility. Make use of it if family friction doesn't resolve itself with attention.

Student-Advisor Relationship Problems

What happens if your advisor takes another job? First question: Is she going to a better place? If yes, find out if she'll bring you along. If she will, determine how much time this will set you back. Will you have to take courses or retake qualifier or comprehensive exams? How long will it take to get the lab running? What resources (e.g., library, computer) might not be available in the new place?

If your advisor's job is a step down or if you believe your graduation will be significantly delayed, you have options. If you're beginning your studies, you can switch to another advisor who is already in the department. Don't wait around for a replacement for your old boss unless he's already been hired. Academic hiring is notoriously slow and you do not want to wait around, doing nothing. If you're ABD (All But Dissertation), you may still receive your degree from your current institution (and with the advisor you've been working for) with or without relocating. You may have to pick up an on-campus co-advisor. If your research is lab-bound and you aren't done with experiments, it might be better to move.

What happens if your advisor dies? You'll have to go somewhere else if she was the only faculty member working in your subdiscipline. See if you've finished enough work to earn a master's degree. If other faculty members in your subdiscipline can guide you through the dissertation and onto a job, then stay. Otherwise, find another advisor somewhere else.

What if you want to fire your advisor? In almost all student-advisor relations, you'll have spats that, if left alone, will just blow over. If, however, you have the same spat twice, this means trouble and you need to deal with it. Just remember that this is an unbalanced power relationship and you have the lower wattage. In many cases, it's like the old-fashioned parent-child relationship (and make no mistake—you're the kid). Also remember that a dispassionate discussion of the problem is much more productive than a screaming match. Finally remember that your apprenticeship is officially over as soon as you graduate (it's not like your advisor is family) and that you can endure a lot for a short time.

After a spat, allow some time—but not too long—for tempers to cool. Try to figure out what you're doing or not doing that bugs your advisor. Is her complaint justified? If so, figure out how to fix it. If not, determine how to present your case in a non-confrontational manner. Actually, any behavior or circumstance is rarely entirely justified or unjustified. Look at both sides and see if you can come up with a plan where both of you have a valid point. Then sit down in private with your advisor to resolve the dispute, and as soon as the meeting is over, implement the plan.

Let's take an all-too-common example from students in experimental science and engineering. Your advisor is getting more and more agitated because you haven't presented convincing data from a critical set of experiments. It's not like you haven't been trying. You're having a difficult time getting the experimental procedure to work. The blow-up occurs on Monday after a weekend when the advisor was working in the lab and you weren't.

First, realize that it isn't the missed time; it's the lack of results that really bugs your advisor. If you don't have the results, there'd better be a demonstrable increase in the time you spend trying to get the results, or your motivation to be a scientist will be called into question. Second, your advisor may not be aware of the amount of time that you have spent on failed experiments. Or maybe it's the type of experiment that takes a long time (i.e., weeks) from start to finish. Instead of trying to think of a compelling excuse for not being in the lab over the weekend, tell your advisor your problems with the procedure. Ask her or someone even more familiar with the technique to conduct the experiment. Watch and take notice when she does something different from what you were doing. If it's a long procedure, remind your advisor of that fact and ask if there is a more efficient way to conduct the experiment or if you could be doing other experiments while you're awaiting the results. Then demonstrate your renewed commitment by spending more time in the lab (especially at times when your advisor is around).

The same confrontation can be applied to the humanities and non-experimental social sciences. Just exchange the word "library" for "laboratory" and "chapters of the dissertation" for "data."

But maybe it really isn't your fault. Relationships, even those with uneven power distribution, are give and take, and you've reached the end of giving (in) and taking (abuse). Just maybe your advisor really is a hypercritical, anal, compulsive, sadistic, control-freak workaholic or worse. As a reality check, ask your advisor's other apprentices if they feel the same way. Talk to your director of graduate studies (if you trust him or her) or someone outside the department. Universities usually have an ombudsperson assigned as a listening post and advisor. This person may be associated with the college, graduate school, or student affairs. Finally, talk to a professional psychologist. Most universities have a psych service associated with the student health center. Present your complaint in an objective, unemotional way, and take the advice.

What are the ramifications of firing your advisor? First, you'll have to find another advisor; if you're trying to stay in the same institution, this'll be difficult.

Professors, in general, don't like getting caught between warring parties. Besides, your ex-advisor is likely to be bad-mouthing you among her colleagues. If you find a faculty member who will take you in, you will still lose precious time remodeling your research to fit the interests of the new advisor. Finally, you've managed to generate an enemy in your profession even before you are a full member.

Before making the drastic decision to fire your advisor, ask yourself if your advisor's behavior is illegal or just extremely aggravating. Harassment—be it based on sexual advances, race, ethnicity, age, or sexual orientation—is against the law. Nasty comments concerning work ethic, efficiency, motivation, writing ability, oral communication, or even basic competency are not. If your advisor's behavior is illegal, get evidence and start complaining up the ladder (from the director of graduate studies to the chair to the college dean to the graduate dean to the provost to the president to your lawyer) until something happens. Give everyone on the ladder a week or two to act before going to the next step.

If your advisor's behavior is illegal or driving you crazy, you should quit. One thing you can do, after discussing the problem with the director of graduate studies or university representative, is to request a leave of absence for a year. Get out of town immediately. Spend a week or two relaxing and planning for the immediate future. Rehashing the past is wasting time. Then tie up any bureaucratic loose ends: withdraw from courses, withdraw from the program, say good bye to the DGS, send a brief note (no venting, no finger-pointing) to your advisor, pack up and get out of town. If, over the course of the year, you still want to pursue a graduate degree, consider a program in different university.

If the relationship is "merely" extreme, chronic aggravation and you have no easily accessible substitute advisor, hunker down and work like hell to graduate as quickly as possible. Political prisoners and POWs had it much worse and survived to tell their tales. Read a couple of their stories if it makes you feel better. Try to fend off the negativity by changing your behavior (at least) around your advisor and avoiding unnecessary contact (i.e., attend mandatory lab meetings but work different hours in the lab).

What if your advisor fires you? First, leave the premises without firing off any nasty comments. Second, determine if this was a hasty, emotional outburst that will cool quickly or whether this outcome had been simmering for quite some time.

After 24 hours, have the DGS determine if this is fixable or not. If not, determine what you might need to do to salvage a master's degree and apply to graduate school elsewhere. A poor second choice is to stay in the same department with a different advisor.

Research Problems

All researchers eventually hit a brick wall in their research. Part of the maturation process is to know (as poker players are fond of saying) "when to hold them and when to fold them." If you aren't getting data, try a different approach. If you are getting data but it contravenes your original hypothesis, proceed with a new hypothesis. As a last resort, abandon the project for another. This isn't a failure on your part. It means that you and the world aren't ready with the ideas or equipment . . . yet. If you quit at the beginning of a project, you can move on without losing a huge time investment. On the other hand, if you put a considerable amount of work into the project, consider backing up to the point where you were getting good results. Then think of a different question or hypothesis to pursue. Research is not necessarily a linear process.

For those of you who find these roadblocks pathologically frustrating, this is a good time to determine exactly why you thought that research was an attractive career choice. No one has fun being stymied, but if it negatively consumes all aspects of your life, then head to the career and placement center and use the other skills that you developed in college for a more self-rewarding professional life.

Bureaucratic Problems

All organizations have a chain of command, and problems are more easily solved with fewer ramifications if you work up the chain. For problems in academe, the chain of command goes something like this: It all begins at the nitty-gritty level with your advisor, then goes to the director of graduate studies, then the chairperson of the department, then to the academic dean, then to the graduate school, then to the provost, and finally to the chancellor/president. If your problem is your advisor, reread the previous section on student-advisor relations. If your problem has to do with policies and rules, start with your departmental secretary. Ask him if other students have had the same problem and if and how they successfully got their way. Armed with this information, go to your advisor and enlist her aid. Generally, faculty members carry more weight (and have more friends in the bureaucracy) than graduate students, and if they carry the ball, there's a better chance you'll be successful. If your advisor isn't around, go up the chain to the DGS.

Be tenacious, but be polite. Be persistent, but don't be a pain in the butt. If you have a good case, things may go your way. Just make sure your case is solid and your attack on policy is both just and important. If you chronically stay in some bureaucrat's face, you'll achieve a bad reputation, which will undermine your cause (and any future causes).

CHAPTER V

Preparing for the Job Market

If you didn't skip over Chapter III's section on self-assessment, then you'll have been preparing for three years to enter the job market. First, an overview of the types of jobs PhDs are trained to take.

ACADEMIC JOBS: TENURE-TRACK FACULTY

Most of you entered graduate school because a teacher or teachers turned you onto the profession. Being a professor is prestigious and stimulating; teaching and research are noble pursuits. But you may not have appreciated academe's diverse niches...

Research Universities

Because you're earning a PhD, you are by definition in one of about 300 public or private research universities. The university has undergraduate students, professional students (in law, business, medicine, education, or agriculture, for example), graduate students doing research for masters and doctoral degrees, and faculty who need to divide their attention among teaching, research, and service. Of course, you cannot be expected to devote 24 hours a day to each of these functions (although, as an assistant professor, it may feel that way).

Research-extensive universities (as defined by the Carnegie Foundation; CarnegieFoundation.org/classification/index.html), of course, accentuate research. If you're in experimental science or engineering, you will be expected to receive and maintain research support from outside—generally federal—sources. Humanities and fine arts do not require funding, but you may need fellowship support anyway in order to do your research and publication. Social sciences and mathematics are somewhere in between with regard to grant support.

The higher you go up the "academic quality" ladder (see the NRC survey, Maher, B. *Research Doctorate Programs in the United States*, National Academy Press, 1995), the more the "quality" (i.e., the revolutionary potential) of your research matters. You may say—and rightfully so—that it is extraordinarily difficult to demonstrate your research potential in the measly six years before tenure, but this is the expectation and this is why few assistant professors earn tenure at the upper-crust institutions. At the high end of the spectrum, teaching must be acceptable (no chronic complaints from the undergraduates who took your course) and committee assignments few (full professors don't really expect to hear from and rarely listen to assistant professors on committees anyway.)

The research productivity-to-quality and teaching excellence-to-quantity ratios tend to tip as you go down the list of research universities in the NRC survey. A good way to gauge your long-term prospects is to ask the dean and the department chair at your job interview what percentage of assistant professors make tenure and what you have to do to earn it. Should you turn down a job at Harvard or Stanford just because the tenure rate is low? No. Just go into the job with your eyes open. This exalted platform will help you make valuable professional contacts, get grants, and present your research among significant players. If you sense that you are not matching up to the senior faculty's expectations, take your grant money, hefty publication list, course curricula, and contacts to an institution that is impressed with your credentials. If you don't like the odds at a prestigious university or you don't like to move, then go down the list of schools ranked in academic quality. If you can get a job at Princeton, you'll be able to get a job elsewhere.

What you need in your CV

Evidence of research potential is first and foremost. Therefore, presentations of your work at national meetings are important for all fields. Your cover letter must stress how your research interests match those of the teaching and research requirements in the job announcement. Your letters of recommendation must address the quality of your dissertation work and your research potential. Multi-year graduate fellowships (NSF or Javits), field research grants (Fulbright, NSF dissertation improvement grants) and dissertation-year fellowships (Newcombe, Spencer, SSRC) demonstrate the marketability of your ideas. For scientists, engineers, and social scientists, one or two first-author publications in reviewed journals are important demonstrations of your research productivity. Never mind if your advisor's name also appears as a coauthor (even though you might have done almost all of the work). Remember that you were using your advisor's money and space to do the work and his name may have helped get the manuscript accepted. It may be a bit much to ask for a book or even a publisher's contract on the CV of a fresh PhD in the humanities, but it helps to have a dissertation topic that is obviously attractive to publishers. Perhaps part of your dissertation can become a monograph or a chapter in someone else's book. Perhaps you can publish articles in refereed journals. For those of you who graduate within six years, this publication list is a lot to assemble in such a short time. That is why the postdoctoral fellow position was invented for many fields (see page 175).

As far as teaching goes, in science and engineering, it helps that you assisted in laboratories or gave guest lectures in your subdiscipline. In math, social science, and humanities, it would be good if you had experience as an instructor in the lower-level courses in your discipline. A large amount of varied experiences in teaching isn't necessary to land an interview. Departmental service is nice but inconsequential. Lots of service and teaching without a corresponding amount of publications is detrimental.

Finally, it helps if someone on your dissertation committee likes your work and knows a well-regarded faculty member at the hiring institution. If you aren't in a department with National Academy members wandering the halls, then find a star in another school to serve as the outside member of your dissertation committee. Of course, it's even better if *you* have met faculty members in the hiring department (which is why it's so important to present your data at national meetings).

Where to look

Your advisor and other faculty members who know your work may have heard about prospective jobs. So ask around. The second-most obvious places to look are the professional societies to which you belong. Many of these organizations post jobs in their magazines and web sites and sponsor job interviews at their national meeting. Next, more general publications in your field may list openings. Finally, and especially if you are anchored to a particular site, call the department and ask or look for job postings on the department's (or the university's human resources) web site.

Professional Schools

Occasionally, economists and psychologists find jobs in business schools, and sometimes PhDs from academic fields will find jobs in a law school. More commonly, biologists, biochemists, bioengineers, psychologists, and biophysicists find work in the basic science departments of medical, allied health, veterinary, dental or nursing schools. Many of these institutions are big research engines, yet their mission is to train practitioners and not researchers. Furthermore, professional school training rarely involves courses in pedagogy or experience in front of the classroom. For these reasons, doctorates are attractive.

This doesn't mean that the practitioners love and trust you, however. Many of your fellow faculty peers and most of the administration will hold a professional degree. They know how hard it was to get into the professional school and how hard it was to succeed. They understand the importance of practical training and technology. They are less interested in abstract theories or basic science. And the students who you will be teaching, by and large, are more interested in learning what will be tested on the boards rather than testing the unknown. For this tough environment, it might be good to come armed with a combined degree, such as an MD/PhD or a JD/PhD. Sometimes getting your PhD in a professional school environment is enough.

What you need in your CV

You'll need everything that is listed above for research universities. It also helps if you have a combined degree or at least got your PhD from a professional school. Taking your postdoctoral years in a professional school is another good way to build credibility and a network.

Where to look

Your advisor, other faculty, and professional publications will be your best shot. If the faculty has little experience with professional schools, they probably won't have contacts, which is why a postdoc in the environment is so important. Not only do you develop a network within the system, you will discover job opportunities before they ever get out in the public.

Master's-Focused Institutions

Most big public universities have branch campuses that serve their communities largely with undergraduate courses (often at night), certificate programs, and advanced professional programs. Many private and public colleges have also gotten into research master's programs. Obviously, this is a mixed bag of schools with varied missions. In order to be competitive in the hiring process, you must determine what the department's expectations are for you. If you are expected to conduct research with undergraduates and master's students, then how are the laboratories equipped? Are you expected to get your own research dollars? If you get a grant, will you get a break in your teaching-load? How many publications are expected six years down the road to tenure? Most of these campuses are undergraduate-classroom focused, and they will expect a lot of good teaching, inexpensive research experiences for graduate and undergraduate students, and service to the department.

What you need in your CV

In order to get your foot in this door, it helps to have varied teaching experiences (several different courses at different levels) and a dissertation topic that relates to the job announcement. (If the department wants someone in Twentieth Century History, your dissertation in physical anthropology won't cut it.) It also helps if your research is relatively inexpensive to run, lends itself to undergraduate experience and master's thesis work, and doesn't require long field-research trips off campus.

Where to look

At this level of college, your dissertation committee members' network may be running a little thin. Ask anyway. Perhaps one is collaborating with a professor at the master's-focused school or maybe a doctoral student at your school works there now. If your dissertation committee is of little help, it is attendant upon you to develop your own network. For instance, some enlightened schools have "Preparing for Future Faculty" (PFF) programs where research university graduate students do an internship in a master's-focused institution. If a PFF program does not exist, then look around for possible adjunct positions at these schools. If you do a good job and the faculty like you, you'll have your foot in the door for the next available position. Of course, these schools also advertise permanent and temporary appointments in professional journals (especially *The Chronicle of Higher Education*) and their websites. If you know where you want to live, call the local schools or check out their web site job postings.

Four-Year Colleges

Again, there is a wide range of missions among these 1,700 schools. They may specialize in everything from engineering to fine arts. Most of these schools, however, are private and accentuate a liberal arts education. Here, the sole focus is on undergraduate education. Most don't neglect research, especially if it involves undergraduates and is relatively inexpensive. Research grants are rare but collegiality—that is, fitting in and getting along—is important. The quality of your research, teaching credentials, and baccalaureate pedigree become more important the higher up on the list of top national liberal arts colleges.

What you need in your CV

Top national liberal arts colleges can be as snooty as the top private research universities. Pedigree is important. How do you find out if any school seems to be obsessed with where you got your undergraduate and graduate degrees? Look at the faculty listing in the undergraduate bulletin or departmental web site. If the faculty all came from the Ivy League and you received your entire education in Nebraska, it's going to be a tough sell. Assuming that your pedigree matches or exceeds that of the search committee members, they'll be looking for experience in developing and teaching varied and interesting courses. These departments are small, and you will be expected to teach a range of courses. A big plus in your CV will be evidence that you have developed some innovative and obviously interesting courses. In the top colleges, you will be expected to be research-productive as well. If you need a lot of money to do your research, you are looking in the wrong place for a job.

Where to look

The same advice provided for those interested in master's-focused universities applies here. Maybe your advisor has a connection; maybe an alumnus from your school teaches there now. Your own network, developed as a temporary instructor in the four year college environment may be stronger. Do not forget your undergraduate contacts if you graduated from a liberal arts college. Perhaps your alma mater is searching for a faculty member, or maybe one of your old teachers knows of another college that is looking to hire.

Community/Junior Colleges

The mission of this educational system is much like branch campuses of major state universities: serve the community. The difference is that the 2,000 junior colleges award associate degrees while most branch university campuses award both associate and baccalaureate degrees. The student body is an eclectic mix of young and old students; some interested in professional training (like dental hygiene) and some interested in ultimately earning the baccalaureate. The students range from being highly motivated individuals to those who only attend because their parents made them. Most of the students enroll at the junior college because they are restricted to the area. Your teaching load here will be very high (five sections a semester); research expectations, very low.

What you need in your CV

Because of the nature of the school, you will be teaching a narrow selection of 100- and 200-level survey courses. Therefore, you should have experience with teaching the introductory courses in your discipline. Past experience in the field (like a job in the private sector, a K–12 teacher, or junior college instructor) is a big help. An obvious commitment to the community also sends the right message. The search committee is looking for someone who understands and appreciates the community college system—which is very different from that of a research university—and who isn't going to leave after a year of chronic whining about the junior college environment.

Where to look

Community colleges are more likely to advertise in *The Community College Times* and broad professional publications such as *The Chronicle of Higher Education*; the American Association of Community Colleges (AACC.nche.edu) has web listings. Community colleges are more likely than universities to post jobs in the local newspaper through the school's human resources department or in general web search engines, some of which are listed on page 94.

In Summary...

All academic search committees are looking for the following:

*   Someone whose teaching and research experience match the department's needs as expressed in the job announcement.

*   Someone who will fit into the departmental culture.

*   Someone who can relate to the students.

*   Someone who won't quit after a year or two for a "better" job.

ACADEMIC JOBS: TEMPORARY

In many fields, it may be difficult or impossible to walk immediately from commencement line to a tenure-track job. For jobs at top national research universities, you may need a postdoc just to have the credentials to be competitive. A UC—Berkeley study indicated that both their English literature and biochemistry graduates averaged three years in temporary positions before landing a permanent academic job. The difference between these two disparate groups is that English Lit PhDs survived on annual teaching contracts while biochemists got postdoctoral appointments in research.

However, temporary teaching and research appointments aren't restricted to one discipline or another. You should first determine where you want to get your first "permanent" job and choose a postdoctoral appointment that will help you get there. If you want to get a position in academe, government, or the private sector that accentuates research, then a postdoctoral fellowship is what you need (this goes to humanities doctorates and social scientists as well). If you are primarily interested in teaching, then temporary academic teaching positions will help you get that job (engineers and scientists, take note).

Postdoctoral Research Appointments

Most of these temporary jobs are in experimental science, but postdoctoral research opportunities exist in engineering, the social sciences, and the humanities. In experimental basic science, the postdoc is essential for a job in a research setting. For others, it's a second chance on the merry-go-round to grab for the brass ring. In other words, if you didn't get that dream job in a top national research university upon graduation, here is an opportunity to buff up your CV in order to be more competitive the next time you apply.

If your academic pedigree is ordinary, this is a good chance to improve your standing by getting a postdoc in a top research university. If you want a job in a professional school, here is an opportunity to gain experience and contacts. If you want to obtain credentials in a cross-disciplinary field, this is the way to get it. Simply choose a postdoc in a place that you want to be.

Most of the postdoctoral research appointments are in academic settings (like research universities and medical and veterinary schools), but industry and federal labs have also gotten into the game to a limited degree. So if you want a government or private sector job, look there for a postdoc if you can't find a permanent job.

In academe, the faculty sponsor usually supports the postdoc on research grants, but try to get your own funding. You will have more freedom of action with your own fellowship salary, you will be more attractive to potential faculty sponsors if they don't have to pay your upkeep, and the award will look very good to a faculty search committee when you hit the job market. The fellowships may be local (awarded by the sponsoring university) or national. The local offerings may not be advertised. Finding a national postdoctoral fellowship is discussed below.

What can you gain from a postdoctoral appointment? The answer is time. Time to present and publish your dissertation research. Time to begin new research projects. Time to learn new techniques and concepts in your field or in a closely related discipline. Time to develop an extended network of peers and senior faculty who can write letters of recommendation. A postdoc also provides an opportunity to have an inside shot at any jobs that come available at your sponsoring institution.

What does a potential faculty sponsor expect from an applicant? Faculty on the hunt for a postdoc are looking for an experienced researcher/scholar who will help the faculty member maintain her research program. If the sponsor is paying your salary, you will be expected to participate in a particular research project. Therefore, you will need to have in your CV some evidence of research productivity and experience in the methods needed for the project. If you have your own fellowship, you will be given a little more freedom to do what you want within the confines of the sponsor's expertise and laboratory equipment.

Please note the difference between faculty sponsor and mentor. As a postdoc, you're a junior colleague rather than a student. A sponsor will provide advice and direction, but you may have to ask for it first. Your sponsor will add an important letter of recommendation for future jobs, so it pays to impress him/her. Always remember that you are using your sponsor's name, space, equipment, and supplies to do your research, and acknowledgment (in publications and presentations) and gratitude are in order. For example, George Kohler was a postdoc in Cesar Milstein's lab when he discovered how to produce monoclonal antibodies. Even though Milstein wasn't even in town when the critical experiments were conducted, George has always stated that he could not have done the work if he had not been in the right place at the right time. Both scientists received the Nobel Prize in Medicine for uncovering the way to produce monoclonal antibodies.

Where to look

First, you need to determine what you still need to learn in order to enhance your career in research. You also need to look at holes in your CV for a job at a professional school, research university, government, or industry. Second, you need to find a faculty member who will sponsor you and who works at your desired type of institution. You may know already who this is from the literature review you conducted for your dissertation research. Third, go to your dissertation research advisor and ask his advice. If you are in a field where postdocs are common, your advisor will have a pretty good idea where you should go, and he will help you to get there. Just make sure the sponsor and location fit what you need. If your advisor's picks aren't what you want, go back, explain what you are looking for, and suggest alternatives.

Whether your graduate advisor is active in your postdoctoral search or not, you need to generate a list of government agencies and foundations that might be interested in funding your postdoctoral research. Some of these are listed in Appendix A. Some will be found in searchable online databases such as www4.nationalacademies.org/pga/rap.nsf, Recruit.ScienceMag.org, Post-docs.com, and HigherEdjobs.com. Don't forget the Community of Science and other search engines that your university may have subscribed to; many postdoctoral appointments are advertised in professional society publications and web sites (*Science* magazine and its *Next Wave* career-development magazine, for example). Your advisor or a new faculty in your department may know of others.

If you are taking the lead on finding a postdoctoral position, write to the top three potential sponsors that you listed above. Tell them what your research interests are and how they might connect to theirs. Ask them if they would be interested in being a sponsor for the fellowships that you discovered. Then ask if there might be other postdoctoral funding sources at their institution (or elsewhere) that you could apply for. Do all of this in less than two pages. Include a CV and the contact information for your advisor (telephone, e-mail, mail address). Then make sure that you inform your advisor that so-and-so might call about you concerning a postdoc. If your advisor doesn't know who so-and-so is, be sure to brief him on the potential sponsor's accomplishments and why you two are such a good fit.

Temporary Faculty Positions

Call them adjuncts, gypsy faculty, lecturers, or one-year sabbatical replacements, these are all temporary faculty appointments. The longer the appointment, the better it is—otherwise you spend all of your time teaching and looking for the next job. Benefits vary from none to some. A temporary appointment does, however, offer a quick way to get a lot of teaching experience and keep you in the academic game. Keep a close eye on the jobs opening in your temporary employer's institution (the faculty is surely watching you). Therefore, you need to exude dedication to the profession and collegiality without being a pest. No one wants a clingy, fawning, and obviously desperate person as a fellow faculty member. You need to appear confident without being arrogant. No one wants a snob as a colleague either. Bottom line: Excite the students and keep your opinion to yourself around faculty issues.

Who does the search committee look for to fill these jobs? They look for someone who can step right in and teach the courses that they define in the job description. If your research and especially past teaching experience does not match their posting, either don't waste time applying or come up with a cover letter that convinces the committee that you meet their needs.

What can you expect? Lots of teaching without much faculty guidance. You'll be busy planning lectures, grading, and talking to undergraduates. Every successful temp is expected to do that. If you want to be considered for a permanent job, do something extra for and in the department. Assist with student projects and publications. Attach yourself to a faculty member's lab to help with undergraduate research. Offer to invite and host a speaker for the departmental seminar series. Don't be pushy. Don't advocate revolutionary measures. If they rebuff your new idea or offer of help, back off and try something else in a month. The key here is to get to know and be liked by the regular faculty. If you feel hypocritical about the aforementioned activities because you really don't much like the environment, then it is time to look for another job.

Where to look

You find these temporary academic positions in the same places that permanent positions are posted. It also pays to look around your department and university for likely openings because of sabbaticals, transfers, or negative tenure-decisions. Check with your advisor and the chairman of the department.

Postdoctoral Teaching Appointments

If you're on a postdoctoral research fellowship and you want a permanent academic job, it would be good to get some teaching experience. Just remember, you are being paid for doing research, so don't overdo the teaching bit and be sure to keep your faculty sponsor informed.

If you have a temporary teaching job, you had better keep your research fresh so that you remain marketable for the tenure-track position. This is a good time to publish all or parts of your dissertation. In the summer, you might even have time to develop new projects.

The best of all worlds is the postdoctoral position that purposely blends both teaching and research. The teaching load is reduced to one or two sections per semester in order for you to have the time to do research and publish. Furthermore, these positions often carry contracts for two or three years. You may be junior fellow of a university society, or you may be a university postdoctoral teaching fellow that is sponsored by the institution or a foundation. Sometimes the fellowship program follows a theme. Most of the time, it requires a close relationship with a faculty sponsor.

Needless to say, many of these postdoctoral positions are even more coveted than second-tier, tenure-track jobs. If you are productive during the fellowship, you not only will have a well-fortified CV and a larger network of players in your field, you'll get a head-start on tenure. In order to get one of these blended postdoctoral positions, you'll need significant teaching and/or research credentials (if you have a strong research record but not much experience in teaching, this is a good reason for applying for the fellowship). Besides the basic credentials, you'll need to spark the interest of a host institution faculty member in your research.

Where to look

Postdoctoral programs are occasionally advertised in *The Chronicle of Higher Education*. Your PhD granting institution may even have such a program that you can apply to. It's advantageous, however, to look elsewhere for a postdoc where you can broaden your network and learn new approaches to research. Often, these gems aren't advertised at all.

Even if an announcement for a teaching postdoctoral fellowship magically appears in the campus mail, you'll have to find someone at the host institution who might be interested in your work and is willing to work with you. This will require a web search of faculty members and a library search of their publications. Your advisor and other faculty in your department may also know a couple of good potential sponsors at the host institution. When you contact one of these faculty members, indicate you're interested in collaborating with them on a research project that would benefit from their experience and send along a CV and the contact information for your advisor. If the first person isn't interested, maybe the next one on your list will be.

Academic Administration

Who better appreciates your advanced degree than an academic institution? Student affairs, undergraduate admissions, the graduate school, library archives, cross-cultural and minority-affairs offices, information technology, and your own departmental offices are fertile ground. And the best way to find out about—and get—such jobs is to have worked there as a graduate student. Of course, a PhD in academic leadership or higher administration is nearly as good as a couple of years practical experience on the job. If you love the academic environment but don't want to get on the tenure track, administration might be a good career. Just remember, you won't be treated with the same respect as the regular faculty, nor will you have the job security of tenure. Furthermore, you will find advancement limited to middle management. Top jobs (academic dean, provost, chancellor, vice president, and president) are reserved for tenured faculty, so it's best to enter academic administration after achieving tenure in your discipline. You'll go further and you'll have a home if you tire of being (or fail as) an administrator.

To make yourself competitive for a potential position in academic administration, you need experience on the job and experience with the people hiring you. In addition to that, demonstrate the skills you learned from your graduate student experience: efficiency, organization, good oral and written communication skills, and the demeanor to be collegial with faculty and staff. If you want to get into this line of work upon graduation, start working in the office during your graduate student days.

Where to look

Besides career and job-search websites, the school's HR department posts many of the entry-level positions. *The Chronicle of Higher Education* posts some junior and many senior appointments.

ACADEMIC JOBS: WEBSITES

Once you find the job on these sites, it's best to apply for the job directly through the school. Before you put a lot of time into the application, be sure to call to make sure that the position isn't already filled. Access your professional society website for discipline-specific job postings.

www.aacc.nche.edu: Lists community college sites.

www.academic360.com: Links to other academic jobs databases such as www.higheredjobs.com.

www.academiccareers.com: A good site for finding administrative, tenure-track, and postdoctoral appointments.

www.apnjobs.com: A worldwide academic position network.

www.bayareaherc.org: An academic job database for the San Francisco area. Look for similar venues in the area that you want to move to.

http://chronicle.com/jobs: Jobs in education from K to research university and research-related jobs outside academe.

www.edu-directory.org: Lists schools by state (helpful if you know where you'll be living).

http://engineering.academickeys.com: An academic resource for engineers.

www.grad.nd.edu/agsccu and **www.ajcunet.edu:** Search engines that advertise jobs in Catholic colleges and universities.

www.h-net.org/jobs: Academic jobs for students in the humanities and social sciences.

http://higheredjobs.com: Everything from executive positions to postdocs and other temporary postdoctoral appointments.

www.newscientistjobs.com: A worldwide source of academic jobs in the sciences.

www.nextwave.org: Science magazine source for information and job listings.

NON-ACADEMIC JOBS

Why were you interested in becoming a professor in the first place? Maybe because...

- You're smart.

- You enjoy being around smart people.

- Given a choice, you'd opt for prestige over money (but it would be nice to have both).

- You think that teaching and research are noble pursuits.

- You want to have the independence of a small business owner but the safety of a large organization.

Academe, believe it or not, hasn't cornered this market.

If research excites you, the government and the private sector offer plenty of R&D jobs for PhDs. The biggest obstacle to getting these jobs is building the network you need to get in. If your advisor doesn't have industry or government contacts, she may not be able to help you—this means you have to develop your own contacts. Several approaches can help once you determine what sort of job you want (and in which sector):

- Ask the alumni associations from both your undergraduate and graduate institutions if they maintain an active list of alums who have indicated an interest in mentoring a graduate.

- Apply for an internship. Most of these summer jobs are business- or undergraduate-oriented, so it might take some digging to find an appropriate position. Many of the internships are full-time for a short period (for example, the summer); others are a day or two per week over the academic year. The contacts and experience that you derive from an internship will be invaluable tools to help you find a job.

- If writing is your thing, do freelance work on topics that you can research locally.

Government Jobs

Federal, state, and local governments have need for recent PhDs in R&D, policy, and administration. For instance, the federal government has a large national laboratory system (e.g. Center for Disease Control, Argonne Laboratories, National Institutes of Health, Sandia Labs) that sponsor research in everything from astrophysics to Lyme disease. Each of these laboratories is under federal agency control (for example, by the Department of Health and Human Resources, the Department of Energy, or NASA). After a couple of years of research in graduate school, you'll know the labs that will be interested in your work. Don't overlook state and local laboratories in environmental/consumer protection, parks and wildlife, mental/public health, art curators, city planning offices, solid waste management, etc.

The legislative branch of government needs scientists and engineers to help formulate policy; so do the lobbies trying to influence legislation. The environment, public health, international development, and agriculture are just four hot topics today. Don't forget state legislatures who have local concerns.

PhDs are hired for regular positions in the executive branch and civil service. For example, the National Science Foundation, the National Institutes of Health, Department of Education, Department of State, and the U.S. Patent Office are a few organizations that appreciate the knowledge a doctorate confers.

Where to look

Check online: Searching for "government jobs for PhDs" generally yields results. The Office of Personnel Management (USAJobs.-opm.gov) collects employment opportunities from hundreds of government offices; you can also try GovernmentJobSearch.com or www.Ph.D.s.org/index?section=6. If you're really connected (or uniquely qualified) and youwant a political postdoc, you can try for a fellowship with the White House WhiteHouse.gov/fellows/). And don't forget the state governments: California, for example, (CSUS.edu/calst/Programs/jesse_unrah.html) and New York State (Senate.state.ny.us) senates have postgraduate fellowships. If you aren't a U.S. citizen, look to your own country—Canada, for one, offers management internships (IDRC.ca/awards/ecintrn.html).

Private-Sector Jobs

The private sector also has a large R&D operation (e.g., biotech, pharmaceuticals, computer science and engineering, telecommunications). Many industries also hire PhDs as managers of technical projects and departments (e.g., environmental compliance). Others use PhDs as consultants (e.g., manufacturing, city planning, brokerage and law firms). The industry representatives will be at your professional meetings and funding your professor's work. They won't be difficult for you to find if you're in the appropriate field. If you are drawing a blank, then perhaps your research area is not commercially lucrative.

What if you're not a scientist or an engineer with obvious R&D channels? Policy development also depends on research experience, as well as experience with writing clear and concise prose. These local jobs listings are in your phone book under "government."

What do you have to interest the private sector? Plenty. Sit down and list your skills and abilities.

- Modern language skills

- Computer (software) expertise

- Analytical/intellectual skills

- Technical skills in research methods (library, statistics, interviewing, science or engineering technology)

- Oral communication skills

- Writing/editing skills

What you need in your CV

The qualifications that you need for R&D positions are much the same as for a research university, only without the teaching experience. In other words, technical experience, presentations and publications, and research potential as described by your advisor and other references are important.

For non-research positions, the fact that you have a doctorate in the field may be the most important criterion. It will be up to you to convince those hiring that your formal education and research experience give you the knowledge to help with policy development and/or administration. It also helps if you, your advisor, and/or your other references have used the agency in the past. For example, if a position opens up to direct the NSF graduate fellowship program, it would be nice if you had been an NSF fellow as a graduate student or at least got a NSF dissertation improvement award. Since only 900 of these fellowships are awarded per year, the more likely possibility is that faculty in your department have gotten NSF grant support or given consultation services to the organization. If they know you, get them to write a letter of reference.

One experience that industry wants and feels that graduate education fails to provide is teamwork. Dissertation research by design is your original idea and effort. This doesn't mean that you haven't worked in a team, even if it is only a team consisting of you, your advisor, and the dissertation committee. In experimental engineering and science and certain subdisciplines in social science, large projects are often attacked by many individuals working together. Be sure to discuss in your cover letter—and perhaps mention in your resume—your experience in working with teams. Your advisor may also want to discuss your group dynamic.

It always helps if you have previous experience with the potential employer or a past job in the industry. This is why an internship is so important, especially for those of you who went to graduate school right out of college. If you are interested in government R&D, you can fashion an aspect of your dissertation research that would benefit from working for a short time in a particular government lab. Suggest to your advisor how beneficial it would be for you to spend a summer or semester at the federal facility. You need your advisor on your side, since it is likely that he/she will be your contact with the government lab and may be paying you while you are away.

Another important aid to getting a non-academic job is to have someone on the inside who can help you. Look around the department for faculty who know someone in the industry or government lab of your choice. Check with your Career Development and Placement Office. They may have a list of recruiters. The center may also have career fairs. As with most institutions, the center may be focused on undergraduate placement, but be persistent and the staff should help.

Where to look

The answer depends on what you have to offer and what you want to do. A good place to begin the search is the series of articles in *The Chronicle of Higher Education* called "Beyond the Ivory Tower." For an archive of articles, go to http://chronicle.com/jobs/archive/advice/beyond.htm. The Internet is also a good place to start looking for jobs. For instance, the Woodrow Wilson National Fellowship Foundation (Woodrow.org) runs non-academic job postings for doctorates who don't want to continue with research or teaching. The Environmental Careers Organization (ECO.org) has a non-academic placement service as well. Needless to say, newspapers published in the area that you want to relocate are invaluable. The problem won't be finding job postings; it will be in deciding what you want to do and if your network can get you in the door.

If teaching floats your boat, consider high schools, prep schools, junior colleges, and the training divisions in large corporations. This is a good career choice if picking a place to live is more important that making a lot of money. Educational credentials are important in areas that have lots of teachers. It would be wise to sneak in a couple of education courses while you are in graduate school if secondary or continuing education is your Plan B. Every state will have different requirements, so find out what you need once you settle on a place. If the school is desperate for teachers, you may be able to start the job and accumulate the credentials during subsequent summers.

Each public school district, prep school, or parochial school hires its own teachers. Find a place that you want (or need to) live and call the administration. You may have to start as a temp; you may have to collect teaching credentials; you may start in some "undesirable" schools within the district, but without a doubt, you'll have an important job.

If You Need More Direction...

If academic or R&D jobs appear to be unattractive career options, perhaps you need to fold up the map and start all over. Start by listing the skills that make you interesting to employers and your potentially marketable interests. Then assess your desires. What drives you: money, fame, or pleasure? Finally, determine what feeds your sense of self-worth. Is it what you have? How you are perceived by others? Service to others? Then run, don't walk, to your school career development center and ask for help. If you tell them you are a graduate student, they might blow you off. Tell them you're a postgraduate in search of a direction. Take their tests and listen to the counselors. If their advice makes sense, write it down and then come back to talk some more. Take all of the workshops that the office offers for non-academic employment (even if it is geared to undergraduates), look for internships or part-time jobs that appear to be interesting, and attend the local career fairs.

If you've decided to opt for an alternate career, should you bother to get the PhD? That depends on how you answer the following: How much time do you have left to get the degree? Will the degree help you climb the ladder you have just chosen? Will you feel like a total loser if you leave the program? If you have more than a year of work to go, if the title has no (or negative) cache for your newly chosen profession, and if you are positive about your future direction, then get started on your new life now. If you don't want to burn the bridge completely, ask for a year's leave of absence.

CHAPTER VI

Hunting for Work

Now that you know the types of careers out there and where to find them, you need to know the steps to landing the job you want.

MAKING THE FIRST CUT

It doesn't matter how personable you are—the first cut for almost any job is largely based on a written presentation of your credentials. The three most important parts to this phase of job hunting are the cover letter, your *curriculum vitae* (CV) or resume, and your letters of recommendation. An example of an academic job announcement, a cover letter, and CV are provided in Appendix A. An example of a cover letter and resume in response to a non-academic job appears in Appendix B. Each element is described in detail below.

Cover Letter

The purpose of your cover letter is to show a search committee that you have all (or most) of the qualifications listed in the job announcement. A lot of blood, sweat, and political considerations went into composing the announcement, and search committees are rarely in the mood to entertain your alternative ideas. Mention where you read the announcement. Address each qualification and determine which of your experiences or courses apply. Some announcements present a laundry list of qualifications. Try to prioritize the list by the type of hiring institution, the position of the qualification in the announcement, and obvious qualifiers such as "PhD in hand is required" versus a "PhD in hand is preferred."

Some job announcements are vague. Either the faculty never resolved their issues or they are fishing for the best candidate out there. Try to figure out their teaching needs from the announcement or from a phone call to the search committee chair. Look through the course catalog to determine what you can teach, especially courses that are currently not being offered. Discover research interests of the faculty in the same way you did when you were trying to determine where to go to graduate school. See if there are any possible research collaborations waiting to happen.

Once you address the needs of the department, you can then discuss what else you can bring to the table. Tailor these comments to the type of hiring institution. For example, if you are applying to a research university, discuss research projects and methods that are not directly associated with your dissertation—especially research that might interest several faculty members. If you are applying to a teaching institution, discuss new courses, ideas for undergraduate research projects, and departmental and university committee work in which you've already participated.

You may discuss community ties or other geographical reasons for wanting the job, but most institutions prefer applicants who are more interested in what the school does and not where it is. You dare not discuss personal issues or concerns at this point; your cover letter is a two-page sales document attempting to match the school's needs with your talents.

Curriculum Vitae

The academic equivalent of the resume, your CV summarizes your professional life in bullet points. The elements of a CV include contact information, educational background, honors and awards, teaching and relevant professional experience, certificates/credentials, and research output, including any presentations and publications. Optional elements include a statement of current and future research interests, teaching philosophy, and reference contact information. Appendix B contains an example.

Contact information

This includes your name, professional mailing address, fax, telephone numbers, and e-mail address. If you haven't already, this might be a good time to invest in a cell phone, especially if you have trouble getting messages from labmates, officemates, or roommates. Don't put down a contact number that you rarely check for messages. You don't have to include personal items here—or anywhere, for that matter—such as age, disabilities, or family status. You should put down your home address and phone if you spend more time there than on campus.

Education

Starting with the most recent, list the academic institutions attended, degree, and years attended (or date that the degree was conferred). This is a good time to give the title of your dissertation and graduate advisor name. If you are a postdoc, start with your current institution and sponsor name. If there are gaps, be sure to tell elsewhere in the CV—under "professional experience," perhaps—or in the cover letter what you were doing during the gaps.

Honors and awards

Start with national graduate prizes, travel and research grants, and/or fellowships and then move onto university and departmental awards you received in graduate school. Finally, list only national undergraduate awards (Phi Beta Kappa). You may want to provide a one-sentence description for each award.

Teaching experience

Start with courses you designed and taught by yourself, then progress onto the lecture courses where the curriculum was set. Finally, add in the tutorials, discussions, or laboratories you assisted in. Be sure to indicate the level of the course and perhaps the number of times that you taught it. You might want to briefly describe the course content, especially if it isn't obvious from the title and if you are applying to a teaching institution.

Research/professional experience

List relevant, recent, and long-term professional experiences. Leave out little jobs which don't show that you can do the potential job or that don't explain big gaps in your professional life. You will need to indicate the years spent in each job that you list. A very brief explanation of your duties might be in order if the job title doesn't adequately describe it.

Certificates

If you've collected certificates in, say, teaching (a nice item for college jobs), teaching college writing, English as a second language, computer applications, academic leadership—or other professional credentials like CPA, JD, allied health specialties—by all means, include them on your CV, especially if they enhance your marketability for specific job openings.

Research output

List in chronological order and sort by importance. Start with the most important: refereed publications (books, monographs, book chapters, and journal articles), then unrefereed publications (articles, essays, reviews, encyclopedia entries, vanity press), and finally presentations. The publications should be in a consistent format common to a book or journal in your field. In other words, members of the search committee should be able to look the material up in the library. Be clear of your place in the list of coauthors. As for presentations, home-department seminars and guest lectures only indicate an impoverished CV.

Optional entries

You should have handy several items in the event that the hiring institution wants them. The most obvious is a list of three to five references with contact information (office mailing and e-mail addresses, telephone numbers). Your dissertation advisor and postdoctoral sponsor should be listed at the top. Second, the hiring institution, especially if it is a research university, may want a statement of future research plans. There's no need to get overly detailed or technical: Provide just enough for the committee to know that you have your own research ideas and what sort of facilities, library holdings, and research travel you'll require. Third, especially if the hiring institution is undergraduate-focused, you may have to provide a "teaching philosophy." This has nothing to do with Aristotle or Kant. The committee wants to know what your educational goals are for the classes that you have taught (and will teach) and how you set the relationship with your class. How are these goals manifested in the curriculum, readings, assignments, and tests? What pedagogical methods do you use to get the class involved with the material? How do you establish a teacher-student relationship? (Hint: The goals and rapport will be different between lower-level and higher-level undergraduate courses and between undergraduate- and graduate-level courses.) Next, the search committee may ask for an abstract of your dissertation. Usually, the abstract is the last part that you write, but if you haven't finished the dissertation yet, do the best that you can. Just make sure that by the end of the one- or two-page abstract, the reader will know what you did, how you did it, and why it is important. Finally, in this age of false credentials, the committee may request an official transcript of your graduate education. Bug the registrar until you know your transcript is in the mail.

Resume

Upon graduation, your CV and resume may be the same length. If you become a successful researcher, however, your CV will grow with the number of presentations and publications. A resume, however, remains at one or two pages. In the beginning of your job hunt, you'll be scrimping for entries to fill one page. Later on, you'll have to pick and chose what to include—and you'll probably keep different versions of your resume—depending upon the job to which you're applying. If Procter & Gamble, for example, is looking for a research chemist, it cares more about your technical expertise than your teaching experience.

The essentials to a resume are contact information, education, professional experience, skills, and other activities, especially community service. Unlike a CV, resume items are usually placed in reverse chronological order. Be concise and arrange your resume so that the important items stick out—for example, *what* you did is more important than when you did it, so lead with the skill and put the dates later. Personal information—age, sex, ethnicity, home address—is unnecessary, with the possible exception of citizenship. Appendix C provides an example.

Letters of Recommendation

Obviously, your postdoctoral sponsor, if you have one, and your graduate advisor, need to be on the list. For academic positions, you will need to fill in one to three other recommendations with faculty members who know your graduate or postdoctoral research and teaching. Most non-academic recommendations are made over the phone to your current supervisor.

Your references will do a better job recommending you if you provide them with the job announcement, your CV, and any other relevant materials. You may also want to give them a topic to accent: your teaching, your research, your service, your collegiality.

In other words, you may want to tailor the letters according to the job. If it is a pure research position, have most of your references address your research findings and potential and your ability to work in teams. If it is a pure teaching position, have most of your references discuss your classroom prowess, your ability to engage undergraduates, your service to the department, and collegiality. For a tenure-track position in a research university, you need both types of letters. For academic administrative jobs, you'll probably need the appropriate experience in order to be credible—for example, designing the department's website is helpful for getting a job in the information technology office. You will need to get a letter from your supervisor. Go up as high on the administrative ladder as comfortably possible for the recommendation. Letters dealing with a previous job in academic administration, government, or the private sector will also be important for non-academic jobs if they are asked for.

If it looks like you'll be taking a temporary position upon graduation, it's not a bad idea to ask your references to write a generic "Dear colleague" letter. Then, when you find that ideal tenure-track job announcement three years later, your references won't have to dredge up old memories. They'll simply dust off their old letter, add your more recent achievements, and tailor the letter to the job announcement. As a poor second choice, you could use your institution or an electronic dossier service—but these letters will have a stale, generic flavor to them. The poorest choice of all—but better than nothing—is for you to collect letters from your references. These obviously aren't confidential and don't carry the same weight as a signed-and-sealed letter of recommendation, but any letter is better than none, and they'll come in handy if you're in a hurry to complete an application.

Personal Website

While it's extremely convenient to post your CV and optional materials online on your personal website, remember that the Internet is mostly public domain and anyone can browse through your professional life: Don't post items like your personal address, phone number, and social security number. And remember, that if you're posting your CV online, present it professionally—no party pictures, political rants, or aberrant links.

MAKING THE SECOND CUT

On review by the search committee, up to 90 percent of the job applications never make the final cut. The lucky few applicants who remain viable may still be too many to bring on campus for an interview. Some selection committees may make further cuts based on phone interviews, video conferences, or face-to-face interviews at professional meetings. Because of time constraints (often less than 30-minute interviews), your preparation will be the same for all of these.

First, you need to have a three-to-five minute statement of your dissertation research (or postdoctoral and dissertation research). Provide enough background to make the research question interesting, briefly describe the methods used to get the data or develop the idea, give the important results, and define overall importance of your findings. Throw in the names of your advisor and other faculty who helped you. Be prepared for follow-up questions concerning the work and its publication plans. The interviewer may not be in your subdiscipline, so avoid jargon and do not assume anything.

You need a short description of future research projects. Be prepared to answer follow-up questions regarding your need for equipment, space, library facilities, and time for field research. Since it's easy to scare away a possible employer with a long list of research needs, conduct some background research on the school's commitment to research, its facilities, and its leave policies. Furthermore, compile a list of possible funding sources for your research—and mention your prior successes in raising money for your research.

You'll also need to describe the courses you've taught and how you taught them, and be ready to answer questions concerning new courses that you might be interested in teaching. Make sure to touch upon the specific job announcement requirements.

Answer the question "Why do you want to come work with us?" In an interview at a research university, you could mention a professor or two with whom you might be able to collaborate, or you could talk about the research facilities that you could use. In a college interview, you might wax poetic about teaching and influencing undergrads. Have nice things to say about the institution's geographical location and setting. If you're having difficulty finding something nice to say, reevaluate your desire for the job.

Finally, compile your own questions concerning the school, the department, the faculty, and the environment. Interviewing is a two-way street: Both parties want to come away feeling that they've made a good deal, both for the institution and the individual faculty members. Ask about salary and benefits. Ask about cost of living. Ask the interviewer what she likes about the place. Ask about the nature and interests of the undergraduate and graduate students. Ask about help available with grant writing and teaching.

You don't have to answer questions about your ethnic origin, religion, sexual orientation, disabilities, or marital state. However, if you think it'll help your cause, you might mention relevant facts during the interview—for example, if you're a Catholic applying for a job at the Catholic University of America, or if you're married but your spouse already has a job lined up.

Both phone and personal interviews at meetings may involve more than one person. Perhaps none on the search committee will be experts in your subdiscipline. You will have to make your work accessible and interesting to them. Write each member's name down if you can. This will be easy in a phone interview, but it's more important in the personal interview to make eye contact with each interviewer and give firm—not crushing—handshakes than it is to remember their names.

It's not just the answers you give that get you past the second cut. Interviewers will be gathering impressions of you from several sensory inputs. For both types of interviews, project a confident, clear, and relaxed tone of voice. If you've done your background research and realize that the institution wants to fill the job opening as much as you want to fill it, you'll probably be more comfortable and more spontaneous. For video conferences or personal interviews, make sure of the place and time and arrive at the interview site with time to spare. For phone interviews, sequester yourself in a quiet, locked space where you won't be interrupted by your dog, kids, or drunken roommates.

A major difference between phone and in-person interviews is that you can be naked in the bathtub for the former, but you'd better be professionally attired and coiffed for the latter. Interviews at professional meetings are all about first impressions. If you arrive looking like Britney Spears or Marilyn Manson, don't expect a call back.

MAKING THE FINAL CUT

If you get the call for a campus visit, you've made it to the final cut.

Usually, the committee is down to three applicants. Campus visits are grueling affairs consisting of a job talk, interviews with individual faculty members and senior administrators (like the academic dean) and "social" events. You may also have to prepare an undergraduate lecture and meet with groups of graduate or undergraduate students.

A campus visit usually begins early, ends late, and may last a couple of days. Usually, you make the travel arrangements (they pay) and the host institution makes the room reservations. It's best to arrive the previous day and get a good night of sleep. If you're flying, wear suitable interviewing clothes and carry on a change of shirt/blouse and underwear—along with your job-talk material and toiletries—just in case the airline loses your checked luggage. Before you arrive, know your schedule, or at least the starting time and contact person, and know where you'll be staying.

From the moment a departmental representative meets you at the airport, you'll be on stage. Be positive, be upbeat, look refreshed, look confident. Your behavior will rub off on the interviewers. Use good table manners, be courteous and respectful to everyone, and for decorum's sake, don't drink too much alcohol.

Faculty interviews are a series of 15 to 30 minute sessions. A few faculty will know your research in detail; others, much less so. You'll have to pitch your answers accordingly. The most important thing to remember, even though it is the fifteenth time you have described your research or teaching experiences, is to be enthusiastic without going overboard. Remember that the interview isn't all about you. Turn the tables on the interviewers by asking them about their research, the courses they teach, their opinions about the students, and the local environs.

The importance of the job talk cannot be overestimated. Most faculty and students will gauge both the quality of your research and your ability to teach from this 45 minute performance. Make sure that your slides project well. Remember that most of the audience is not familiar with your subdiscipline, so avoid jargon, define abbreviations more than once, and avoid being overly technical. Don't assume everyone intuitively recognizes the importance of your research question. The same goes for your results. Make sure that you practice the talk until you can give it without constantly looking at your prepared notes. More than likely you'll know more about the research you are presenting than anyone else in the room. Keep that in mind while appearing confident, relaxed, and enthusiastic all at the same time.

A good outline for the job talk starts with a historical background to establish context and importance followed by a clear, concise purpose statement. This should take 25 percent of the allotted time. Next, describe your results. Unlike most journal articles that describe materials and methods in one section, you should group a result with a particular methodology. After explaining each result, summarize what you've learned. The results section should comprise about half of your talk; with the remaining time, you should make conclusions, discuss their potential importance, and describe possible future work.

Usually, there's time after your talk for audience questions. If you've been practicing in front of your peers, you'll already know most potential queries. Inevitably, though, somebody will throw the occasional curve ball. Some are good questions that you won't know the answer to. Simply respond, "Excellent question, but I'll get back to you after I've looked over my reference material." Some questions are off the wall; respond with "I don't think I understand your question. Can we explore this after the session?" And some questions may be confrontational. Keep your responses on an intellectual level. Point out the different approaches you took and controls you used to derive the same result. If it's true, acknowledge that your findings are at variance with others, but state that your evidence (which is supported by several others in the field) indicates that your conclusion is correct. Stick to your guns with regard to your methods and findings—after all, if you concede these, the audience will have wasted 45 minutes listening to you—but maintain a calm, thoughtful manner. You can afford to be more generous if someone disputes one of your more speculative discussion points. Respond with something along the lines of "It's possible, but I'd like to look at the evidence for your point of view once again before I concede mine."

Many colleges will also want you to give a lecture in an undergraduate class. Find out the topic, the level of course, the assigned readings, and the amount of preparation that the students have on the topic before you design the lecture. When in doubt, assume that the students do not know the background to the lecture. Make the lecture self-contained—that is, begin and end the topic within your allotted time—and pitch it to the level of the text or readings. If you can, supply alternative opinions to those offered in the text. It may be difficult to establish a rapport when you don't know the names of the students, so unless you're especially gifted in getting undergraduates to talk, don't base your lecture on the Socratic method. Do, however, break up the session with time for questions. Most of the faculty members, sitting in the back, are gauging your presence, your organizational skills, and your enthusiasm, so content is less important than performance.

NEGOTIATING AN OFFER

Congratulations! Someone appreciates your talents and wants you to come to work with them. But don't pack your bags quite yet. Now is the best time for you to negotiate the best package possible. Once you accept the job, you'll have considerably less leverage, until you can prove you are invaluable. You'll need to negotiate your academic year salary, possibilities for summer funding, research and office facilities, relocation expenses, temporary university housing or help with buying a home, release time for research, teaching load, a job for your spouse, and your start time.

Of course, it's always better to have more than one institution courting you. Even if that's untrue, it's a good negotiating stance to appear like you are; obstinate arrogance, however, is no attitude to cop. When the faculty member calls to make the offer, demonstrate interest and say something nice about your visit and the institution (resist gushing even if this is your dream job, or you'll lose all leverage.) Then launch right into the particulars of the job offer. This isn't the time for extended negotiations. You just want their opening offer. Write their answers down; in all of the excitement, you will forget.

First Contact Questions

What will my academic year (nine-month) salary be?

Your starting salary is the basis for future raises, which are usually a percent increase over last year's salary. To determine if a salary offer is in line, look at *The Chronicle of Higher Education Almanac*, which annually publishes average salaries in most academic positions. Just remember that the average salary of an assistant professor means someone in that rank for about two to three years (who has earned two or three raises). Also check the cost of living in the area to determine if the salary will meet your needs as a professional family person—and not as a wretched graduate student.

What summer funding possibilities do you offer (faculty positions only)?

Sometimes departments will offer to pay for your first summer at the same rate as you received during the academic year. Often, you may be able to supplement your academic year salary by teaching summer courses. Finally, institutional and outside granting agencies often provide a summer salary in association with research grants. Of course, if you have a job in the government, academic administration, or the private sector, you'll have 12 months of work and pay per year and maybe a couple of weeks of vacation.

What will my initial teaching assignments be (academic jobs only)?

There's more than meets the eye when the faculty representative says "2–2." Does that mean two sections of the same course each semester? Two different (one-section) courses per semester? Two courses per semester, each with multiple sections? The major time-eater is the preparation for teaching a course for the first time; find out how many new preps per semester you'll be doing for the first couple of years (if you taught the same or similar course as a graduate student, that's not new prep). The second largest time-eater is individual student contact. You will need to find out the number of sections per course that you are responsible for and the total number of students you will be teaching each semester. Next, find out what laboratory sections, tutorials, or discussion groups are associated with the course. These are major time-drains. Finally, find out what assistance you will have with staff, graduate students, or undergraduates teaching the course.

Why should this matter—after all, isn't teaching why you were hired? Not really. Teaching *well* both inside and outside the classroom is what you should have been hired for. Furthermore, all universities and most colleges will expect you to conduct research and publish your findings. A very high teaching load affects the quality of your formal and informal instruction and the quantity of your research. Therefore, keeping the new preps down to one a semester and the student load manageable (less than 50 per semester) would be ideal. If you're responsible for more than that, ask how much evidence of research productivity is needed to earn tenure.

Finally, determine the courses you'll teach. A steady diet of the same 100-level survey course for non-majors (like English Composition or Introduction to Biology) will make you intellectually anorexic. Sprinkle in special courses for undergraduates, standard upper-level courses, and graduate offerings—some, your very own creations. Just remember the warning concerning new prep time...

How can the department and school help me in my research?

If you are a scientist or engineer, you probably toured your putative laboratory space during the campus visit. If you need some additional space (like a cold room or dedicated tissue culture area), now is the time to speak up. If the space needs to be renovated for your work, ask now. Once you sign the contract, you will be last in a long faculty line requesting more space or renovations.

Ask what capitalization budget you can expect. Don't assume that the equipment that you saw in the lab during the campus visit will be there when you arrive. Sometimes everything disappears with the departing faculty member; sometimes the remaining faculty will descend like vultures on a recently vacated lab (and you'll be lucky to find paint on the walls). Figure out what equipment and supplies you need for the next three years of research, and figure out which specialized equipment you'll need in the teaching labs that you will be responsible for. Then go to the catalogs and find out how much all of this stuff costs—and you'll instantly become more appreciative of your graduate advisor and postdoctoral sponsor. Once you've assembled your list, have your advisor or sponsor look at it. You will be expected to present this equipment-and-price list to the hiring department. Some of it may already be in the department, some of it will be bought on your capitalization account, and some you may have to borrow until your first grant comes in. If you're an experimentalist being courted by a research university, you won't shock them with your request for a $200,000 capitalization budget (though they can still say no). If you're being courted by a teaching institution, that $200,000 request may have just priced you out of a job. Be reasonable and flexible in either case. Another item faculty applicants in science and engineering often overlook is library subscriptions to important journals in your field. If the institution's library doesn't hold the journals you need, ask them to order them.

If you're in arts and letters, the library was probably the first place you looked for research materials on the campus visit. Again, if you need a collection, a monograph series, books, and journals to do your work, ask if the library will buy them (you'll make friends too—the librarians will appreciate the fact that anyone considered them during the hiring process). Don't forget your other research needs such as personal computers, printers, software, or databases. Of course, if you need to conduct field research, you should discuss release time and possible departmental and college resources to support travel.

It doesn't matter which field you'll soon be a functioning faculty member of—you need an office. A member of the hiring team may have pointed out an office during your visit; find out if the space they showed you will, in actuality, be your office. Verify that it is a single-occupancy office. Find out if it is wired for telephone and the campus computer network. Make sure that book cases, desks, and chairs come standard. These may sound like dumb questions, but the faculty rep who is negotiating the deal will be happy to say, "Yes, of course" every so often.

What are the employee benefits?

The biggies are health insurance and retirement. For health insurance, you need to know out-of-pocket expenses and any clauses concerning pre-existing conditions. For retirement, find out how much your employer will contribute to your 401(k) plan or how long you have to be in the system for the state retirement package. For non-faculty positions, find out how much vacation time per year you'll get.

How about my spouse?

Sometimes it's not all about you. If your spouse is on the job market, see if you can come as a package deal. Optimally, both of you will get tenure-track positions. Or one of you may end up with the faculty position and the other getting something else. If that happens, both of you can use this opportunity to improve your CVs enough to eventually *both* attain permanent faculty positions.

Do you cover moving expenses?

Determine if temporary faculty housing is available for your arrival. It's much more relaxing to find a place to live if you aren't holed up in a motel. If you are getting a job on either coast, ask if the institution offers any programs to help faculty buy a house. Finally, ask how much the relocation allowance will be. Even if you can pack everything in the back seat of your car, you'll incur moving expenses, including travel and temporary lodging, until you find a place to live.

When do I have to make a decision?

You need time to evaluate the answers to these questions—and you may want to shop around to other places where you've interviewed. Ask for a week or two to make your decision. The school may press for a quicker answer, but asking for two weeks isn't unreasonable, especially if they haven't yet answered all of your questions.

So... when do I start?

Most academic appointments begin with the academic year. But what happens when that postdoctoral fellowship you applied for back in November becomes available? A year of pure research where you can get parts of the dissertation published and begin the next project will be invaluable when you come up for tenure. Ask your hiring department if you can defer the faculty appointment for a year to take the temporary position. Tell them that you will be happy to sign the contract and that the fellowship will make you a better researcher when you arrive on their campus.

What if you're done and are staring down the barrel of a penniless summer? If it's still early spring, you might be able to sign up to teach a summer course, either with your new employer or your old graduate institution. It's pretty rare to get a couple of months off to travel, visit, and veg out, so take this time to recharge your batteries before you start the next job if you can afford it. At least get enough of a gap between graduation and starting the job to find a place and unpack your boxes.

More than likely, non-academic employers may want you right away. At least make them wait until you defend your dissertation.

Second Contact Question

Can you offer me a larger salary?

No matter what your research into salaries indicates, ask if the department has any latitude to offer a larger salary. Their counter question, of course, will be "What do you want?" Your answer should be prefaced with comments about average salaries for assistant professors, the cost of living, your student loans, a desire to buy a home and raise a family followed by a reasonable counter-offer (no more than $10,000 higher than their original offer). Don't let the conversation snag on this topic. If the faculty representative says "maybe," move onto the next item. If the faculty member says "no," help this person fill the gap between their offer and your desire by moving onto the next topic—the average raises for assistant professors over the last three years, for example. While the past is no guarantee for the future, it might help fill the gap between their offer and your need.

By the second contact, you should know if you are in the running elsewhere. If you didn't get everything that you requested at the first school, ask for another day or two to make a decision. Then contact the other institutions to see if they are ready to make an offer. If they delay you with vague promises, they're either uncertain about hiring you or their first choice is stringing them along (just like you're doing elsewhere). The gamble, of course, lies with choosing the job at hand or the vague possibility of another.

If the first school comes back with everything you ask for, be prepared to give them an answer during this second call. After all of the running around you put the faculty rep through, you'd better have a good reason to say "no."

CHAPTER VII
Q & A with PhD Recipients and Candidates

We interviewed recent PhD recipients and current PhD candidates at several of the most highly selective schools in the country. We asked them about their experiences: getting in, getting adjusted, and getting the most from their programs. To illustrate the similarities and differences among various student experiences, we sought out students from a diverse range of fields. PhD candidates in the following disciplines gave generously of their time and advice in responding to the questions we posed:

- Art history

- Bioengineering

- Computer science

- English

- Religious studies

- Sociology

We've maintained the anonymity of each respondent and removed any identifying information from the responses below. Each response is identified only by the respondent's field of study.

Do you have any tips for writing a successful statement of purpose?

Art history: Be very clear about your goals and how the specific program you are applying to is the best place to achieve them. This means writing a different statement for each program you apply to. Elaborate your view of the strengths of the school, the department, and particular faculty members. When outlining your purpose be careful to strike a balance between a thoughtfully developed set of prior interests and a desire to expand your horizons. You are not meant to know what your dissertation will be about before you enter years of predoctoral coursework; you should, however, explain why you are interested in and well-suited to undertake a sustained course of study in a broad area of specialization—i.e., modern architecture, critical theory, or South Asian visual culture. Be as articulate and straightforward as possible; no matter how sophisticated you think a jargon-ridden letter looks, the committee will be frustrated and unimpressed by overly complicated wording.

Bioengineering: The statement of purpose should be thought of as your vision for the next four to seven years. Because graduate study is such a long-term endeavor, it is not likely you will be able to spell out your research plans down to the smallest detail. Instead, it is more useful to address the anticipated impact of your research on the scientific field of relevance to you, as well as the expected impact of the research program to which you are applying on your personal development. In this latter point, it is advisable to be specific about particular research activities at the school to which you are applying.

Computer science: Graduate school is all about research. If you have significant research experience, your statement of purpose should demonstrate your ability to do research and talk about it. In particular, explain the project you worked on and the results.

English: There's no magic formula for writing a good statement, just perhaps some general principles to keep in mind. First, don't attempt to impress people as it's rather easy to see through. Second, write about yourself—this is about why you're doing what you're doing. Third, while the statement shouldn't be a specific research proposal, work in specific details, both about your past academic career (special courses of interest, etc.) and future plans (particular facets of your field that interest you). Fourth, tailor each statement towards each institution—why are you choosing to apply there? What do they offer? Why would this suit you? Finally, use the word limit to your advantage and try not to go over it—it's an excuse to polish up what you have, and, after all, the statement of purpose is another piece of your writing that will be seen by the admissions committee.

Religious studies: I think when writing a statement of purpose you want to be broad and specific at the same time—you want to show that you have specific research interests that you'd be able to dive into immediately, but you also want to show that you're flexible. After a year or two of coursework it's more than likely you'll no longer be all that interested in what you first thought you'd work on. Also, if you sound too dead-set on a topic and there's no professor who wants to work with you on it, you've got pretty much no chance of getting in.

Sociology: Personal statements for undergraduate applications are all about showing excellence and breadth [of experience]. Undergraduate schools are looking for students who can contribute to the academic, social, and cultural aspects of college life. Personal statements for graduate school applications are very different. Academic prestige at research universities is all about research and publication. To that end, departments are looking for individuals who are going to produce high-quality research. A statement of purpose should highlight your research experience and potential as well as the match of your particular, unique interests to those of faculty members in the department. Remember, you are selling yourself as an eventual high-powered researcher who will reflect well on the department that "produced" you.

For your recommendation letter, did you opt to ask a tenured professor who didn't know you that well, or an adjunct professor who knew you very well? To what degree do you attribute your application success to that decision?

Art history: My recommendations were written by tenured professors who knew my work well. If you cannot find big-name clout and familiarity with your work in a single reference, balance your portfolio by soliciting references from both camps. It is imperative that you secure at least one letter from a sympathetic faculty member, whatever the rank, who is keen to help you achieve your goals and will commit the time to customize a strong letter for each particular application.

Bioengineering: The most effective recommendation is one from a faculty member who knows people on the admissions committee at the school of your choice. This occurs more commonly in graduate admissions than undergraduate because the graduate school admissions committee is usually made up of professorial faculty who will have interacted with the professors at your home institution via research conferences, collaborations, etc. Tenured faculty will tend to know and be known by more people on those admissions committees than adjuncts, so, in this respect, I think a recommendation letter from a tenured professor can be more valuable. However, if they don't know you well enough to fill a page-long evaluation, their letter can do more harm than good. For this reason I suggest getting to know the tenured faculty in your department outside the classroom during your application year. The earlier you do this, the less forced the interaction will feel.

Computer science: It's much better to choose a professor who knows you well and can speak specifically about why you will make a good researcher. Admissions committees have to read a ton of recommendations—ones that speak generally about a student don't help them.

English: Usually institutions will ask for more than one recommendation letter, which gives you the chance to go for both an adjunct and a tenured faculty member. When in doubt, always choose a professor who knows you and your work well, regardless of their status. There's always an obvious difference between a form letter and one written by someone who clearly knows you.

Religious studies: My recommenders were: a PhD student who had led my study abroad program the year before, a non-tenure-track visiting professor, and a tenured professor who didn't know me all that well. All very less-than-ideal. The professor at UVA that I was hoping to work under, however, personally knew the first two. So although they weren't tenured, or even close to being so, they probably ended up being more helpful.

Sociology: I had three letters of recommendation, two from associate professors and one from an adjunct professor. All of them new me reasonably well—I had taken small classes with all three—and one of them knew me very well as I had been a research assistant for him. As with any recommendation letter, it's easier for the writer to say specific things about you if they know you well, and the more specific a letter is, the more informative readers will find it. There may be benefits to having specific people write letters for you in specific cases, but I do not think a letter's effect is directly related to the tenure status or "famousness" of the writer. I do think a letter from a faculty member who knows someone on the faculty at the prospective institution is helpful—particularly if this contact is on the admissions committee—because the letter writer's comments will have added credibility. The readers will know how that writer writes (Are they particularly prone to hyperbole? Are they known for identifying research talent?), which will allow them to place the recommendation in context. Personal networks also allow the informal exchange of additional information or recommendation beyond the letter itself.

How should one go about finding an advisor?

Art history: Spend time with a number of professors during their office hours and assess to what extent each is accessible, supportive (intellectually and tactically), and interested in your projects. All these qualities are essential in an advisor, though they may be difficult to find in one professor. It may be wise to cultivate more than one advisor, whether officially or unofficially. This might come in handy as a hedge, should you need to switch advisors down the line; as a diversification strategy, should you need to balance profs who provide big-name clout and hands-on support; or as a simple networking tactic. Remember that your advisor(s) will be your chief representative(s), speaking up for you in faculty meetings and writing letters of recommendation that will be essential to every grant and application you write during your doctorate and in the years beyond. Socializing with more advanced students and alumni is the best way to glean candid assessments of how well different advisors perform for their advisees. Find out how supportive your potential advisors were during comprehensive exams, the dissertation phase, and the career search.

Bioengineering: I strongly believe that the process of finding an advisor should occur even before your application is sent. The easiest route to graduate school admission is to have a faculty member at the school to which you are applying who wants to work with you. This happens by making contact with professors with whom you share academic interests. A quick search of the Web will give you an idea of which professors at a given school are working in your area. E-mail contact is the most convenient and, for the student, the least intimidating method for making initial contact. Faculty will usually have an idea of whether they will be taking students the following year, and if your research interests are a match. Once you've found that match, you've basically achieved the goal.

Computer science: If you're going to a school with a small department, you should already have two or three possible advisors in mind. Take their classes, schedule meetings with them to discuss their research plans, and go to lunch with them. Also, get to know their grad students—they can give you a sense of what it's like to work with them.

I don't know much about large departments, but I get the impression that classes become a particularly important means for finding an advisor.

Religious studies: This is a little different for me because there are only two Tibetan Buddhism professors I have to choose from. Even still, I don't know who my advisor will end up being. I'm sure it's something the three of us will sit down and discuss, but, in the long run, I feel like it won't end up making much of a difference since I'll be working with both of them anyway.

Sociology: This may vary by department and by individual style. Some people try to take classes with potential advisors to get to know them in a formal context. Others just show up at office hours and talk it over. Either way, you'll probably want to talk to other graduate students—especially those already working with a certain faculty member—to get a sense of what it is like to work with him or her and what to expect out of the advisor-advisee relationship with that person.

Is it possible to switch advisors? How is that generally done?

Art history: Of course it is structurally possible. If you can't get out from under someone diplomatically and/or on your own steam, a switch can be arranged through the Director of Graduate Studies or Dean of Students.

Bioengineering: Switching advisors can be tricky, depending on funding issues. In science and engineering, it is common for the advisor to be responsible for paying the student's living stipend in addition to normal research expenses. In this case, leaving an advisor would also mean abandoning your financial support. Therefore, switching advisors requires that you have another faculty member lined up who is willing to take on the added financial burden. Once this issue is settled, the amount of red tape involved in making the switch will vary from one institution to the next. A last point to note is that switching advisors may mean starting a new research topic. If you have already devoted a few years to one project, are you willing to drop that line of work and start over from scratch?

Computer science: Yes. It's just a matter of talking to both professors.

Religious studies: For me it'll be very easy to switch advisors, if I decide to do so. When Tibetan Buddhism professor number two was hired, number one—who, until then, was my advisor by default—sent an e-mail to all of his students, saying that if anyone wanted to switch to the other guy, he'd be more than happy to make that happen. I imagine in some departments some bad blood could result from such a switch, but I haven't run into a situation like that.

Sociology: Switching is much like the initial search. You'll want to see if you can form some relationship with the new advisor, or at least meet him or her to discuss the possibility, before making the switch. I would avoid going without an advisor for too long, if possible. Not only do advisors provide work-related advice, they also provide institutional recognition, needed signatures and approvals, access to resources, and some potential representation in discussions (both formal and informal) among faculty in the department.

How do PhD students choose dissertation topics?

Art history: Laboriously and over a prolonged period. During your coursework you will endeavor to gain an overview of your field of specialization. As this picture becomes more complete, it will be easier to see both topics of special interest and exploitable lacunas in the present scholarship. In order to define and claim your territory you will need to work closely with your advisor(s) to ensure that your topic is unclaimed and makes a significant contribution to the field. The topic should be interesting enough to sustain years of attention but also manageable in the required timeframe with available archival resources.

Bioengineering: The dissertation topic in science and engineering is often tied to the research topics for which the advisor currently has funding (e.g., from NIH, NSF, etc.). Smaller details, such as research methods to be used, are usually refined in consultation with the advisor.

Computer science: As far as I can tell, we wander into them. The first couple years are usually spent taking classes and doing smaller research projects, often as part of a professor's long-term research agenda. It's quite common for a grad student to branch off from one of these projects into a related problem that becomes his or her dissertation.

Religious studies: It depends on the student. Some students enter graduate school with a clear idea of what they want to do for their dissertation and end up doing it. Some—most, I think—come up with the topic in their third or fourth year, often after doing a master's paper/exam on a similar topic. Others who have difficulty coming up with their own topic have one given to them by their advisor, based either on what he knows of them, or on something he personally would like to see investigated.

Sociology: There is a great deal of variety on this front as well. Some people know what they want to study from day one. In some ways this is helpful, particularly if you have a like-minded advisor from the start. You can choose courses and adapt other departmental requirements toward preparation and planning for your dissertation. Others are not as clear at the start. These people will develop ideas from coursework, in response to papers or presentations they read or hear, and from conversations with advisors, other faculty, and even other graduate students. This can be a time-consuming process, however, so if your goal is to finish graduate school quickly, it's better to have a solid sense of your research interests before you arrive.

What happens if a candidate doesn't pass the general exams?

Bioengineering: This varies from one institution to the next and even among departments at a single school. In some departments, for example, the average student fails the general exam the first time and a second exam is taken by almost everyone. In other departments, failure is uncommon but a re-take is permitted, though possibly contingent upon the completion of a supplemental course. If someone fails the general exam twice, there is usually no additional recourse.

Computer science: At [my school], they usually give the candidate a second chance to pass "quals," which consists of a research talk. It is very uncommon for a candidate to fail "quals." Like other schools with small departments, [my school] has a policy of only accepting students it expects to succeed. After a second failure, the candidate is asked to leave the department.

Religious studies: I think they spend more time preparing, then try again.

Sociology: In my department, if you fail generals the first time you are allowed to take them again a semester later. Failing twice rarely happens. If it does, it may be the end of the road for the student, though there are almost always exceptions to the rules. There are formal petition processes in place that would allow a student to explain an extenuating circumstance and try again. I think a third try, however, would probably be the last. A general rule of thumb about the way things work in academia: There are lots of rules, regulations, and deadlines, but almost all of them have some flex.

How might a student who doesn't initially receive an ideal financial aid package go about obtaining a better package?

Art history: Many students start their programs without ideal or even adequate packages. I had no funding when I was admitted, but was able to obtain solid scholarships in subsequent years. Securing funding is an ongoing process, so be prepared, no matter what your initial award, to write a number of grants each year. Although the grim facts are rarely advertised, graduate students in the humanities are likely to spend some semesters or years without adequate funding. Even if your initial package offers guaranteed support to degree completion (I have never heard of such a case, by the way), it may take some time to find decent-paying employment after you graduate. Thus when you are considering your financial prospects, you have to consider not only five to seven years of predoctoral funding, but also the possibility up to three years of career searching, relieved only by low-paid adjunct teaching positions and/or postdoctoral fellowships. The regrettable reality is that individuals who have no financial safety net to fall back upon should not embark on a course of study such as this.

Bioengineering: This can be difficult. Usually, the best option is to apply for external support such as the graduate fellowships offered by NIH, NSF, DoD, DoE, etc. Faculty members are not known to take on students who they cannot support initially.

Computer science: I'm afraid I couldn't say, outside of applying for fellowships.

Religious studies: Look for other sources of funding within the university. A student who's offered $8,000 per year from the Religious Studies Department, for example, might be able to earn $12,000 per year working as a writing tutor or in some other department in the university.

Sociology: This I'm not really sure about. Most schools offer the opportunity to teach—either as a teaching assistant or as an actual course instructor—as a way for graduate students to support themselves. There are also lots of research projects going on in various departments, many of which require some "grunt work"—collecting or coding data, doing library searches, performing other tasks. These faculty projects—especially those that have received grant funding—are good places to find work for pay. In a perfect world, you'd find research assistant work in an area of interest to you and have access to the data for your own use in the future. Finally, there are three types of grants available: departmental, institutional, and external. These come in all shapes and sizes, with a wide variety of requirements and restrictions. Lately I feel like I've seen a lot more grant offers for studying non-U.S. nations and societies than for studying the U.S., but that may be a misperception on my part. Keep an eye out for opportunities from various research institutes, both on and off campus, and talk to your advisor for other suggestions.

What types of outside funding are best to pursue?

Computer science: Traditional sources are NSF fellowships and the Hertz fellowship. More recently, the Department for Homeland Defense started offering fellowships to grad students in related fields.

Religious studies: This really depends on your field. I've been fortunate enough to get a lot of money from the federal government through fellowships that support students studying less commonly taught languages. For people in other disciplines, I have no idea. Two things to consider are how much a particular grant/fellowship is for and how many years it's for. Getting a fellowship that's good for two or three years can save a person the trouble of having to scramble for funding every year.

Sociology: See my answer to the previous question. I don't think I have more to add, other than I hear that National Science Foundation grants tend to be larger—but more competitive—than many others.

Does teaching take up a lot of time? Do you have any time management tips?

Art history: Teaching is very time-consuming, but it should be that way. Anyone who pursues a humanities doctorate purely out of a desire to do research should rethink their career choice. Teaching is the foundation of scholarship and should be treated as a worthy goal rather than a necessary means. Nevertheless, teaching can also serve your research, for the process of articulating and discussing your knowledge with undergraduates will force you to organize and clarify your thoughts. Endeavor to obtain teaching assistantships in fields that your comprehensive exams will cover and for specific courses that you will teach after graduation.

Bioengineering: I did not teach as a graduate student.

Computer science: Teaching and grading, in particular, take up a lot of time. Introductory courses are especially time consuming. I would suggest teaching more advanced courses when possible. Also, try to get grading done as early as possible—there's nothing more annoying than grading for a deadline.

Religious studies: I haven't had to do any teaching yet.

Sociology: Yes, but that's not always a bad thing. Your worth will be judged primarily by your research output, but, if you pursue an academic career, you will almost certainly be teaching at some point. Getting experience now is worthwhile. Teaching is also a good source of funding, and if you can find a course that is in your particular subfield, you will get to carefully read material relevant to your own work. Teaching also offers a welcome diversion from your research work; spending all of your time focused on research can burn you out. Be careful, though. Teaching can become the ultimate source of legitimate procrastination. You can always spend more time on your teaching responsibilities. Set some limits on how much time you will spend. And do not feel pressured to respond instantly to student e-mails. If you set up regular times for providing feedback to students and opportunities for asking questions, those should be your primary slots for dealing with student concerns.

Do you have any tips for post-graduation job placement success?

Art history: Start insanely early and build your resume with publications and speaking engagements. Go to all relevant conferences and network as much as possible.

Bioengineering: Your advisor plays a key role in your post-graduation job placement success, especially if your goal is to land a job in academia. The adage, "It's who you know" rings especially true in this case. Often the only difference between the candidate who gets the job and the one who doesn't is that the hiring committee knows the successful candidate (or his or her pedigree) better than the other. While this might seem unfair, hiring committees often receive hundreds of applications for a single position. A candidate who is known by the hiring committee will naturally stand out from the rest. For this reason it is so important for your advisor to help get your name out to his or her colleagues and create a "buzz." Of course, at the end of the day, you have to prove there is substance behind the hype; however, with hundreds of applications not everyone will make it to the proving stage.

Computer science: It's important to have publications at the big conferences and to meet influential people in your field.

Sociology: I haven't gotten that far just yet, so I don't have much to offer. Having seen a number of job talks, however, I would say it's very important for you to work on your public speaking skills well before you go into the job market. A brilliant idea presented poorly is not going to get you a job in a tight market, especially at departments that see junior faculty members as potential teachers of introductory courses that need to attract undergraduate majors. Additionally, I've heard that "working the network" of faculty you know who know faculty elsewhere is a big bonus in at least getting your application a second look.

What are alternative (i.e., non-academic) careers that graduates of your program pursue?

Art history: Museums, commercial galleries, and publishers (of art criticism or other subject matter) offer the primary career alternatives. However, an MA rather than a PhD would suffice for these. There is no point in writing a dissertation if you do not want to teach and research at the university level.

Bioengineering: The biotechnology sector is rapidly expanding, providing many opportunities in industry for PhD graduates.

Computer science: Research labs (e.g., Sun, IBM) are a frequent target.

Religious studies: Graduates of my program who haven't gone into academics have ended up at NGOs, working for the CIA, and as translators for various organizations, most of them religious. Being near-fluent in Tibetan gives us easy access to certain niche occupations. Those niches are very niche-like, however, and are always relatively obscure.

Sociology: I can't think of any good specific examples at the moment, but I know of people considering jobs in think-tanks, politics (campaigns, Congressional staff positions, elected positions), government work (the Census Bureau), and even marketing and consulting jobs.

Are there special perks of being a PhD student that some might not know about? Anything in particular you would recommend taking advantage of?

Bioengineering: Depending on your advisor, you will often have the freedom to set your working hours. This is especially valuable if you have a family and would like the flexibility to participate in daytime events with your children. Also, research sometimes hits a wall and it is good to just leave the lab and try again the next day. This is usually your prerogative when setting your own hours.

Attending research conferences becomes a great excuse to travel the world. I have had the chance to see places that I never would have had I decided to go straight into industry instead of pursuing a PhD.

Religious studies: Theoretically, being a PhD student could help with the ladies, but that hasn't been my experience. It has been my experience, however, that it helps win over their mothers.

One of the best things about being a PhD student is how much free money you're entitled to. We get to travel to Asia for free every summer, just because we're PhD students. You need to ask people about these sorts of things, then take full advantage of them.

Sociology: Student life is remarkably flexible in terms of time. You set your own hours, so if mornings aren't your thing, work afternoons and evenings. Depending on the institution, there are also a lot of unique cultural events and opportunities on and around college campuses that you don't really find elsewhere. In addition, if you find ways to meet people in other departments, you can really broaden your intellectual horizons through very interesting informal cross-disciplinary conversations. Some schools also offer unique opportunities to get involved more heavily with undergraduate life, as undergraduate thesis advisors, residence hall directors, and organizational advisors. If you enjoy college life and the stimulation of lively undergraduate activity, these can be great opportunities to get involved and to give something back to a new generation of students. And, of course, grad student bars have wonderful atmospheres.

The flexibility issue has a downside, though. PhD work follows you everywhere, at all times. Because you could be working at all times, on all days, you may often feel like you should be working at all times, on all days. Add to this the fact that others in your department who feel this pressure will work virtually nonstop and you can really start to feel concerned if you're not doing the same. It can be a rather overwhelming sensation at times, and you can find yourself working long, hard hours without feeling like you're making a lot of progress. This is a tension that lots of graduate students (probably almost all of them, really) deal with during their graduate careers. Keep in mind that this can happen, and be willing to talk to people (other graduate students and junior faculty can be especially helpful) to see how they have dealt with it.

What was the smartest move you made during your program? What was the smartest move you wish you had made?

Art history: Stay open-minded and honest enough to constantly reevaluate your goals, motivations, interests, and happiness; be willing to adapt to the vicissitudes of your personal life, your department and field, and the job market.

In choosing a program, consider that a department or school that prioritizes teaching, mentorship, and community may have advantages over one with a more prestigious name or roster of professors.

Foster sociability and solidarity among your fellow graduate students rather than succumb to competitiveness. Your peers will provide you with feedback, moral and intellectual support, and a social network that will keep you sane during grad school and keep you in the loop once everyone has graduated and is dispersed throughout academia. Don't be intimidated to fight for issues that are important to graduate students; insist on proper mentorship, a living wage, and guidance in professional development and the job search. None of these are a given at the administrative level and graduate students need each other to insist upon them.

Bioengineering: I think my smartest move was getting to know several faculty members on campus besides my own research advisor. Not only do other faculty members often have great insight into research problems, they can also be reference-letter writers—and most academic jobs require four or five references! Looking back, I wish I had not stressed so much about first-year classes and general exams. They really had no bearing on the success of my PhD program.

Computer science: I wish I had gotten my classes out of the way as soon as possible. If you're coming straight out of college, you might be tired of classes and eager to get involved in research, but, later in your career, you will find it tiresome to continue taking classes.

Religious studies: Coming to Tibet has probably been my smartest move. I'm not sure if there's anything I could have done better. Everything so far has been working out perfectly for me, and I mean that.

Sociology: My smartest move was getting involved in a brand new research project from the start. While the project has been a huge time commitment, I have learned more about the research process through my involvement with it than I have in any of my courses or research assistant work. Finding an engaging project with good faculty is a great way to develop intellectual ideas, get access to data, find funding, and gain valuable practical research experience. The project I've been on has also given me the chance to travel to a number of places I had never been to and meet a variety of fascinating people outside academia as well as within.

I wish I had come in with a more concrete sense of what I wanted to study. Developing my interests along the way has been an interesting but challenging process. A clearer sense of academic interest from the start would have streamlined my path through graduate school, and maybe put me on track to finish six months to a year sooner.

CHAPTER VIII

A Word about Master's Degrees and Master's Degree Programs

The benefits of having a master's degree are numerous and varied. For starters, master's-level employees tend to earn more. According to Salary.com's 2003 calculations, individuals with master's degrees earned an average of $53,000 per year—$10,000 more annually than their bachelor's degree-holding counterparts. When that master's degree happened also to be a professional degree (such as an MBA), average earnings soared to $81,000. (That category also included non-master's professional degrees, such as the JD.) It's intuitively obvious: Education pays.

Master's degree programs also afford students the opportunity to specialize in their fields at a level that undergraduate programs typically don't. They further offer the opportunity to conduct original research and to report findings from that research in master's theses. Throughout the investigative process, there are also numerous opportunities to publish.

Having expertise in an area of specialization–not to mention publications–may also help aspiring PhD students gain admission to top programs. Does this mean that all prospective applicants should get master's degrees before seeking out a doctorate? Of course not! Each year PhD programs accept lots of students with bachelor's degrees, and those students go on to receive "incidental" master's degrees on the way to the PhD. (Typically those are awarded after students successfully complete General Examinations, but regulations vary by degree program and institution.) Master's degrees are not usually express prerequisites to PhD programs. They are, however, especially helpful when the proposed field of graduate study differs significantly from the undergraduate curriculum that has been completed.

Finally, it's worth noting that not all master's degrees are created equal. Some are terminal professional degrees, while others are not. The MFA, for instance, is a terminal degree: Once individuals have earned an MFA, their educations are considered complete, and they are (theoretically, at least) eligible for any position in their field—often including teaching at the university level–provided they have the necessary experience and other relevant credentials. Conversely, the MS, for instance, is an advanced degree but not a terminal one; MS-holding individuals will often need PhDs or other doctorate-level degrees before all positions in their field may (again, theoretically) be open to them.

Master's Degree Programs

In what follows, you'll find listings of master's degree programs. Each includes a description of the degree (in a nutshell, what it is and what the program is like), necessary undergraduate coursework (how to make yourself a well qualified applicant), funding options (in the form of fellowships, assistantships, scholarships, and loans), and descriptions of the career paths (both traditional and nontraditional) that are open to individuals who hold the degree.

It's worth noting that a number of schools offer joint-degree programs (such as the JD/MBA or MPH/PhD). In those cases, undergraduate coursework requirements as well as funding options and even degree requirements may vary from what would be typical for discrete programs. In such instances (and as a rule of thumb, always!) check the specific requirements for each program to which you apply.

Master of Accountancy (MAcc)

Brief description
The Master of Accountancy is a one-year, non-thesis graduate program designed to prepare students for careers in public accounting. Beyond the advanced-level training that MAcc candidates receive, they also benefit from an additional opportunity to complete the 150 credit hours (undergraduate coursework included) that are a prerequisite for the Certified Public Accountant (CPA) exam. A number of schools offer both on-campus and distance learning MAcc degree programs.

Undergraduate coursework
Due to the highly specialized nature of the graduate curriculum and CPA exam, an undergraduate degree in accounting is typically required. (More than half of the four-year colleges in the United States offer accounting as a major!) Undergraduate coursework in accounting covers subjects such as calculus, finance, economics (macro- and micro-), statistics, taxation, accounting information systems, and business ethics, all of which are necessary preparation for advanced study in the field.

Funding your MAcc
Students typically fund their MAcc degrees by obtaining various forms of financial aid, including scholarships, student loans (for which U.S. citizens and eligible

noncitizens must complete FAFSA forms), and assistantships. Note that aid options may vary depending on whether the program is completed on campus or online.

Career paths

Graduates often find careers as professional accountants for the government, private industry, and nonprofit organizations; many ultimately launch their own firms. Annual salaries for seasoned professionals often exceed $80,000, and the hours— save the months leading up to April 15th–are generally reasonable. Those who pursue nontraditional related career paths may opt to become actuaries, auditors, bank officers, benefits administrators, statisticians, venture capitalists, financial analysts, investment bankers, management consultants, traders, or even entrepreneurs.

Master of Applied Anthropology (MAA)

Brief description

The Master of Applied Anthropology is a two-year program that focuses on the application of anthropology to human conflict issues throughout the world. Those who pursue this degree tend to be problem solvers who want to work on a global scale to resolve conflicts that involve cultural diversity, poverty, gender, class, and other influential social variables. As the emphasis of this degree is placed on using the skills acquired in the world outside of academia, this is considered a professional rather than a liberal arts degree.

Undergraduate coursework

Since anthropology covers such a broad range of both the humanities and sciences, MAA candidates come from all realms of study, though most can show substantial evidence of undergraduate anthropological interest.

Funding your MAA

In some instances, schools will not offer financial aid to students who do not wish to pursue a PhD, so be sure to check with your school regarding financial packages for master's candidates before accepting. Typical packages include scholarships, student loans, fellowships, and teaching and research assistantships.

Career paths

Though salaries aren't high—$47, 550 on average—anthropologists tend to have a high degree of satisfaction with their careers. While some graduates pursue a PhD with the intention of one day teaching, many others decide to enter the public and private sectors as practitioners, advertising executives, museum curators, archaeologists, diplomats or foreign-service officers, and social workers.

Master of Architecture (MArch I, MArch II, or MArch III)

Brief description

The Master of Architecture is a one- to 3.5-year program. The MArch I is primarily for students whose bachelor's degrees are not in architecture specifically, but rather in a related discipline. In particular, the MArch I degree is geared toward students who have not completed the five-year bachelor of architecture degree. MArch II is for students who have completed the five-year bachelor of architecture degree. Typically, the MArch II entails one or two years of study. Finally, the somewhat less common MArch III degree program usually requires 3.5 years of study. Many MArch III programs do not require students to have previous academic training in architecture. In all cases, MArch students explore not only the history and theory of architecture, but also the technical, social, ethical, and aesthetic concerns that come with the design and construction of a building. Additional coursework in design, mathematics, computer science, and structural engineering will also be required. Most programs require a thesis or final design project. Only about 110 schools in the nation offer NAAB-accredited professional programs in architecture, so admission to these programs is highly competitive. Once the professional architecture program has been successfully completed and three years' work experience obtained, the aspiring architect may take the Architectural Registration Exam (ARE).

Undergraduate coursework

As just noted, MArch programs are extremely competitive, so you'll likely need to submit a very convincing portfolio of creative work to gain entrance. If possible, a five-year BArch degree is ideal. Crucial coursework includes mathematics (trigonometry, analytic geometry, and calculus), physics, design fundamentals, architectural design, architectural theory, architectural structures, construction, and computer graphics.

Funding your MArch

Once admitted, students often find themselves in the running for a veritable bevy of scholarships and fellowships—but make sure to check with your department, as you may have to apply for each award separately! If all else fails, there are always those stalwart student loans (for which U.S. citizens and eligible non-citizens must complete FAFSA forms).

Career paths

With successful architects earning more than $99,800 per year, it's no surprise that this field is booming in both supply and demand for innovative minds and designs. Those who opt not to continue their studies at the doctoral level often find employment in architecture and engineering firms, as design, building, or construction managers, interior designers, teachers, planners in the public or private sectors, and some even go into business for themselves.

Master of Arts (MA)

Brief description

The master of arts is typically a two-year (but may be a one-year) graduate course of study in humanities or social science. Typically, students undertake this course of study before applying for a doctorate, but some opt to pursue it so they may explore the subject of their choice in greater depth.

Undergraduate coursework

Applicants must have completed a BA and are expected to display a high level of proficiency in their area of study, particularly in reading, researching, and writing. Most schools require GRE (general exam) scores, as well. For programs in biochemistry/cell and molecular biology, biology, chemistry, computer science, literature in English, mathematics, physics, or psychology, GRE subject tests are typically also required.

Funding your MA

Students typically fund their MA through a combination of financial aid sources such as merit- and need-based scholarships, teaching fellowships and assistantships, and student loans.

Career paths

Most students get an MA in order to fulfill the academic prerequisite for a PhD, which itself is a prerequisite for teaching at the university level. However, there are options besides academia for those who choose to hold at an MA. Thanks to a curriculum consisting largely of research, writing, and analytical thinking, most graduates find themselves well-equipped for careers in teaching, business, government, nonprofit work, administration, journalism, advertising, and countless other related and unrelated professions.

Master of Arts in International Economics and Finance (MAief)

Brief description

The Master of Arts in International Economics and Finance is a one- to two-year terminal degree designed to train economists in the analysis of business, economic, and financial policy on an international level. In contrast to an MBA, this degree is less concerned with the management than with the application of standard economic theory and econometric methods to firms and financial markets worldwide.

Undergraduate coursework

While you'd expect an undergraduate degree in economics or business to be necessary, those who have an interest and talent for international economic issues and graduated with degrees in other fields may also apply. Demonstration of strong analytical skills is key, however. Be sure to check your school's admission requirements, as GRE and/or GMAT scores are often required.

Funding your MAief

Students often fund their MAief through a series of public and private scholarships (make sure to get in touch with private businesses and financial corporations to ask about what they can offer you—the way they see it, giving you money to study is an investment in their future), and student loans.

Career paths

Entry-level position salaries for recent MAief graduates tend to start at $50,000 on average, and there's no shortage of companies and organizations that are keen to hire analysts. Graduates often take positions as researchers, consultants, or tax analysts for consulting companies; fixed income or equity analysts in asset management companies; analysts or associates in investment banking; project managers, budget analysts, or policy analysts in private, government, and non-profit sectors; and there are always those who find faculty positions.

Master of Arts in Religion (MAR)

Brief description

The Master of Arts in Religion is a two-year program for students who have completed an undergraduate major or minor in religion. The program emphasizes theology, ethics, and biblical studies, and prepares students for teaching in public and private schools or undertaking doctoral studies in this field. A number of schools offer both on-campus and distance learning MAR degree programs.

Undergraduate coursework

Depending on where you apply, an undergraduate degree with a major or minor in religious studies will probably be required, as is a solid background in the humanities and social sciences. Besides coursework in religion, undergraduate study should include courses in anthropology and relevant foreign languages.

Funding your MAR

Students typically fund their MAR degrees by obtaining various forms of financial aid, including scholarships, student loans, and assistantships. Note that aid options may vary depending on whether the program is completed on campus or online.

Career paths

Like many advanced degrees, the MAR is a labor of love—and while good jobs can be found, those seeking top-dollar paychecks may want to look elsewhere. Those who seek spiritual enlightenment, however, should be more than happy with their options. Many students who wish to become clergy members go on to study religion at a higher level, while others opt to teach theology in public and private institutions. Some take educational jobs in places of worship, while others work a variety of secular jobs, having undertaken an MAR for personal rather than professional reasons.

Master of Arts in Teaching (MAT)

Brief description

The Master of Arts in Teaching is a professional degree designed specifically to prepare students for a teaching career in a particular area of study (say, English, history, math, or science) in grades 7–12. The MAT focuses on teaching as a clinical profession, and the degree itself functions as a training ground for future teachers, giving them skills and knowledge that can be applied directly to any classroom environment while also offering apprenticeships with working professionals so they may get an idea of what to expect as practitioners.

Undergraduate coursework

Students are expected to have an undergraduate degree in the field of study (or closely related field of study) in which they intend to teach.

Funding your MAT

In a move to attract more teachers to understaffed schools (as is the case in New York City, among others), some cities have begun offering substantial scholarships for MAT candidates who are willing to sign a contract to teach in that city for anywhere from two to five years. In addition to this, there are other scholarships and fellowships available, and as always, prospective MAT degree candidates may apply for student loans.

Career paths

When a degree has this level of professional focus, it isn't outside the realm of reason to claim that 99.9 percent of graduates go on to teach, largely in the public school system. Okay, that may be a slight exaggeration—but seriously, this is a program tailor-made for individuals who want to teach, and as graduates that's exactly what they tend to do. With an ever-increasing need for teachers and improving salaries, this is one path to a career that promises to be highly rewarding.

Master of Business Administration (MBA)

Brief description

The Master of Business Administration is a professional degree that trains students in management and strategy, accounting, economics, marketing, finance, organization, and decision sciences, in order to prepare them for leadership roles in the highly competitive and unpredictable world of business.

Undergraduate coursework

While an undergraduate degree in business or a related field of study is definitely recommended, it isn't necessary (though do make sure you've taken a few statistics and calculus courses). For MBAs in particular, work experience (and success) can—and often does—offset an imperfect undergraduate curriculum; the average age of entering candidates is typically late 20s. One thing that is absolutely necessary is your GMAT score. Be sure to check with your school for any additional requirements.

Funding your MBA

Students typically fund their MBA degrees by obtaining various forms of financial aid, including scholarships, student loans, and assistantships. Note that aid options may vary depending on whether the program is completed on campus or online. For MBA programs in particular, students are more likely to take on large loans (which they're very likely to get), since post-graduation earning potential is so high. (Graduates from Columbia Business School in 2004 earned an average starting salary of $143,682.)

Career Paths

High salaries and technology have been the two driving factors behind the increasingly competitive world of business management and administration. You could say: The higher the salaries, the more attractive the jobs. The better the technology, the fewer people needed to run a business. But there always needs to be someone in charge, and most graduates find jobs and good salaries across a wide array of finance, banking, consulting, energy, transportation, marketing, and technology firms in the public and private sectors.

Master of Business and Organizational Leadership (MBOL)

Brief description

The Master of Business and Organizational Leadership is geared toward working professionals who want to apply to positions with advanced managerial and leadership responsibilities. Akin to the MBA, the MBOL concentrates on the role and implementation of leadership and influence in successful business ventures.

Undergraduate coursework

Students are expected to have an undergraduate degree in business or related field of study. Since this is a program designed for professionals, those applying should have three to five years of job experience on average (check with your school to make sure).

Funding your MBOL

Students typically fund their MBOL degrees by obtaining various forms of financial aid, including scholarships, student loans, and assistantships. Note that aid options may vary depending on whether the program is completed on campus or online.

Career paths

Since most students undertake an MBOL after several years of working in business administration, they tend to have a good idea of where they're headed after graduation, often returning to their previous—or current, as the case may be—employer to work in a higher managerial position.

Master of City Planning (MCP)

Brief description

The Master of City Planning is a two-year professional degree that is designed to provide students with an understanding of the history, theory, fields, and sub-fields of city planning, while also training them in the fundamentals of city planning, such as urban design, urban economic development, community development and housing, environmental planning and policy, and land-use planning.

Undergraduate coursework

Admissions tend to favor those with an undergraduate degree in urban studies (or a similar program) who display a proficiency in both the creative and practical aspects of city planning. Depending on the school to which you apply, GRE scores may also be necessary.

Funding your MCP

There are many opportunities for students to secure funding for their degree through scholarships, paid internships (also a great way to ensure a job after graduation!) and student loans.

Career paths

After graduation, around 75 percent of MCP holders are employed by local and state government agencies that handle transportation, housing, and environmental protection. In the private sector, jobs are bountiful in engineering, scientific, and architectural services, and also for planners involved in technical, management, and scientific consulting.

Master of City and Regional Planning (MCRP)

Brief description

The Master of City and Regional Planning is a two-year professional degree similar to an MCP in that it is designed to provide students with an understanding of the history, theory, fields, and sub-fields of city planning, while also training them in the fundamentals of city planning, such as urban design, urban economic development, community development and housing, environmental planning and policy, and land use planning. However, with the MCRP a strong emphasis is placed on both urban land use planning (physical planning and urban design) and environmental planning (natural systems and development impacts).

Undergraduate coursework

As with the MCP degree, admissions tend to favor those with an undergraduate degree in urban studies (or a similar program) who display a proficiency in both the creative and practical aspects of city planning. Depending on the school to which you apply, GRE scores may also be necessary.

Funding your MCRP

There are many opportunities for students to secure funding for their degree through scholarships, paid internships (also a great way to ensure a job after graduation!), and student loans.

Career paths

After graduation, most of MCRP holders are employed by local and state government agencies that handle transportation, housing, and environmental protection. In the private sector, jobs are bountiful in engineering, scientific, and architectural services, and also for planners involved in technical, management, and scientific consulting.

Master of Criminal Justice (MCJ)

Brief description

The Master of Criminal Justice is a professional degree designed for individuals in the criminal justice field who want to expand their leadership and managerial abilities, prepare for further criminological studies, or pursue a career teaching criminal justice.

Undergraduate coursework

Applicants to the MCJ must have an undergraduate degree, and in most cases, take the GRE (check with your school). As this degree is designed largely for current law enforcement professionals (though pre-professionals are also encouraged to apply), evidence of experience in your field of study is looked on favorably.

Funding your MCJ

Students typically fund their MCJ degrees by obtaining various forms of financial aid, including scholarships, employer tuition reimbursement, and student loans. Note that aid options may vary depending on whether the program is completed on campus or online.

Career paths

Crime doesn't pay, but criminal justice does. Jobs are on the rise (and competition is heating up) as are salaries and after graduation students can expect to earn $51,000 per year on average in a variety of positions in any field of law enforcement imaginable. Students tend to take jobs with major organizations—ATF, CIA, DEA, FBI, U.S. Marshalls, Secret Service, Coast Guard, INS, police departments nationwide—or work as private investigators or on private security details. Other jobs include crime scene investigators, forensic psychologists, court clerks, paralegals, and court reporters.

Master of Divinity (MDiv)

Brief description

The Master of Divinity is a three-year professional degree in divinity. It is the minimum academic requirement for ordination, designed to provide students with the necessary foundation to take on a leadership role in a church or ministry, or to prepare students for further academic study (PhD, ThD, and DMin).

Undergraduate coursework

Applicants must hold an undergraduate degree, preferably in liberal arts with some evidence of religious study, and must usually include a "religious autobiography" detailing the applicant's history and interest in religion. Relevant foreign language study and proficiency is also important.

Funding your MDiv

Students often fund their MDiv through a combination of scholarships, fellowships, grants, and student loans.

Career paths

With a degree in ministry, most students (not surprisingly) take quickly to ministering after graduation. And while yearly salaries hover around $30,000, job satisfaction is high. MDiv graduates who opt not to continue with their studies find careers largely in churches as ministers, chaplains, counselors, and educators. Other organizations that typically hire graduates include hospitals, grant making and social advocacy organizations, armed forces, public and private schools and universities, and charitable foundations.

Master of Education (MEd)

Brief description

The Master of Education is a one- or two-year degree program designed to offer professional teachers and educators the opportunity to further their knowledge and understanding of education in order to work better in the classroom or apply to higher educational positions. Many teachers are required to apply for this degree by state law. Teachers with master's-level degrees also earn more each year!

Undergraduate coursework

Students are required to have an undergraduate degree, and in most cases, must present GRE scores. As this is a degree geared toward professionals, evidence of teaching experience is recommended.

Funding your MEd

Students look to scholarships, grants, fellowships, and as always, student loans to fund their degree. In some cases, school districts will fund or subsidize study.

Career paths

For most students, this degree is a necessary step in advancing to a higher position (often administrative) within their schools or receiving a raise. Many therefore return to teaching on completing the program. Even for those who entered the program immediately after completing their BA degrees, finding a job as a teacher is more than possible, thanks to an increasing job market and the contacts made while working in the classroom during MEd study. Some students go on to pursue EdD degrees; these individuals often become school/district administrators or education policy makers.

Master of Engineering (MEng)

Brief description

The Master of Engineering is a two-year coursework-based professional degree that is offered as an alternative to the traditional research-based Master of Science; there is no project or thesis requirement for the MEng. It is ideal for students who, due to professional responsibilities, do not have the time for research.

Undergraduate coursework

Applicants must have an undergraduate degree in engineering or closely related field (math or science—anything else is stretching it). In some instances, GRE scores are also required so be sure to check with your school beforehand.

Funding your MEng

Students most often fund their MEng degrees by obtaining various forms of financial aid, including scholarships, student loans, and assistantships.

Career paths

Businesses depend on engineers to provide innovative and economical solutions to their product problems, and given the age of technological wonder we live in, the demand for talented and well-educated engineers is higher than ever. From petroleum to telecommunications to everything in between, MEng graduates are able to find good jobs in a market that provides some of the highest average starting salaries around.

Master of Fine Arts (MFA)

Brief description

The Master of Fine Arts is a two- to three-year terminal degree in writing, film, acting, or studio art. Unlike the MA, there is less focus on academic study and more on actual artistic output, with most classes functioning as workshops and seminars dedicated to the furthering of artistic endeavors. A thesis or final project is required.

Undergraduate coursework

Applicants to the program require an undergraduate degree and a portfolio of creative work in the area of intended study. Competition to MFA programs is intense, and a strong portfolio, artistic experience, and a rigorous undergraduate curriculum are a must. Outside experience (in the form of publications, professional productions, and exhibitions) are also crucial. Depending on the school, GRE scores may be required.

Funding your MFA

Students often fund their MFA through a combination of scholarships, teaching fellowships, grants, and student loans. Some scholarships may be awarded based on the strength of the portfolio—the more they want you, the less you're likely to have to pay.

Career paths

Well, no one ever got into art to make money, right? Though this degree may not offer the seemingly gold-paved path to fortune that others might, it should be noted that it does give students the opportunity to focus on their art for at least two years, and to learn from the masters of their craft—and maybe even to secure a multimillion-dollar book/film deal in the process. In any case, graduates do find jobs—well-paying ones even—in fields more varied than would be thought possible (freelancing, consulting, performing, writing, acting, and so forth). Since the MFA is a terminal degree, many graduates often go on to teach at the university level.

Master of Forensic Sciences (MFS)

Brief description

The Master of Forensic Sciences is a specialized professional degree designed to integrate scientific practices and methods with law enforcement issues. By learning to apply the laws of science along with social theory and law to crimes, students are prepared for careers as both sleuths and crime solvers.

Undergraduate coursework

Students are typically required to have an undergraduate degree in science with a concentration in the field of forensics that they want to study.

Funding your MFS

Students largely fund their degrees through student loans.

Career paths

Interest in this field has skyrocketed in recent years, thanks in part to a little show called "CSI." As a result, the job market for MFS graduates is both competitive and lucrative. Most find employment with crime labs operated by private industry or with the local, state, or federal government. Others decide to work in the field with law enforcement agencies as crime scene investigators, while for those who want to eventually teach or become forensic anthropologists, entomologists (you might be shocked by how much insects at a crime scene reveal!), or pathologists, this degree serves as a prerequistite for further academic study.

Master of Health Administration (MHA)

Brief description

The Master of Health Administration is a professional degree designed to train students for management careers in health policy, economics, and project and program implementation within the health care industry. By approaching health care from a business perspective, students learn to implement a wide range of techniques and perspectives in dealing with organizational, policy-based, economic, financial, and managerial issues involving any health services enterprise.

Undergraduate coursework

Students must have an undergraduate degree (virtually any field of study is acceptable, though an interest in business or health care is important), and in most cases GRE scores are required, as well.

Funding your MHA

Students fund their degree through a combination of fellowships, internships, teaching or research assistantships, grants, and student loans. Note that aid options may vary depending on whether the program is completed on campus or online.

Career paths

Graduates often find careers in a variety of positions—such as project, process, and quality management, business and policy development, clinical program evaluation, analysis and evaluation—with pharmaceutical companies, biotechnology companies, medical device and diagnostic firms, health insurance plans, hospitals, managed care organizations, and consulting firms, earning on average $67,430 per year.

Master of Health Science (MHS)

Brief description

The Master of Health Science is a specialized degree that offers an alternative to the MPH by allowing students to engage in advanced study and research or professional advancement in the health care area of their choice. It is designed both for students with little health care experience and current professionals who want to begin or advance their public health careers

Undergraduate coursework

Students must have an undergraduate degree (any field of study is acceptable, though preference is given to those who specialized or have experience in business or health care; some students without much experience may be required to complete certain prerequisite courses) and in most cases GRE scores are required as well.

Funding your MHS

Students tend to fund their degree through a combination of fellowships, internships, teaching or research assistantships, grants, and student loans. Aid options may vary depending on whether the program is completed on campus or online.

Career paths

Students who were previously (or are continually) employed in the health care industry return to take on higher-level leadership roles. Other graduates often find careers in a variety of positions—such as project, process, and quality management, business and policy development, clinical program evaluation, analysis and evaluation—with pharmaceutical companies, biotechnology companies, medical device and diagnostic firms, health insurance plans, hospitals, managed care organizations, and consulting firms. Students earn an average of $67,430 per year.

Master of Industrial Design (MID)

Brief description

The Master of Industrial Design is a two- to three-year project-based degree that focuses on the creation, development, and design of products and their relation both to the manufacturer and to society as a whole. Students are trained in identifying consumer need and interest along with the heeding technical, economic, ethical, environmental, and safety concerns involved with industrial design. The program places an emphasis on teamwork and cooperation in order to create a product that is not only aesthetically pleasing, but also functional and appealing to consumer demand.

Undergraduate coursework

Students must have an undergraduate degree (preferably in industrial design, although those with degrees in other fields are often provisionally accepted and required to complete certain prerequisites before beginning their MID), and evidence of professional or personal interest in industrial design is recommended.

Funding your MID

Students tend to fund their degree through a combination of fellowships, scholarships, teaching or research assistantships, grants, and student loans.

Career paths

With design jobs on the rise, graduates can expect to earn $52,310 on average right after graduation. Those who crave independence in their vocation can take comfort: One out of three industrial designers is self-employed. MID graduates find careers with corporate design offices in manufacturing companies, independent design consulting firms, governmental agencies, and educational institutions, where they work in a varied range of roles, including communications, equipment, toy, electronics, exhibit, furniture, vehicle, interior, and product or packaging designers.

Master of Landscape Architecture (MLA)

Brief description

The Master of Landscape Architecture is a professional degree that focuses on the creation, development, and design of outdoor and indoor landscape areas. Students are trained to consider all elements and concerns involved in the shaping or reshaping of the natural world, including environmental ethics, communication, design development, project management, building materials and technology, and ethical conduct.

Undergraduate coursework

If applying to the professional degree (MLA I), students simply need an undergraduate degree. If applying to the post-professional degree (MLA II), students need an undergraduate degree in landscape architecture. Evidence of experience or significant interest in landscape architecture in not required, but it is recommended.

Funding your MLA

Students tend to fund their degree through a combination of fellowships, scholarships, teaching or research assistantships, grants, and student loans.

Career paths

An independent bunch, more than 26 percent of landscape architects are self-employed in an ever-expanding job market. Hiring is up, salaries are up, and graduates who crave a more collaborative environment find work with a number of private, public, and academic organizations, most often in architectural, engineering, and planning firms, or with regional, municipal, federal, and state agencies. And for those who prefer academia to the office, there's always teaching.

Master of Laws (LLM)

Brief description
The Master of Laws is an advanced postgraduate law degree that usually takes one year to complete. The program allows students who come from all areas of law—both professional and academic—to specialize in the particular area of law of their choosing.

Undergraduate coursework
In most cases—though there are occasionally exceptions for foreign applicants—students need a Juris Doctor (JD) degree from an American Bar Association-approved law school.

Funding your LLM
Students fund their LLM through a combination of scholarships, teaching fellowships, research assistantships, grants, and student loans.

Career paths
Most LLM graduates pursue careers in law in the area of their specialization, starting as associates with legal firms and working their way up the proverbial ladder to partner, private practice, or a nomination to judgeships. Competition for positions is growing fiercer thanks to a growing job market and attractive salaries ($94,930 per year on average), so the LLM distinction makes a difference when applying to firms.

Master of Liberal Arts (MLA)

Brief description
The Master of Liberal Arts is an interdisciplinary degree designed for students who want to explore in detail their intellectual interests by creating their own course of study within the arts and sciences. The degree program can take anywhere from two to five years, depending on whether the program is full-time or part-time.

Undergraduate coursework

Students must have an undergraduate degree and show evidence of significant interest in the area they intend to study.

Funding your MLA

Students tend to fund their degree through a combination of scholarships, teaching fellowships, grants, and student loans.

Career paths

The MLA is largely a personal interest degree, meaning that students often undertake it for intellectual rather than professional fulfillment (though in some cases graduates use the degree to advance to a higher position in their line of work). As most graduates enter the program after already finding careers, they tend to return to their previous jobs in every type of occupation and industry. Many also use the degree as a springboard to study at the doctoral level.

Master of Library Science/Master of Library and Information Science (MLS/MLIS)

Brief description

The Master of Library Science is a two-year professional degree designed to train students in the cataloging, classification, and preservation of books, as well as how to manage library resources and identify information needs for people of all ages and backgrounds. Given the increasing technological capacities to store and retrieve information, qualified reference librarians with electronic aptitude are in demand. Note: The Master of Library and Information Sciences (MLIS) is essentially the same degree as the MLS, as it differs only in the name the university gives it.

Undergraduate coursework

Applicants to the program require an undergraduate degree (typically, but not necessarily, in English), and in most cases GRE scores are also needed.

Funding your MLS

Students tend to fund their degree through scholarships, grants, and student loans.
Career paths

MLS graduates go on to work wherever libraries are used, information services are needed, or cataloging is necessary. Though jobs aren't necessarily on the rise, an expected exodus of retiring librarians will give any future graduate a very good shot at employment. Many students find work as an academic, law, music, public, or fine arts librarian with academic, public, and government institutions. Others go into medical or media cataloging or become researchers for information services providers. A word of advice: Many employers prefer to hire students who are graduates of MLS programs at any of the 56 schools accredited by the American Library Association.

Master of Music (MM or MMus)

Brief description
The Master of Music is a two-year degree in music with an emphasis on personal musical performance (rather than theory) across an array of majors including composition, conducting, jazz, opera, individual instruments, and many more.

Undergraduate coursework
Applicants to the program require an undergraduate degree (typically in music, but an outstanding audition and impressive array of performance experience will ultimately trump the undergraduate degree program) and can expect to audition for admission into the program. Also, depending on what specific major the applicant intends to study, proficiency in a particular foreign language may also be required.

Funding your MM or MMus
Students often fund their degree through a combination of scholarships, grants, and student loans.

Career paths
Music, as with any art-based degree, is a labor of love, and employment can often be seen more as pitfall than possibility. This isn't to say making a living as a professional musician is impossible, but be ready for a competitive and at times uneven job market. For those who make it, job satisfaction is high. For a more stable career, many graduates continue their studies in music at the doctoral level in order to become professors or instructors, and many give private lessons throughout their studies.

Master of Occupational Therapy (MOT)

Brief description

The Master of Occupational Therapy is the entry-level degree for the occupational therapy profession. Students investigate human development post-injury or post-illness and learn the many components of rehabilitation. Many ultimately specialize in a particular field; OT of the hand, for example).

Undergraduate coursework

Applicants require an undergraduate degree (though students of any major may apply, there are science-based prerequisites that are mandatory for those seeking admission). Work or volunteer experience in occupational therapy is encouraged (in some programs mandatory), and GRE scores may be required.

Funding your MOT

Students most often fund their degree through a combination of teaching fellowships, grants, and student loans.

Career paths

Employment is on the rise, and with the 2007 deadline approaching for the MOT to become the minimum educational requirement for the profession, recent and future graduates can look forward to steady work and rising wages ($54,660 per year on average). For graduates who opt to enter the workforce rather than continue with their studies, most find jobs in hospitals, occupational therapy or physician's offices, home health care services, nursing homes, private practice, and government agencies.

Master of Philosophy (MPhil)

Brief description

The Master of Philosophy is typically awarded to PhD candidates who have completed all required coursework but have yet to complete and defend their doctoral dissertations (known as ABD—All But Dissertation). (It is also an independent one-year master's program in the UK.) The Doctor of Philosophy program is designed for students who want to explore education in any field in greater depth while honing their research and teaching skills, all with the goal of developing into successful educators and scholars.

Undergraduate coursework

Applicants to the program sometimes have a master's degree in the area they intend to study. GRE scores (both general and, as applicable, subject tests) are also required. Demonstrated aptitude in the area of study is key.

Funding your MPhil

Students often fund their MPhil through a combination of scholarships, teaching fellowships, grants, and student loans.

Career paths

As this is somewhat a transitory degree, most students go on to defend their dissertations and gain their PhD; afterwards, they often join university faculties as full-time, tenure-track professors or researchers. Other graduates, usually those with science-based degrees may decide to put their educations into practice outside of academia and work in their fields with organizations, institutions, or simply as private practitioners.

Master of Professional Studies (MPS)

Brief description

The Master of Professional Studies is a terminal interdisciplinary degree that is used for programs of study that do not adhere to traditional categories, such as interactive telecommunications, organizational studies, or certain social science programs. An emphasis is placed on developing leadership abilities for use professionally in organizations that deal with highly complex political and social issues.

Undergraduate coursework

Applicants are required to have an undergraduate degree and in most cases, GRE scores are needed, as well.

Funding your MPS

Students often fund their MPS through scholarships, teaching fellowships, grants, and student loans. Note that aid options may vary depending on whether the program is completed on campus or online.

Career paths

As the MPS program is designed to train a student in the necessary professional skills for a particular occupation, it's no surprise that many graduates go on to work in a managerial capacity in the specific field of their educational undertaking. Examples of industries are homeland security management, human resources, health and safety management, waste management, and more. Other graduates decide to continue with their studies at the doctoral level in the pursuit of further education or job advancement.

Master of Project Management (MPM)

Brief description

The Master of Project Management is a terminal professional degree that prepares technically qualified individuals for responsible management roles in construction, urban planning, and architecture and engineering design. Students are trained in the fundamentals of successful scheduling, risk analysis, human resources, budget, and conflict management.

Undergraduate coursework

Due to the highly technical nature of the MPM, an undergraduate degree in engineering or a closely related field (evidence of similar work experience is encouraged, especially if the degree isn't in engineering) and in some cases, GRE scores are required.

Funding your MPM

Besides personal savings, private grants and loans, the main source of funding for MPM students tends to be student loans. Aid options may vary depending on whether the program is completed on campus or online.

Career paths

Since this degree tends to be one that working professionals undertake in order to further their careers, most return to their previous company to work in a higher capacity (with a substantial pay raise) as supervisors or managers largely in engineering or scientific firms. Continuing education on the doctoral level is an option as well, and with a growing job market it pays well to be well educated.

Master of Public Administration (MPA)

Brief description

The Master of Public Administration is a professional degree that trains students to become skilled and successful leaders or managers in the public service field through the development and implementation of public policy, projects, and programs while keeping any budgetary, organizational, and human resources issues in mind.

Undergraduate coursework

While most applicants pursued an undergraduate major in the social sciences, anyone with an undergraduate degree may apply provided they show an aptitude and interest in public administration. Work experience in the public sector or undergraduate coursework in economics, American government, and statistics is recommended. In most cases, GRE scores are necessary.

Funding your MPA

Students often fund their degree through a combination of scholarships, teaching fellowships, and student loans. Aid options may vary depending on whether the program is completed on campus or online.

Career paths

Thanks to a specialized degree is an ever-growing field, MPA graduates are in demand and most often find work in business or education administration, nonprofit organizations, and local, state, and federal government, in specializations involving community development (planning and development), agriculture, health care, law enforcement, policy analysis, and public and private education.

Master of Public Health (MPH)

Brief description

The Master of Public Health is a professional postgraduate degree designed to educate working professionals in the five core public health areas: health services administration, biostatistics, epidemiology, behavioral sciences/health education, and environmental health sciences, in order to undertake and successfully handle any public health issues that may arise in their eventual careers.

Undergraduate coursework

Applicants are required to have an undergraduate degree (not necessarily with a health emphasis, though most schools require a minimum number of science and math classes), evidence of either academic or professional postgraduate experience in public health, and in most cases, GRE scores.

Funding your MPH

Students usually fund their degree through a combination of scholarships, grants, and student loans. Note that aid options may vary depending on whether the program is completed on campus or online.

Career paths

Either way you go—academic or professional—get ready for long hours but big rewards. Many students who enter the MPH program are enrolled in other health-related degree programs or plan to apply for doctoral-level studies after graduating. Many students enter the work force and find jobs in a wide array of administrative positions in health care as researchers, consultants, medical directors, and advisors to public, private, and government health care providers, pharmaceutical manufacturers, and insurance companies.

Master of Public Policy (MPP)

Brief description

The Master of Public Policy is a professional degree that trains students to become skilled and successful leaders or managers in the public service field through the development and implementation of public policy, projects, and programs while keeping any budgetary, organizational, and human resources issues in mind. Similar to the MPA, the MPP focuses more on analyzing the political, economic, quantitative, organizational, and normative aspects of complex problems in public policy.

Undergraduate coursework

While most applicants pursued an undergraduate major in the social sciences, anyone with an undergraduate degree may apply provided they show an aptitude and interest in public administration. Work experience in the public sector or undergraduate coursework in economics, American government, and statistics is recommended. And in most cases, GRE scores are necessary.

Funding your MPP

Students usually fund their degree through a combination of teaching fellowships, scholarships, grants, and student loans.

Career paths

Graduates find work in education administration, nonprofit organizations, and local, state, and federal government, in specializations involving community development, agriculture, health care, law enforcement, and policy analysis.

Master of Sacred Theology (STM)

Brief description

The Master of Sacred Theology is a second-level professional degree designed to build on a student's academic foundation for entrance to a doctoral program or offer further theological instruction to ordained ministers. It is comparable to the Master of Theology degree, though it places a more pronounced emphasis on the practical—rather than the academic—aspects of theology.

Undergraduate coursework

Applicants must have a Master of Divinity or related degree is required. In some cases GRE scores may be required (usually dependent on the last degree earned), so be sure to check with your school for their specific admissions criteria.

Funding your STM

Students tend to fund their degrees through a combination of scholarships, teaching fellowships, student loans, and other forms of financial aid.

Career paths

For many graduates the STM is a required part of their journey toward a doctoral degree, while for others it offers a way of exploring the many facets of their professional field in greater depth, afterwards beginning or resuming careers as ordained ministers or religious educators.

Master of Science (MS)

Brief description

The Master of Science is generally a two-year graduate course of study in an area of science (which ranges from fields diverse as biotechnology to real estate), most often pursued before applying for a doctorate, but sometimes undertaken by those who wish to study the subject of their choice in greater depth.

Undergraduate coursework
Applicants must have completed a bachelor of science degree and are expected to display a high level of proficiency in their area of study, particularly in mathematics, research, and writing. Most schools require GRE scores as well.

Funding your MS
Students typically fund their degree through a combination of financial aid sources, such as merit- and need-based scholarships, teaching fellowships and assistantships, and student loans (for which U.S. citizens and eligible non-citizens must also complete FAFSA forms).

Career paths
Most students undertake an MS with the understanding that they will complete a PhD in their subject of study. After earning this degree, most remain in academia to teach, though many gain employment in fields as varied as imaginable. In recent years, science-based careers have skyrocketed and show no signs of relenting—forgive the cliché—but the sky truly is the limit in this sector.

Master of Science in Foreign Service (MSFS)

Brief description
The Master of Science in Foreign Service is a two-year degree program designed to prepare students for careers in international affairs. Specifically, the curriculum involves both the theory and practice of foreign service, as the degree is very professionally-oriented.

Undergraduate coursework
Applicants are required to have an undergraduate degree and history of high academic achievement. Other important criteria for admission are evidence of academic interest and professional work in international affairs. GRE scores are also required. Ultimately, background checks are likely before job offers may be made.

Funding your MSFS
Students usually fund their degree through a combination of scholarships, teaching fellowships, and student loans.

Career paths

As the MSFS degree is designed for students seeking careers in that specific field of study, it should come as no surprise that graduates most often enter the workforce immediately after the commencement ceremony. Many take positions with national and foreign government agencies, NGOs, and private corporations. As you would expect of such a degree, up to 75 percent of those who go into Foreign Service gain employment overseas. Of those who remain in the United States, the majority work with the government and are based out of Washington, DC.

Master of Science in Nursing (MSN)

Brief description

The Master of Science in Nursing is the most common professional degree in nursing, designed to develop leaders in health promotion, patient advocacy and health care innovation at local, national, and global levels. This is a required degree for becoming an advanced-practice nurse, such as clinical nurse specialist or nurse practitioner, or for undertaking doctorate-level study in nursing.

Undergraduate coursework

Applicants typically have a bachelor of science in nursing (in some cases with a minimum cumulative GPA of 3.0; in all cases with a strong background in mathematics and science), submit GRE scores, and though not required, professional nursing experience is recommended.

Funding your MSN

MSN students most often fund their degree through a combination of student loans and other forms of financial aid.

Career paths

For many graduates this degree is a stepping stone to doctorate-level study in nursing, which in turn leads to advanced leadership positions or careers as nursing educators. For those who enter the workforce after graduation, the majority find employment as health care practitioners in hospitals and nursing care facilities in both the public and private sectors. Most graduates have little trouble securing a position, as the supply of qualified nurses far dwarfs the demand.

Master of Social Work (MSW)

Brief description
The Master of Social Work is a professional degree designed to prepare students for leadership roles in community, advocacy, planning, and administrative organizations that deal with all aspects of human needs. This degree has replaced the bachelor's of social work as the minimum educational requirement for work in this field.

Undergraduate coursework
Applicants are required to have an undergraduate liberal arts degree and evidence of substantial interest or work in social issues. In some cases, GRE scores may also be needed, so it's best to check with your school to be certain of their specific requirements.

Funding your MSW
Students tend to fund their degree through a combination of scholarships, grants, students loans, and other forms of financial aid. Note that aid options may vary depending on whether the program is completed on campus or online.

Career paths
With employment on the rise (particularly in rural areas where qualified individuals are hard to come by), MSW graduates are enjoying prosperity in the workplace, even though the salary (on average $34,000–$40,000) leaves something to be desired. Social workers report a good deal of personal satisfaction. Nine out of ten jobs are found in social assistance industries, such as state and local government agencies, and also in health care facilities.

Master of Theology (ThM)

Brief description
The master of theology is a postgraduate degree that is typically pursued after the completion of a master of divinity and involves further in-depth theological study. Comparable to a master of sacred theology degree, the ThM is most often undertaken by ordained ministers who seek to further their education, or by students who wish to pursue their doctorate.

Undergraduate coursework

Applicants must have a master of divinity, a bachelor of divinity, or a master of theological studies. there may also be certain language requirements, such as Hebrew or Greek, so make sure to check with your school for their specific requirements, as they may vary.

Funding your ThM

Students tend to fund their degree through a combination of scholarships, teaching fellowships, student loans, and other forms of financial aid.

Career paths

For many graduates, this degree is a required part of their journey toward doctoral theological studies, while for others it is a way of exploring the many facets of their professional field in greater depth, afterwards beginning or resuming careers as ordained ministers or religious educators.

Master of Urban Planning (MUP)

Brief description

The Master of Urban Planning is a two-year professional degree that qualifies graduates to work as urban planners and instructs them in all aspects of the economic, physical, and social development of residential and commercial areas both large and small—simply put, it's the science of building successful cities.

Undergraduate coursework

Admissions to this degree favor those with a wide field of undergraduate study (involving social studies, architecture, etc.) and who display a proficiency in both the creative and practical aspects of urban development. GRE scores may also be required, so make sure to check with your school before applying.

Funding your MUP

Students fund their degree through scholarships, assistantships, student loans, and other forms of financial aid.

Career paths

Despite the fact that the MUP is a terminal degree, many MUP graduates choose to study urban planning at the doctoral level. Those who enter the professional world after graduation find a competitive field thanks to burgeoning academic interest, increased building, and rising salaries. This shouldn't deter you however, as many find good jobs as urban planners with local government or private firms in their field of concentration, such as land use, environmental planning, housing, community development, economic development, international development, urban design, transportation planning, or geographic information systems.

Master of Urban and Regional Planning (MURP)

Brief description

The Master of Urban and Regional Planning is a two-year professional degree that is a variation on the Master of Urban Planning degree. Like the MUP, this degree qualifies graduates to work as urban and regional planners, instructing them in all aspects of the economic, physical, and social development of residential and commercial areas both large and small—the main difference being an expanded scope that includes regional as well as urban areas.

Undergraduate coursework

Admissions to this degree favor those with a broad-based field of undergraduate study (involving social studies, architecture, etc.) and who display a proficiency in both the creative and practical aspects of urban and regional development. GRE scores may also be required, so make sure to check with your school before applying.

Funding your MURP

Students fund their degree through scholarships, assistantships, student loans, and other forms of financial aid.

Career paths

Despite the fact that the MURP is a terminal degree, many MURP graduates—like their MUP counterparts—choose to study urban and regional planning at the doctoral level in the hope of pursing professional enhancement or educational qualification. Those who join the workforce after graduation find a competitive field thanks to burgeoning academic interest, increased building and development, and rising salaries. However, this shouldn't deter you, as many find good jobs as urban and regional planners with local government or private firms in their field of concentration, such as land use, environmental planning, housing, community development, economic development, international development, urban design, transportation planning, or geographic information systems.

Appendices

APPENDIX A

Ten Writing Tips for Graduate-Level Work

Good writing almost never comes easily. Some tips to help you stay on track:

1. **Remember Your Goal**

   Don't lose sight of your ultimate purpose for writing.

   - **A letter to a potential postdoctoral sponsor or a fellowship application should...**

     Convince the reader that your research ideas are valid (are they reasonable?) and feasible (can the project be done within the funding period?). Furthermore, you must provide evidence that you're qualified to undertake the project.

   - **A cover letter for a job should...**

     Convince the search committee that you fit the job description.

   - **Your dissertation or a scholarly publication should...**

     Clearly lay out your research and conclusions without overselling your arguments. Write precisely.

2. **Don't Get Paralyzed**

   Remember the Chinese proverb "A long journey begins with a single step." Take your writing one step at a time and don't let its size paralyze you into inactivity. Construct your outline. Begin with the part you know best. Set aside a place and time that you can write for two or three hours *every* day—every day. If you become blocked, move to a different section of the work or edit what you have already done.

3. **Study Two or Three Similar Works**

   Examine the overall structure, presentation, and style of other people's writing—other writers' perspectives can only help your own.

4. Set Deadlines

Specific goals break a seemingly unassailable work into manageable chunks. Work out a timeframe with your advisor—and stick to it. Respect your agreed-upon deadlines.

5. Keep It Comprehensible

Even if you're writing a journal article or dissertation, not every reviewer will understand your subdiscipline's jargon. Define the important terms that you use throughout the text.

6. Keep It Legible

Your readers should be able to finish your document without eye strain. Set the font at 10 to 12 points, use a serif typeface, and keep one-inch margins. Single-spaced line breaks are fine, unless you're otherwise directed. If you go over the page limit, reject the temptation to break these rules. Edit instead.

7. Use Concise Sentences and Active Voice

If your sentences go on for more than three lines, start planting periods.

8. Present a Coherent Structure

Just don't get carried away with sub-sub-sub sections. Number or letter your sub-sections. Bold your headings. Indent to set off blocks of information. That should be enough.

9. Allow Time for a Second (or Third) Pair of Eyes

Give yourself enough time before the deadline to get one or two people to carefully review your work. Your advisor and someone outside of your subdiscipline will be good editors.

10. Listen to Criticism

If your colleagues, advisors, and friends don't understand what you are trying to say, you can be sure a distant reader won't either. Keep revising until your critics' red marks disappear.

APPENDIX B

Postdoctoral Award Opportunities

INDEX OF AWARDS BY DICIPLINE

ALL DISCIPLINES

Engineering/Mathematics

HUMANITIES

Academy of Motion Picture Arts and Sciences

American Academy in Rome

American Antiquarian Society

American Antiquarian Society

American Historical Association (AHA)

Andrew W. Mellon Foundation

Archaelogical Institute of America

College of Liberal Arts and Sciences of the University of Illinois—Urban-Champaign

Columbia University Society of Fellows in the Humanities

Cornell University Society for the Humanities

Cornell University Society of Fellows in the Humanities

DAAD (German Academic Exchange Service)

Davis Center for Russian and Eurasian Studies at Harvard University

Dibner Institute for the History of Science and Technology

Dumbarton Oaks/Harvard University

Getty Research Institute for the History of Art and the Humanities

Scientific/Medical Research

SOCIAL SCIENCES

The subsection labeled "Amount" refers to stipend amounts only. It does not include such additional funds as health benefits, professional development allowances, relocation allowances, institutional allowances, research allowances, etc.

Academy of Motion Picture Arts and Sciences

Award: Don and Gee Nicholl Fellowships in Screenwriting

Summary: International competition with the purpose of identifying and encouraging talented new screenwriters.

Amount: $30,000

Tenure: 1 year

Contact Info:

Nicholl Fellowships in Screenwriting

Academy Foundation

1313 North Vine Street

Hollywood, CA 90028-8107

Website: www.oscars.org/nicholl/index.html

Award Area: Humanities

American Academy in Rome

Award: Rome Prize Fellowships in Classical Studies

Summary: Fellowships in the following fields: Architecture, Design, Historic Preservation and Conservation, Landscape Architecture, Literature, Musical Composition, Visual Arts, Ancient Studies, Medieval Studies, Renaissance and Early Modern Studies, Modern Italian Studies.

Amount: Up to $21,000

Tenure: 6–24 months

Contact Info:

American Academy in Rome

7 East 60th Street

New York, NY 10022-1001

Website: www.aarome.org

Award Area: Humanities

American Antiquarian Society

Award: Mellon Post-Dissertation Fellowships

Summary: Fellowship is to provide time and resources to extend research and/or to revise the dissertation for publication in American history and culture through the year 1876.

Amount: $30,000

Tenure: 1 year

Contact Info:

Mellon Post-Dissertation Fellowships

American Antiquarian Society

185 Salisbury Street

Worcester, MA 01609-1634

Website: www.americanantiquarian.org/mellon.htm

Award Area: Humanities

American Antiquarian Society

Award: Mellon Postdoctoral Research Fellowships

Summary: Fellowship is to provide time and resources to extend research and/or to revise the dissertation for publication in American history and culture through 1876.

Amount: Up to $40,000

Tenure: 9–12 months

Contact Info:

Mellon Post-Dissertation Fellowships

American Antiquarian Society

185 Salisbury Street

Worcester, MA 01609-1634

Website: www.americanantiquarian.org/mellonpostdoc.htm

Award Area: Humanities

American Australian Association (AAA)

Award: Education Fellowships Program

Summary: Fellowships from the United States to Australia (and vice versa) for well-defined research projects in the life sciences and medicine, with particular interest in the fields of oceanography/marine sciences and stem cell research.

Amount: Up to $20,000

Tenure: 1 year

Contact Info:

Director of Corporate Relations and Education

American Australian Association

599 Lexington Avenue, 18th Floor

New York, NY 10022

Website: www.americanaustralian.org/Educational/usa-australia.php

Award Area: Scientific/Medical Research

American Cancer Society

Award: Postdoctoral Fellowships

Summary: Supports the training of researchers who have just received their doctorates to enable them to qualify for an independent career in cancer research (including basic, preclinical, clinical, psychosocial, behavioral, and epidemiologic research).

Amount: $40,000 for first year; $42,000 for second year; $44,000 for third year

Tenure: 1–3 years

Contact Info:

American Cancer Society, Inc.

Extramural Grants Department

Research Department

1599 Clifton Road, Northeast

Atlanta, GA 30329-4251

Website:

www.cancer.org/docroot/RES/content/RES_5_2x_Postdoctoral_Fellowships.asp?sitearea=RES

Award Area: Scientific/Medical Research

American Council of Learned Societies (ACLS)

Award: CSCC National Program for Advanced Study and Research in China

Summary: Supports research on China or the Chinese portion of a comparative study. Research is in the People's Republic of China.

Amount: Unspecified

Tenure: 4–12 months

Contact Info:

Office of Fellowships and Grants

American Council of Learned Societies

633 Third Avenue

New York, NY 10017-6795

Website: www.acls.org/csccguid.htm

Award Area: Social Sciences

American Councils for International Education— ACTR/ACCELS

Award: Title VIII Combined Research and Language Training (CRLT) Program

Summary: Support and language instruction for those seeking to conduct research in Belarus, Central Asia, Russia, the South Caucasus, Ukraine, and Moldova.

Amount: $5,000–$25,000

Tenure: 3–9 months

Contact Info:

Outbound Programs/Title VIII CRLT ProgramAmerican Councils for International Education: ACTR/ACCELS1776

Massachusetts Avenue, Northwest, Suite 700

Washington, DC 20036

Website:

www.americancouncils.net/program.asp?PageID=121&ProgramID=13

Award Area: Social Sciences

American Educational Research Association (AERA)

Award: Postdoctoral Fellowship Program

Summary: Research topics may cover a wide range of education policy-related issues.

Amount: $40,000 per year

Tenure: 2–3 years

Contact Info:

AERA Grants Program

5662 Calle Real, #254

Goleta, CA 93117-2317

Website: www.aera.net/fellowships/?id=87

Award Area: Social Sciences

American Federation for Aging Research (AFAR)

Award: AFAR Research Grant Program

Summary: The major goal of this program is to assist in the development of the careers of junior investigators committed to pursuing careers in the field of aging research.

Amount: Up to $60,000 per year

Tenure: 1–2 years

Contact Info:

American Federation for Aging Research

70 West 40th Street

New York, NY 10018

Website: www.afar.org/grants.html

Award Area: Social Sciences

American Heart Association

Award: Predoctoral and Postdoctoral Fellowships

Summary: Awarded for investigations in all areas of cardiovascular disease and stroke.

Amount: Predoctoral: Up to $26,000 per year; Postdoctoral: Up to $51,036 per year

Tenure: Up to 3 years

Contact Info:

Attn: Affiliate Research Services
Division of Research Administration
American Heart Association
7272 Greenville Avenue
Dallas, TX 75231-4596

Website: www.americanheart.org/presenter.jhtml?identifier=3001355

Award Area: Scientific/Medical Research

American Historical Association (AHA)

Award: Fellowship in Aerospace History

Summary: For research in any aspect of the history of aerospace, including cultural and intellectual history, economic history, history of law and public policy, and the history of science, engineering, and management.

Amount: $20,000

Tenure: 6–9 months

Contact Info:

Fellowship in Aerospace History
American Historical Association
400 A Street, Southeast
Washington, DC 20003

Website: www.historians.org/prizes/NASA.htm

Award Area: Humanities

American Mathematical Society

Award: Centennial Fellowships

Summary: To help further the careers in research of outstanding recent post-doctoral mathematicians.

Amount: $64,000

Tenure: 1 year

Contact Info:

Membership and Programs Department

American Mathematical Society

201 Charles Street

Providence, RI 02904-2294

Website: www.ams.org/employment/centflyer.html

Award Area: Mathematics/Engineering

American Physiological Society

Award: Postdoctoral Fellowship in Physiological Genomics

Summary: Supports research in genomic advances in the context of the organism with the intention of employing organ system approaches during post-doctoral training.

Amount: $36,000 for first year; $38,000 for second year

Tenure: 2 years

Contact Info:

American Physiological SocietyPostdoctoral Fellowship in Physiological Genomics

9650 Rockville Pike

Bethesda, MD 20814-3991

Website: www.the-aps.org/awards/student.htm

Award Area: Scientific/Medical Research

American Psychological Association (APA) National Institute of Mental Health (NIMH)

Award: Minority Fellowship Program: Mental Health Research Fellowship

Summary: Geared toward training students who have primary interests in research related to the mental health or the psychological well-being of ethnic minorities.

Amount: Varies

Tenure: Up to 3 years

Contact Info:

APA/MFP

MHR Application

750 First Street, Northeast

Washington, DC 20002-4242

Website: www.apa.org/mfp

Award Area: Social Sciences

American Research Center in Egypt (ARCE), U.S. Department of State, Bureau of Educational and Cultural Affairs (ECA), National Endowment for the Humanities, Samuel H. Kress Foundation, William P. McHugh Memorial Fund

Award: Postdoctoral Scholars

Summary: Promotes a fresh and more profound knowledge of Egypt and the Near East through scholarly research and assists in training American specialists in Middle Eastern studies in academic disciplines that require familiarity with Egypt.

Amount: Variable

Tenure: 3–12 months

Contact Info:

American Research Center in Egypt

Emory University, Briarcliff Campus

1256 Briarcliff Road, Northeast

Building A, Suite 423W

Atlanta, GA 30306

Website: www.arce.org

Award Area: Social Sciences

American Social Health Association

Award: ASHA Research Fund (ARF)

Summary: Postdoctoral fellowships in all areas of STD research, including cancroids, chlamydia, gonorrhea, group B streptococcal infection, herpes, HIV, human papillomavirus (HPV), pelvic inflammatory disease (PID), and syphilis.

Amount: $35,500 for first year; $36,000 for second year

Tenure: 2 years

Contact Info:

Manager, ASHA Research Fund

American Social Health Association

PO Box 13827

Research Triangle Park, NC 27709

Website: www.ashastd.org/

Award Area: Scientific/Medical Research

American Society for Engineering Education

Award: Naval Research Laboratory Postdoctoral Fellowship Program

Summary: Research at a naval R&D center or laboratory. Proposals developed closely with the proposed host facility stand the greatest chance of success in the selection process.

Amount: Up to $65,000

Tenure: 1–3 years

Contact Info:

NRL Postdoctoral Fellowship Program

American Society for Engineering Education

1818 North Street, Northwest, Suite 600

Washington, DC 20036

Website: www.asee.org/resources/fellowships

Award Area: Mathematics/Engineering

American Society for Microbiology (ASM) and National Center for Infectious Diseases (NCID)

Award: Postdoctoral Research Fellowship in Infectious Diseases and Public Health Microbiology

Summary: Supports the development of new approaches, methodologies, and knowledge in infectious disease prevention and control in areas within the public health mission of the Centers for Disease Control and Prevention (CDC).

Amount: $37,300

Tenure: Up to 2 years

Contact Info:

ASM/NCID Postdoctoral Research Fellowship Program

Education Department

American Society for Microbiology

1752 North Street, Northwest

Washington, DC 20036

Website: www.asm.org/Education/index.asp?bid=15497

Award Area: Scientific/Medical Research

Andrew W. Mellon Foundation

Award: Mellon Postdoctoral Fellowships in the Humanities

Summary: Fellows will be expected to teach two courses in each year of their residency, at least one which should contribute something to the Dartmouth curriculum.

Amount: $46,750

Tenure: 2 years

Contact Info:

Administrator, Leslie Humanities Center

6240 Gerry Hall, Room 205

Dartmouth College

Hanover, NH 03755-3526

Website: www.dartmouth.edu/~lhc/mellon.html

Award Area: Humanities

Archaeological Institute of America

Award: Olivia James Traveling Fellowship

Summary: For travel and study in Greece, the Aegean Islands, Sicily, Southern Italy, Asia Minor, and Mesopotamia. Primarily for students of the classics, sculpture, architecture, archaeology, and history.

Amount: $22,000

Tenure: 6–12 months

Contact Info:

Fellowships

Archaeological Institute of America

656 Beacon Street, Fourth Floor

Boston, MA 02215

Website: www.archaeological.org

Award Area: Humanities

Arthritis Foundation

Award: Postdoctoral Fellowship

Summary: For research related to the understanding of arthritis and the rheumatic diseases.

Amount: $50,000

Tenure: 1–3 years

Contact Info:

Arthritis Foundation

Research Department

1330 West Peachtree Street, Northwest, Suite 100

Atlanta, GA 30309-20904

Website: www.arthritis.org/research/ProposalCentral.asp

Award Area: Scientific/Medical Research

Baylor University

Award: Postdoctoral Fellowship Program

Summary: To help recent PhD graduates in the humanities, mathematics, science, and education make the transition from graduate programs to professional teaching careers. Postdoctoral fellows will be assigned to a university home department, will have a half-time teaching load, and will be expected to pursue research in collaboration with university faculty.

Amount: Competitive

Tenure: 1 year

Contact Info:

Office of the Vice Provost for Research
Baylor University
1 Bear Place, #97310
Waco, TX 76798-7310

Website: www.baylor.edu/vpr/index.php?id=17297

Award Area: All disciplines

Cancer Research Institute

Award: Postdoctoral Fellowships Program

Summary: For the development of immunological approaches to the diagnosis, treatment, and prevention of cancer. Research must be conducted under a sponsor who holds formal appointment at host institution.

Amount: $40,000 for first year; $42,000 for second year; $44,000 for third year

Tenure: Up to 3 years

Contact Info:

Director of Grants Administration
Cancer Research Institute
681 Fifth Avenue
New York, NY 10022

Website: www.cancerresearch.org/criprogs.html#Fellowship

Award Area: Scientific/Medical Research

Carnegie Institution of Washington, Department of Terrestrial Magnetism

Award: Postdoctoral Fellowships in Astronomy

Summary: DTM research interests encompass extragalactic astronomy, star and planet formation, extrasolar planet detection and characterization, planetary astronomy, and the physical and chemical evolution of prebiotic compounds.

Amount: Unspecified

Tenure: Up to 3 years

Contact Info:

Astronomy Fellowship Committee

Department of Terrestrial Magnetism

Carnegie Institute of Washington

5241 Broad Branch Road, Northwest

Washington, DC 20015

Website: www.dtm.ciw.edu/content/view/65/99/

Award Area: Engineering/Mathematics

Carnegie Institution of Washington, Geophysical Laboratory

Award: Postdoctoral Fellowships

Summary: Research emphasizing interdisciplinary research in fundamental chemistry and physics related to geology, planetology, astrochemistry, and astrobiology.

Amount: Unspecified

Tenure: Unspecified

Contact Info:

Geophysical Laboratory

Carnegie Institution of Washington

5251 Broad Branch Road, Northwest

Washington, DC 20015

Website: www.gl.ciw.edu/employment/postdoc1.php

Award Area: Scientific/Medical Research

Carter G. Woodson Institute for Afro-American and African Studies

Award: Woodson Predoctoral and Postdoctoral Residential Research and Teaching Fellowship

Summary: Residential fellowships to scholars designed to facilitate the completion of dissertations/manuscripts in African American and African Studies and related fields.

Amount: Unspecified

Tenure: Predoctoral: 2 years; Postdoctoral: 1 year

Contact Info:

Selection Committee, Residential Research Fellowships

The Carter G. Woodson Institute

University of Virginia

PO Box 400162

Charlottesville, VA 22904-4162

Website: www.virginia.edu/%7ewoodson/index.html

Award Area: Social Sciences

Center for Afro-American and African Studies at the University of Michigan

Award: Du Bois–Mandela–Rodney Postdoctoral Fellowships

Summary: Established to identify and support scholars of high ability engaged in postdoctoral work on Africa or the African diaspora.

Amount: $42,000

Tenure: 1 academic year

Contact Info:

Du Bois–Mandela–Rodney Fellowship

Center for Afroamerican and African Studies (CAAS)

The University of Michigan

505 South State Street

4700 Haven Hall

Ann Arbor, MI 48109-1045

Website: www.umich.edu/~iinet/caas/

Award Area: All disciplines

Center for International Studies at the University of Missouri—St. Louis

Award: Lentz Postdoctoral Fellowship in Peace and Conflict Resolution Research

Summary: Supports scholarly research on peace and conflict resolution in the international arena, intercultural conflicts, and other settings of conflict and violence.

Amount: $23,400

Tenure: 1 year

Contact Info:

Director, Center for International Studies

University of Missouri-St. Louis

366 Social Sciences and Business Building (MC 58)

1 University Boulevard

St. Louis, MO 63121-4499

Website: www.umsl.edu/services/cis/research/lentz_fellow.html

Award Area: Social Sciences

Center on Religion and Democracy, University of Virginia

Award: Postdoctoral Fellowship Program

Summary: Research will be conducted in thematic two-year cycles. Applicants can be from any discipline, but must be working on a project relating to religion and public life.

Amount: $35,000

Tenure: 2 years

Contact Info:

The Center on Religion and Democracy

University of Virginia

PO Box 400178

Charlottesville, VA 22904

Website: http://religionanddemocracy.lib.virginia.edu/programs/fellow ships.html

Award Area: All disciplines

College of Liberal Arts and Sciences of the University of Illinois—Urbana-Champaign

Award: Mellon Junior Postdoctoral Fellowships

Summary: Funding for research in interpretive methods in the humanities, period studies, histories and cultures, and cultural values.

Amount: $40,000 per year

Tenure: 2 years

Contact Info:

Mellon Junior Postdoctoral Fellowships

University of Illinois at Urbana-Champaign

College of Liberal Arts and Sciences

294 Lincoln Hall, MC 448

702 South Wright Street

Urbana, IL 61801

Website: www.las.uiuc.edu/faculty/mellon/

Award Area: Humanities and Social Sciences

Columbia University Society of Fellows in the Humanities

Award: Mellon Fellowship

Summary: Teaching fellowship for introductory courses in general education: Contemporary Civilization, Literature Humanities, Music Humanities, Art Humanities, and Asian Civilizations.

Amount: $52,000

Tenure: 1–2 years

Contact Info:

Society of Fellows in the Humanities

Heyman Center

Mail Code 5700

Columbia University

2960 Broadway

New York, NY 10027

Website: www.columbia.edu/cu/societyoffellows/fellowship.html

Award Area: Humanities and Social Sciences

Cornell University Society for the Humanities

Award: Mellon Postdoctoral Fellowships

Summary: Teaching-research fellowships in Comparative Literature; English; Feminist, Gender, and Sexuality Studies; and Theatre, Film, and Dance.

Amount: $40,000

Tenure: 1 year

Contact Info:

Program Administrator

Mellon Postdoctoral Fellowships

Cornell University

Society for the Humanities

A.D. White House

27 East Avenue

Ithaca, NY 14853-1101

Website: www.arts.cornell.edu/sochum/html/melloninfo.html

Award Area: Humanities and Social Sciences

Cornell University Society for the Humanities

Award: Society for the Humanities Fellowships

Summary: Thematic research in humanistic disciplines. Theme changes annually.

Amount: $40,000

Tenure: 1 year

Contact Info:

Program Administrator

Cornell University

Society for the Humanities

A.D. White House

27 East Avenue

Ithaca, NY 14853-1101

Website: www.arts.cornell.edu/sochum/

Award Area: Humanities and Social Sciences

DAAD (German Academic Exchange Service)

Award: Leo Baeck Institute—DAAD Grants

Summary: Funded research in New York or Germany on the social, communal, and intellectual history of German-speaking Jewry. Funds for research in Germany or in New York.

Amount: New York: $2,000; Germany: 715- 975 per month

Tenure: 1–10 months

Contact Info:

Leo Baeck Institute

15 West 16th Street

New York, NY 10011

Website: www.daad.org/?p=48513

Award Area: Humanities and Social Sciences

Davis Center for Russian and Eurasian Studies at Harvard University

Award: Postdoctoral, Senior, and Regional Fellowships

Summary: Research in the humanities and social sciences on Russia and the Soviet successor states.

Amount: Postdoctoral: $33,500; Senior: $21,500; Regional: $41,500

Tenure: 1 semester–1 academic year

Contact Info:

Fellowship Program

Davis Center for Russian and Eurasian Studies

Harvard University

625 Massachusetts Avenue

Cambridge, MA 02139

Website: www.daviscenter.fas.harvard.edu

Award Area: Humanities and Social Sciences

Department of Health and Human Services (DHHS), Centers for Disease Control and Prevention (CDC), National Center for Infectious Disease (NCID), Association of Public Health Laboratories (APHL)

Award: EID Postdoctoral Laboratory Research Fellowship Program

Summary: Emphasis on research or development in infectious diseases. Fellowships will be awarded to conduct applied research or development in areas relevant to public health.

Amount: $37,191 per year

Tenure: 2 years

Contact Info:

EID Laboratory Fellowship Program

APHL

2025 M Street, Northwest, Suite 550

Washington, DC 20036

Website: www.cdc.gov/ncidod/eidlfp.htm#eidpost

Award Area: Scientific/Medical Research

Dibner Institute for the History of Science and Technology

Award: Senior and Postdoctoral Fellows Programs

Summary: For advanced research in the history of science and technology.

Amount: $35,000 per year

Tenure: Senior: 1 year; Postdoctoral: 1–2 years

Contact Info:

Program Coordinator

Dibner Institute for the History of Science and Technology

MIT E56-100, 38 Memorial Drive

Cambridge, MA 02139

Website: http://dibinst.mit.edu/DIBNER/Fellows/FellowsProgram.htm

Award Area: Humanities

Dumbarton Oaks / Harvard University

Award: Dumbarton Oaks Fellowships—Junior Fellowships, Fellowships, and Summer Fellowships

Summary: Residential fellowships in Byzantine Studies (including related aspects of late Roman, early Christian, Western medieval, Slavic, and Near Eastern Studies), Pre-Columbian Studies, Mexican, Central American, and Andean South America), and Studies in Landscape Architecture.

Amount: Fellowship and Junior Fellowship: $21,870–$43,000; Senior Fellowship: $230 per week

Tenure: Fellowship and Junior Fellowship: 1 academic year; Senior Fellowship: 6–9 weeks

Contact Info:

Office of the Director

Dumbarton Oaks

1703 32nd Street, Northwest

Washington, DC 20007

Website: www.laspau.harvard.edu/grantee_guide/fantel/grants.htm

Award Area: Humanities

e7 Network of Expertise for the Global Environment

Award: e7 Sustainable Energy Development Scholarship Program

Summary: Focus on advance studies and research in sustainable energy development.

Amount: Masters-level: $20,000 per year; Postdoctoral: $25,000 per year

Tenure: Up to 2 years

Contact Info:

Secretariat for the e7 Network of Expertise for the Global Environment

1155 Metcalfe Street, Suite 1120

Montreal, Quebec

H3B 2V6

Canada

Website: www.e7.org/Pages/O-Schol.html

Award Area: Scientific/Medical Research

Educational Testing Service (ETS)

Award: Postdoctoral Fellowship Program

Summary: Independent research in Princeton, New Jersey, in one of the following areas: psychology, education, teaching, learning, literacy, statistics, computer science, educational technology, minority issues, and testing issues, including new forms of assessment and alternate forms of assessment for special populations.

Amount: $50,000

Tenure: Up to 2 years

Contact Info:

Educational Testing Service
Rosedale Road
Princeton, NJ 08541-0001

Website: www.ets.org/research/fellowships/fel00-post.html

Award Area: Social Sciences

German Marshall Fund

Award: Research Fellowship Program

Summary: Grants for PhD candidates and senior scholars for research to improve the understanding of significant contemporary economic, political, and social developments relating to Europe, European integration, and relations between the United States and Europe.

Amount: Unspecified

Tenure: Unspecified

Contact Info:

German Marshall Fund of the United States
1744 R Street, Northwest
Washington, DC 20009

Website: www.gmfus.org/fellowships/research.cfm

Award Area: Social Sciences

Getty Research Institute for the History of Art and the Humanities

Award: Research Grants for Predoctoral and Postdoctoral Fellowships

Summary: Each year the Getty Research Institute invites applications from scholars working on projects related to a specific theme. See website for theme.

Amount: Predoctoral: $18,000; Postdoctoral: $22,000

Tenure: 9 months

Contact Info:

Attn: Pre- and Postdoctoral Fellowships

The Getty Foundation

1200 Getty Center Drive, Suite 800

Los Angeles, CA 90049-1685

Website: www.getty.edu/grants/research/scholars/pre_post_fellows.html

Award Area: Humanities

Getty Research Institute for the History of Art and the Humanities

Award: Research Grants for Getty Scholars and Visiting Scholars

Summary: Each year the Getty Research Institute invites applications from scholars working on projects related to a specific theme. See website for theme.

Amount: Scholars: Up to $75,000; Visiting Scholars: $3,500 per month

Tenure: Scholars: 1 academic year; Visiting Scholars: 3 months

Contact Info:

Attn: Getty Residential Scholar and Visiting Scholar Grants

The Getty Foundation

1200 Getty Center Drive, Suite 800

Los Angeles, CA 90049-1685

Website: www.getty.edu/grants/research/scholars/scholars.html

Award Area: Humanities

Harry Frank Guggenheim Foundation

Award: Grants for Research

Summary: For efforts to increase understanding of the causes, manifestations, and control of violence, aggression, and dominance, particularly in relation to social change, the socialization of children, intergroup conflict, interstate warfare, crime, family relationships, and investigations of the control of aggression and violence.

Amount: $15,000–$30,000 per year

Tenure: 1–2 years

Contact Info:

Harry Frank Guggenheim Foundation
527 Madison Avenue
New York, NY 10022-4304

Website: www.hfg.org

Award Area: Social Sciences

Harvard Academy for International and Area Studies

Award: Academy Scholars Program Predoctoral and Postdoctoral Fellowships

Summary: Research should combine disciplinary excellence in the social sciences (including history and law) with an in-depth grounding in particular non-Western countries or regions, including domestic, comparative, or transnational issues.

Amount: Predoctoral: $25,000 per year; Postdoctoral: $44,000 per year

Tenure: 2 years

Contact Info:

The Academy Scholars Program
Harvard Academy for International and Area Studies
Weatherhead Center for International Affairs
1727 Cambridge Street
Cambridge, MA 02138

Website: www.wcfia.harvard.edu/academy/

Award Area: Social Sciences

Harvard-Smithsonian Center for Astrophysics

Award: Menzel, Clay, and CfA Postdoctoral Fellowships

Summary: Proposed program should be in an active field of research at the CfA. Fellows are encouraged to formulate and develop their own scientific programs in research.

Amount: Menzel and Clay: $50,000 per year; CfA: $48,000 per year

Tenure: Menzel and CfA: 2–3 years; Clay: 4 years

Contact Info:

Fellowship Program Coordinator

Center for Astrophysics

Harvard University

60 Garden Street, MS 47

Cambridge, MA 02138

Website: http://cfa-www.harvard.edu/postdoc

Award Area: Scientific/Medical Research

Helen Hay Whitney Foundation

Award: Research Fellowships

Summary: Supports early postdoctoral research training in all basic biomedical sciences.

Amount: $41,000 for first year; $42,500 for second year; $44,000 for third year

Tenure: 3 years

Contact Info:

Helen Hay Whitney Foundation

450 East 63rd Street, Suite 1K

New York, NY 10021-7928

Website: www.hhwf.org/HTMLSrc/ResearchFellowships.html

Award Area: Scientific/Medical Research

Hereditary Disease Foundation

Award: John J. Wasmuth Postdoctoral Fellowships

Summary: Support for research projects that will contribute to identifying and understanding the basic defect of Huntington's disease. Areas of interest include trinucleotide expansions, animal models, gene therapy, neurobiology and development of the basal ganglia, cell survival and death, and intercellular signaling in striatal neurons.

Amount: Up to $56,000 per year

Tenure: 1–2 years

Contact Info:

Hereditary Disease Foundation
3960 Broadway, Sixth Floor
New York, NY 10032

Website: www.hdfoundation.org/funding/postdoct.htm

Award Area: Scientific/Medical Research

Hereditary Disease Foundation

Award: Milton Wexler Postdoctoral Fellowship Award

Summary: Support for research projects that will contribute to identifying and understanding the basic defect of Huntington's disease. Areas of interest include trinucleotide expansions, animal models, gene therapy, neurobiology and development of the basal ganglia, cell survival and death, and intercellular signaling in striatal neurons.

Amount: Up to $61,500

Tenure: 1 year

Contact Info:

Hereditary Disease Foundation
3960 Broadway, Sixth Floor
New York, NY 10032

Website: www.hdfoundation.org/funding/wexler.htm

Award Area: Scientific/Medical Research

Humboldt Foundation

Award: Humboldt Research Awards

Summary: Candidates should exhibit superior academic achievement, peer-reviewed publications, specific research plan, and good command of German for humanities and social sciences, or of English for scientists.

Amount: Up to $75,000

Tenure: 6–12 months

Contact Info:

Alexander von Humboldt Foundation

U.S. Liaison Office

1012 14th Street, Northwest, Suite 301

Washington, DC 20005

Website: www.humboldt-foundation.de/en/programme/preise/pt.htm

Award Area: All disciplines

Huntington Library

Award: National Endowment for the Humanities Fellowships

Summary: Applicant must be pursuing scholarship in a field appropriate to the Huntington collections.

Amount: Up to $40,000

Tenure: 4–12 months

Contact Info:

The Huntington Library, Art Collections, and Botanical Gardens

1151 Oxford Road

San Marino, CA 91108

Website: www.huntington.org/ResearchDiv/Fellowships.html

Award Area: Humanities

Huntington Library, Art Collections, and Botanical Gardens

Award: Mellon Postdoctoral Research Fellowships

Summary: Applicants must be pursuing scholarship in a field appropriate to the Huntington's collections.

Amount: $40,000

Tenure: 9–12 months

Contact Info:

The Huntington Library, Art Collections, and Botanical Gardens

1151 Oxford Road

San Marino, CA 91108

Website: www.huntington.org/ResearchDiv/Fellowships.html

Award Area: Humanities

Institute for Advanced Study (IAS)

Award: School of Mathematics Memberships

Summary: Research and study in pure mathematics, combinatorics, mathematical physics, and applied mathematics.

Amount: Unspecified

Tenure: 1 year

Contact Info:

School of Mathematics

Institute for Advanced Studies

Einstein Drive

Princeton, NJ 08540

Website: www.math.ias.edu/

Award Area: Engineering/Mathematics

Institute for Research in the Humanities at the University of Wisconsin—Madison

Award: Friedrich Solmsen Fellowships

Summary: For research in literary and historical studies of the European Classical, Medieval, and Renaissance periods up to about the year 1700.

Amount: Unspecified

Tenure: 1 year

Contact Info:

Institute for Research in the Humanities

University of Wisconsin—Madison

1401 Observatory Drive

Madison, WI 53706

Website: www.wisc.edu/irh/research.html

Award Area: Humanities

Irvington Institute for Immunological Research

Award: Postdoctoral Fellowships in Immunology

Summary: Research of immune system disorders, including cancer, AIDS, diabetes, lupus, multiple sclerosis, and rheumatoid arthritis.

Amount: Junior-level: $42,000 for first year; $44,000 for second year; $45,000 for third year; Senior-level: $45,000 for first year; $46,000 for second year

Tenure: Junior-level: Up to 3 years; Senior-level: 1–2 years

Contact Info:

Fellowship Coordinator

245 Fifth Avenue, Room 2101

New York, NY 10016

Website: www.irvingtoninstitute.org/fellowships.html

Award Area: Scientific/Medical Research

Jackson Laboratory

Award: Postdoctoral Training Programs

Summary: Research includes Cancer, Developmental Biology and Aging, Genomics, Hematology/Immunology, Metabolic Diseases, and Neurobiology and Sensory Deficits.

Amount: Unspecified

Tenure: Unspecified

Contact Info:

The Jackson Laboratory

600 Main Street

Bar Harbor, ME 04609-1500

Website: www.jax.org/education/postdoc.html

Award Area: Scientific/Medical Research

Jane Coffin Childs Memorial Fund for Medical Research

Award: Jane Coffin Childs Fund Fellowships

Summary: Supports research into the causes, origins, and treatment of cancer in the United States.

Amount: $41,000 for first year; $42,000 for second year; $44,000 for third year

Tenure: 3 years

Contact Info:

Administrative Director

Jane Coffin Childs Memorial Fund for Medical Research

333 Cedar Street, LW300-SHM

New Haven, CT 06510

Website: www.jccfund.org/

Award Area: Scientific/Medical Research

John M. Olin Institute for Strategic Studies at Harvard University

Award: Predoctoral and Postdoctoral Fellowships in National Security

Summary: Promotes basic research in the broad area of security and strategic affairs, particularly the causes and conduct of war, military strategy and history, defense policy and institutions, etc.

Amount: Predoctoral: $20,000; Postdoctoral: $35,000

Tenure: 1 academic year

Contact Info:

Olin Institute for Strategic Studies

1033 Massachusetts Avenue

Cambridge, MA 02318-5319

Website: www.wcfia.harvard.edu/olin/index.htm

Award Area: Social Sciences

Leukemia Research Foundation

Award: Postdoctoral Fellowships

Summary: The Leukemia Research Foundation supports research on leukemia and related disorders in such areas as biochemistry, microbiology, virology, molecular biology, and immunology.

Amount: Up to $30,000 per year

Tenure: 2 years

Contact Info:

Medical Grants Administrator

Leukemia Research Foundation

820 Davis Street

Evanston, IL 60201

Website: www.leukemia-research.org/phd/application.asp#post

Award Area: Scientific/Medical Research

Los Alamos National Laboratory

Award: Postdoctoral Research Appointments

Summary: Research in a scientifically-rich R&D environment; opportunities to present, publish, and strengthen national scientific and technical capabilities. Candidates must be nominated and sponsored by a member of the Laboratory's technical staff.

Amount: $63,200–$74,000 per year

Tenure: Up to 3 years

Contact Info:

Postdoctoral Research Appointments

Mail Stop P290

Los Alamos National Laboratory

Los Alamos, NM 87545

Website: www.lanl.gov/science/postdocs/index.shtml

Award Area: Engineering/Mathematics

Lymphangiomyomatosis (LAM) Foundation

Award: LAM Postdoctoral Fellowship Awards

Summary: Fellowships are for the study of the cellular and molecular basis of the abnormal smooth muscle proliferation that occurs in lymphangioleimyomatosis.

Amount: Up to $50,000 per year

Tenure: Up to 3 years

Contact Info:

The LAM Foundation

10105 Beacon Hills Drive

Cincinnati, OH 45241

Website: http://lam.uc.edu/html/proposal.html

Award Area: Scientific/Medical Research

McNeil Center for Early American Studies

Award: Barra Foundation Fellowship

Summary: Fellows are expected to be in residence during the academic year and to participate in the McNeil Center's program of seminars and other activities. The Barra Foundation Fellowship is designed primarily for candidates specializing in Early American art or material culture.

Amount: $18,000

Tenure: 9 months

Contact Info:

The McNeil Center for Early American Studies
University of Pennsylvania
3619 Locust Walk, Third Floor
Philadelphia, PA 19104-6213

Website: www.mceas.org

Award Area: Humanities

Metropolitan Museum of Art

Award: Art History Fellowships

Summary: Research in fields including Asian art; arts of Africa, Oceania and the Americas; antiquities; arms and armor, costumes; drawings, illuminated manuscripts; paintings, photographs, prints, sculpture, textiles, and Western art. Some art history fellowships for travel abroad are also available for students whose projects involve firsthand examination of paintings in major European collections.

Amount: Predoctoral: Up to $30,000; Senior: Up to $40,000

Tenure: 1 year

Contact Info:

Fellowship Program in Art History
The Metropolitan Museum of Art
1000 Fifth Avenue
New York, NY 10028-0198

Website: www.metmuseum.org/education/fellowship.html

Award Area: Humanities

Michigan Society of Fellows at the University of Michigan

Award: Postdoctoral Fellowships in the Humanities and Arts, Sciences, and Professions

Summary: Fellows are appointed as Assistant Professors in appropriate departments and as Postdoctoral Scholars in the Michigan Society of Fellows. They are expected to be in residence in Ann Arbor during the academic years of the fellowship, to teach for the equivalent of one academic year, to participate in the informal intellectual life of the Society, and to devote time to their independent research or artistic projects.

Amount: $47,271 per year

Tenure: 3 years

Contact Info:

Michigan Society of Fellows
University of Michigan
3572 Rackham Building
915 East Washington Street
Ann Arbor, MI 48109-1070

Website: www.rackham.umich.edu/Faculty/society.html

Award Area: All disciplines

Minda de Gunzburg Center for European Studies at Harvard University

Award: James Bryant Conant Postdoctoral Fellowships for German and European Studies

Summary: Research in the fields of European history, politics, economics, society, or culture, with preference given to projects that involve German.

Amount: $40,000

Tenure: 1 year

Contact Info:

Conant Fellowship Competition
Minda de Gunzburg Center for European Studies
Harvard University
27 Kirkland Street
Cambridge, MA 02138

Website: www.ces.fas.harvard.edu/grants/index.html?postdoc

Award Area: Humanities and Social Sciences

The National Academies

Award: Postdoctoral Research Associateships

Summary: Providing postdoctoral scientists and engineers opportunities for research on problems largely of their own choice that are compatible with the interests of their respective sponsoring laboratories.

Amount: Variable

Tenure: 1 year

Contact Info:

Research Associateship Programs

Keck Center of the National Academies

500 Fifth Street, Northwest, GR 322A

Washington, DC 20001

Website: http://www4.nas.edu/pga/rap.nsf/

Award Area: Engineering/Mathematics and Scientific/Medical Research

National Academy of Education, Spencer Foundation

Award: Postdoctoral Fellowships

Summary: Program is designed to promote scholarship in the United States and abroad on matters relevant to the improvement of education in all its forms.

Amount: $55,000

Tenure: 1 year (or 2 contiguous years working half-time)

Contact Info:

The National Academy of Education

500 Fifth Street, Northwest, #1049

Washington, DC 20001

Website: www.nae.nyu.edu/spencer/index.htm

Award Area: All disciplines

National Hemophilia Foundation

Award: Judith Graham Pool Postdoctoral Research Fellowships in Hemophilia

Summary: Research on the biochemical, genetic, hematologic, orthopedic, psychiatric, or dental aspects of hemophilia or von Willebrand Disease. Other topics include rehabilitation, therapeutic modalities, psychosocial issues, women's health issues, liver disease, and AIDS/HIV, as they pertain to hemophilia or von Willebrand disease.

Amount: $42,000 per year

Tenure: Up to 2 years

Contact Info:

Assistant Director of Research

National Hemophilia Foundation

116 West 32nd Street, 11th Floor

New York, NY 10001

Website: www.hemophilia.org/research/jgp.htm

Award Area: Scientific/Medical Research

National Historical Publications and Records Commission

Award: Fellowships in Advanced Historical Documentary Editing

Summary: Provides hands-on experience in historical editing, including transcription, documentary collection, document selection, annotation, proofreading, and indexing.

Amount: $40,000

Tenure: 1 year

Contact Info:

Fellowships

Editing Institute

NHPRC, Room 111

National Archives and Records Administration

700 Pennsylvania Avenue, Northwest

Washington, DC 20408-0001

Website: www.archives.gov/nhprc/apply/program.html

Award Area: Humanities

National Humanities Center

Award: Fellowships

Summary: Residential fellowships for advanced study in the humanities.

Amount: Up to $50,000

Tenure: 1 academic year

Contact Info:

Fellowship Program

National Humanities Center

7 Alexander Drive

PO Box 12256

Research Triangle Park, NC 27709-2256

Website: www.nhc.rtp.nc.us/fellowships/fellowships.htm

Award Area: Humanities

National Institutes of Health (NIH)

Award: Postdoctoral Intramural Research Training Award (IRTA)

Summary: Basic and clinical research free from the demands of obtaining grants and teaching; opportunities to do both, however, are available.

Amount: $38,500–$71,000

Tenure: Up to 3 years

Contact Info:

Center for Scientific Review

National Institutes of Health

9000 Rockville Pike

Bethesda, MD 20892

Website: www.training.nih.gov/postdoctoral/irta.asp

Award Area: Science and Engineering

National Institutes of Health (NIH)

Award: Ruth L. Kirschstein National Research Service Award (NRSA) Individual Postdoctoral Fellowships

Summary: Training in basic, behavioral, or clinical research aspects of health-related sciences.

Amount: $35,568–$51,036

Tenure: Up to 3 years

Contact Info:

Center for Scientific Review

National Institutes of Health

6701 Rockledge Drive

Room 1040, MSC 7710

Bethesda, MD 20892-7710

Website: www.grants.nih.gov/training/nrsa.htm

Award Area: Scientific/Medical Research

National Oceanic and Atmospheric Administration (NOAA) Coastal Services Center

Award: Coastal Management Fellowship

Summary: On-the-job training and education in coastal resource management policy for postgraduate students. Fellowship also provides project assistance for state coastal zone management programs.

Amount: Competitive

Tenure: 2 years

Contact Info:

NOAA Coastal Services Center

2234 South Hobson Avenue

Charleston, SC 29405

Website: www.csc.noaa.gov/cms/fellows.html

Award Area: Scientific/Medical Research

National Radio Astronomy Observatory (NRAO)

Award: Jansky Fellowships

Summary: For research at any of the major NRAO sites. Focus on topics in radio astronomy is desirable, though not essential. Current areas of research include: cosmology; galaxy formation and galactic dynamics; gravitational lenses; theoretical and observational studies of AGN and radio galaxies; the interstellar medium, molecular clouds, and star formation; stellar evolution and circumstellar shells; comets and solar system bodies; and astrometry.

Amount: $49,000+ per year

Tenure: 2–3 years

Contact Info:

Director's Office

National Radio Astronomy Observatory

520 Edgemont Road

Charlottesville, VA 22903-2475

Website: www.nrao.edu/administration/directors_office/jansky postdocs.shtml

Award Area: Scientific/Medical Research

National Renewable Energy Laboratory

Award: Research Participant Program

Summary: Focus on research and development related to NREL's mission. See website.

Amount: Variable

Tenure: Variable

Contact Info:

NREL Human Resources Office

Research Participant Program

1617 Cole Boulevard

Golden, CO 80401-3393

Website: www.nrel.gov/education/rpp.html

Award Area: Engineering/Mathematics

National Science Foundation (NSF); Directorate for Biological Sciences (BIO)

Award: Postdoctoral Research Fellowships in Biological Informatics

Summary: Research and training in developing and using computational, statistical, and other tools in the collection, organization, dissemination, and use of information to solve problems in biology. The research and training plan of each fellowship should address important scientific questions in contemporary biology and include a strong link among computer, information, and computational science and biology and develop and/or apply state-of-the-art informatics tools or approaches to the stated problem.

Amount: $45,000 per year

Tenure: 2–3 years

Contact Info:

The National Science Foundation
4201 Wilson Boulevard
Arlington, VA 22230

Website: www.nsf.gov/publications/pub_summ.jsp?ods_key=nsf04539

Award Area: Scientific/Medical Research

National Science Foundation (NSF); Directorate for Biological Sciences (BIO); Division of Biological Infrastructure (DBI); Directorate for Social, Behavioral, and Economic Sciences (SBE)

Award: Minority Postdoctoral Research Fellowships

Summary: Training and research at the postdoctoral level in a host institution in the areas of biology and social, behavioral, and economic sciences supported by NSF.

Amount: $3,000 per month

Tenure: 2–3 years

Contact Info:

The National Science Foundation
4201 Wilson Boulevard
Arlington, VA 22230

Website: www.nsf.gov/publications/pub_summ.jsp?ods_key=nsf00139

Award Area: Scientific/Medical Research and Social Sciences

National Sleep Foundation (NSF)

Award: Pickwick Postdoctoral Research Fellowships in Sleep

Summary: Provides the funds to enable young researchers to devote full-time professional effort to research related to the study of sleep or sleep disorders.

Amount: $35,568–$45,048 per year

Tenure: 1–2 years

Contact Info:

Pickwick Postdoctoral Fellowship Review Committee

c/o National Sleep Foundation

1522 K Street, Northwest, Suite 500

Washington, DC 20005

Website: www.sleepfoundation.org/activities/index.php?secid=&id=23

Award Area: Scientific/Medical Research

Natural Sciences and Engineering Research Council of Canada

Award: Postdoctoral Fellowships

Summary: Provides support for researchers in science and engineering at a pivotal time in their careers.

Amount: $40,000 per year

Tenure: 2 years

Contact Info:

Scholarships and Fellowships Division Natural Sciences and Engineering Research Council of Canada

350 Albert Street

Ottawa, Ontario

K1A 1H5

Canada

Website: www.nserc.gc.ca/sf_e.asp?nav=sfnav&lbi=3a

Award Area: Mathematics and Scientific/Medical Research

New York University

Award: Remarque Institute Fellowships

Summary: For scholars with interests in contemporary Europe. Preference may be given to candidates whose interests include the study of political, regional, ethnic, religious, linguistic, cultural and economic encounters and conflicts in contemporary Europe, and between Europe and North America.

Amount: Unspecified

Tenure: 1 year

Contact Info:

Director, Remarque Institute

New York University

53 Washington Square South

New York, NY 10012-1098

Website: www.nyu.edu/pages/remarque/

Award Area: Social Sciences

Newberry Library

Award: Mellon Postdoctoral Research Fellowship

Summary: For postdoctoral scholars doing individual research in the library's collections. The Newberry's collections concern the civilizations of Western Europe and the Americas from the late Middle Ages to the early twentieth century.

Amount: $1,200 per month

Tenure: Fewer than 12 months

Contact Info:

Committee on Awards

The Newberry Library

60 West Walton Street

Chicago, IL 60610-7324

Website: www.newberry.org/research/L3rfellowships.html

Award Area: Humanities

Oak Ridge Universities, Oak Ridge Institute for Science and Education

Award: Oak Ridge National Laboratory Postdoctoral Research Associates Program

Summary: Provides support for research and training in a broad range of science and engineering activities related to basic sciences, energy, and the environment.

Amount: Competitive

Tenure: 1–3 years

Contact Info:

Oak Ridge Institute of Science and Education
PO Box 117, MS 36
Oak Ridge, TN 37831-0117

Website: www.orau.gov/orise/edu/ornl/gi-pdRA.htm

Award Area: Scientific/Medical Research

Obert C. and Grace A. Tanner Humanities Center, University of Utah

Award: Obert C. and Grace A. Tanner Visiting Fellowships

Summary: Research support for anthropology, communication, history (including art history), religious studies, ethnic studies, jurisprudence, languages and linguistics, literature, philosophy, women's studies, and historical or philosophical applications of the social and natural sciences.

Amount: $33,000

Tenure: 9 months

Contact Info:

Fellowship Program
Tanner Humanities Center
University of Utah
380 South 1400 East, Room 201
Salt Lake City, Utah 84112-0312

Website: www.hum.utah.edu/humcntr

Award Area: Scientific/Medical Research and Humanities and Social Sciences

Omohundro Institute of Early American History and Culture

Award: Institute / Andrew W. Mellon Postdoctoral Research Fellowship

Summary: Award is to revise the applicant's first book manuscript and the Institute's commitment to publish the resulting study. The Institute's scope encompasses the history and cultures of North America's indigenous and immigrant peoples during the colonial, Revolutionary, and early national periods of the United States and the related histories of Canada, the Caribbean, Latin America, the British Isles, Europe, and Africa, from the sixteenth century to approximately the year 1815.

Amount: $45,000

Tenure: 1 year

Contact Info:

Andrew W. Mellon Postdoctoral Research Fellowship

OIEAHC

PO Box 8781

Williamsburg, VA 23187-8781

Website: www.wm.edu/oieahc/fello.html

Award Area: Humanities

Omohundro Institute of Early American History and Culture

Award: Institute / NEH Postdoctoral Fellowship

Summary: The candidate's dissertation or other manuscript must have significant potential as a distinguished, book-length contribution to scholarship. The Institute's scope encompasses the history and cultures of North America's indigenous and immigrant peoples during the colonial, Revolutionary, and early national periods of the United States and the related histories of Canada, the Caribbean, Latin America, the British Isles, Europe, and Africa, from the sixteenth century to approximately the year 1815.

Amount: $40,000 per year

Tenure: 2 years

Contact Info:

Institute—NEH Fellowship

OIEAHC

PO Box 8781

Williamsburg, VA 23187-8781

Website: www.wm.edu/oieahc/fello.html

Award Area: Humanities

Open Society Institute, Soros Foundation Network

Award: Soros Justice Fellowships

Summary: Innovative criminal justice programs in collaboration with existing organizations in the United States or overseas.

Amount: Unspecified

Tenure: Unspecified

Contact Info:

Program Assistant

The Soros Justice Fellowships, U.S. Justice Fund

The Open Society Institute

400 West 59th Street, Third Floor

New York, NY 10019

Website: www.soros.org/grants

Award Area: Social Sciences

Organization of American Historians (OAH)

Award: White House Historical Association Fellowships

Summary: Focus on projects shedding light on the roles of the White House as home, workplace, museum, structure, and symbol. Work should enhance understanding of how the White House functions.

Amount: $2,000 per month

Tenure: 1–6 months

Contact Info:

White House Historical Association Fellowship

Organization of American Historians

112 North Bryan Avenue

PO Box 5457

Bloomington, IN 47408-5457

Website: www.oah.org/activities/awards

Award Area: Social Sciences

Organization of American States (OAS)

Award: OAS Fellowships

Summary: To promote economic, social, scientific, and cultural development of OAS member states through advanced training of their citizens in the priority areas requested by the countries.

Amount: Variable

Tenure: Unspecified

Contact Info:

OAS Department of Scholarships and Training

1889 F Street Northwest, Seventh Floor

Washington, DC 20006

Website: www.educoas.org/portal/en/becas/acerca.aspx?culture=en

Award Area: Social Sciences

Pasteur Foundation

Award: Postdoctoral Fellowship Program

Summary: Research in Institut Pasteur laboratories in Paris.

Amount: $45,000 per year

Tenure: 3 years

Contact Info:

Secrétariat de la Direction de l'Evaluation Scientifique

Institut Pasteur

25 Rue du Docteur Roux

75724 Paris Cedex 15

France

Website: www.pasteurfoundation.org/PostDoct.html

Award Area: Scientific/Medical Research

Phi Beta Kappa Society

Award: Mary Isabel Sibley Fellowship

Summary: Awarded alternately for original research in Greek or French. Award may be used for the study of Greek language, literature, history, or archaeology, or the study of French language and literature.

Amount: $20,000

Tenure: 1 year

Contact Info:

The Mary Isabel Sibley Fellowship Committee
Phi Beta Kappa Society
1606 New Hampshire Avenue, Northwest
Washington, DC 20009

Website: www.pbk.org/scholarships/sibley.htm

Award Area: Humanities

Princeton University

Award: Society of Fellows in the Liberal Arts

Summary: Program aims to promote innovative interdisciplinary approaches to scholarship and teaching. Postdoctoral (Cotsen) Fellows are appointed for three-year terms to pursue research and teach half-time in their academic host department.

Amount: $60,500 per year

Tenure: 3 years

Contact Info:

Society of Fellows
Joseph Henry House
Princeton University
Princeton, New Jersey 08544

Website: www.princeton.edu/~sf

Award Area: Humanities and Social Sciences

Robert Wood Johnson Foundation

Award: Scholars in Health Policy Research Program

Summary: The Program is intended to foster the development of a new generation of creative thinkers and problem solvers in health policy research within the disciplines of economics, political science, and sociology.

Amount: $74,000 for first year; $77,000 for second year

Tenure: 2 years

Contact Info:

Boston University Health Policy Institute

53 Bay State Road

Boston, MA 02215-2197

Website: www.healthpolicyscholars.org/

Award Area: Social Sciences

Rockefeller Foundation

Award: Rockefeller Foundation Resident Fellowships in the Humanities

Summary: Original research at host institutions that were selected for their potential to promote new work in the humanities.

Amount: $35,000–$40,000 (Varies by institution)

Tenure: 8–10 months

Contact Info:

The Rockefeller Foundation

Resident Fellowships in the Humanities

420 Fifth Avenue

New York, NY 10018-2702

Website: www.rockfound.org/

Award Area: Humanities

Rockefeller Foundation / Joan B. Kroc Institute for International Peace Studies, University of Notre Dame

Award: Rockefeller Visiting Fellowship in the Program in Religion, Conflict and Peacebuilding Program

Summary: The program explores the complex role of religion in contemporary conflicts dealing with three dimensions: comparative religious ethics, intolerance and human rights; interreligious and intrareligious differences, dialogue and conflict resolution; and post-conflict peacebuilding.

Amount: $35,000+ per year

Tenure: 1 year

Contact Info:

PRCP Coordinator

Kroc Institute for International Peace Studies

100 Hesburgh Center for International Studies

PO Box 639

Notre Dame, IN 46556

Website: www.nd.edu/~krocinst

Award Area: Social Sciences

Royal Society

Award: Royal Society USA / Canada Research Fellowships

Summary: Awarded for research in any branch of the natural sciences. Awards are not granted in the areas of the social sciences or clinical medical research.

Amount: $24,000–$32,000 per year

Tenure: 12–36 months

Contact Info:

Royal Society

6 Carlton House Ter.

London SW1Y 5AG

United Kingdom

Website: www.royalsoc.ac.uk/funding.asp?id=2351

Award Area: Mathematics/Engineering and Scientific Research

Rutgers Center for Historical Analysis (RCHA)

Award: Senior and Postdoctoral Fellowships

Summary: Thematic research in historical analysis. See website for annual theme.

Amount: Unspecified

Tenure: Unspecified

Contact Info:

Project Director

Senior and Postdoctoral Fellowships

Rutgers Center for Historical Analysis

88 College Avenue

New Brunswick, NJ 08901

Website: http://rcha.rutgers.edu/

Award Area: Humanities

School of American Research

Award: Resident Scholar Fellowships—National Endowment for the Humanities Fellowships, Weatherhead Fellowships, and Katrin H. Lamon Fellowships

Summary: The program supports scholars who have completed their research and analysis and who need time to think and write about topics important to the understanding of humankind.

Amount: Unspecified

Tenure: 9 months

Contact Info:

Resident Scholar Program

School of American Research

PO Box 2188

Santa Fe, NM 87504-2188

Website: www.sarweb.org

Award Area: Humanities

Smithsonian Institution

Award: Graduate Student Fellowships, Predoctoral Fellowships, Senior and Postdoctoral Fellowships

Summary: Changing fellowships. See website for complete information on application procedures, eligibility and areas of study for dissertation, post-doctoral and senior fellowships, and grants.

Amount: Predoctoral: $20,000 per year; Postdoctoral and Senior: $35,000–$40,000 per year; Graduate: $4,500

Tenure: Predoctoral: 3–12 months; Postdoctoral: 3–12 months; Graduate: 10 weeks

Contact Info:

Office of Fellowships
Smithsonian Institution
PO Box 37012
Victor Building 9300, MRC 902
Washington, DC 20013-7012

Website: www.si.edu/ofg

Award Area: All disciplines

Smithsonian Institution National Air and Space Museum

Award: Postdoctoral Earth and Planetary Sciences Fellowship

Summary: Supports research that concentrates on geologic and geophysical research of the Earth and other terrestrial planets using remote sensing data obtained from Earth-orbiting and interplanetary spacecraft. Research also focuses on global environmental change.

Amount: Variable

Tenure: 1+ years

Contact Info:

Fellowship Coordinator
National Air and Space Museum
MRC 312
PO Box 37012
Washington, DC 20013-7012

Website: www.si.edu/ofg/fell.htm

Award Area: Scientific/Medical Research

Smithsonian Institution Office of Fellowships

Award: Molecular Evolution Fellowships

Summary: Supports research that uses the resources and research opportunities offered at one of the Smithsonian Institution bureaus.

Amount: $30,000 per year

Tenure: 12–24 months

Contact Info:

Office of Fellowships and Grants

Smithsonian Institution

PO Box 37012

Victor Building 9300, MRC 902

Washington, DC 20013-7012

Website: www.si.edu/ofg/fell.htm

Award Area: Scientific/Medical Research

Social Science Research Council (SSRC)

Award: Berlin Program for Advanced German and European Studies

Summary: Supports anthropologists, economists, political scientists, sociologists, and all scholars in germane social science and cultural studies fields, including historians researching the period after the mid-19th century.

Amount: Dissertation project: $1,100 per month; Postdoctoral: $1,400 per month

Tenure: 10–12 months

Contact Info:

Berlin Program

Social Science Research Council

810 Seventh Avenue

New York, NY 10019

Website: http://userpage.fu-berlin.de/~bprogram/

Award Area: Social Sciences

Social Science Research Council (SSRC), American Council of Learned Societies

Award: Japan Society for the Promotion of Science (JSPS) Program for ABDs and PhDs

Summary: Open to all social science and humanities disciplines; applications need not be explicitly related to the study of Japan.

Amount: Up to ¥1.5 million per year

Tenure: 3–24 months

Contact Info:

Fellowships, Japan Program

Social Science Research Council

810 Seventh Avenue

New York, NY 10019

Website: www.ssrc.org/fellowships/japan/

Award Area: Humanities and Social Sciences

Social Science Research Council (SSRC), Japan Foundation Center for Global Partnership

Award: Abe Fellowship Program

Summary: Program encourages international multidisciplinary research on topics of pressing global concern. It seeks to foster the development of researchers interested in policy-relevant topics of long-range importance who are willing to become key members of a bilateral and global research network built around such topics.

Amount: Unspecified

Tenure: 3–12 months

Contact Info:

Abe Fellowship Program

Social Science Research Council

810 Seventh Avenue

New York, NY 10019

Website: www.ssrc.org/fellowships/abe/

Award Area: All disciplines

Society for Neuroscience (SFN), National Institute of Mental Health (NIMH), National Institute of Neurological Disorders and Stroke (NINDS)

Award: Minority Neuroscience Fellowship Program (MNFP)

Summary: Funding to increase the pool of underrepresented minority groups pursuing careers in mental health-related neuroscience research and teaching programs.

Amount: Variable

Tenure: Predoctoral: Up to 3 years; Postdoctoral: Up to 2 years

Contact Info:

Minority Neuroscience Fellowship Program

11 Dupont Circle, Northwest, Suite 500

Washington, DC 20036

Website:

http://apu.sfn.org/content/Programs/DiversityinNeuroscience/mnfp/index.html

Award Area: Scientific/Medical Research

Stanford University

Award: Stanford Humanities Fellows Program

Summary: Designed to give the best recent PhD recipients in the humanities a unique opportunity to develop as scholars and teachers.

Amount: $50,000 per year

Tenure: 1–2 years

Contact Info:

Director, Humanities Fellows Program

Department of English

Stanford University

450 Serra Mall

Stanford, CA 94305-2087

Website: http://fellows.stanford.edu/

Award Area: Humanities

Stanford University Center for International Security and Cooperation

Award: Predoctoral and Postdoctoral Fellowship Program

Summary: The Center invites applications from a variety of disciplines, including anthropology, economics, history, law, political science, sociology, medicine, and the natural and physical sciences. The Center also seeks applications from military officers or civilian members of the United States government, members of military or diplomatic services from other countries, and journalists interested in arms control and international security issues.

Amount: Predoctoral: $20,000; Postdoctoral: $35,000

Tenure: 9 months

Contact Info:

Fellowship Program Coordinator
CISAC
Encina Hall, E210
Stanford University
Stanford, CA 94305-6165

Website: http://cisac.stanford.edu/

Award Area: All disciplines

Stanford University Center for International Security and Cooperation

Award: Science Fellows Program

Summary: Research in nuclear, biological, and chemical weapons and delivery systems; prospects for international control of weapons of mass destruction; strategies for dealing with biological terrorism; information technology and security; nuclear weapons safety/security; ballistic missile defense; energy and security; environmental security.

Amount: Variable

Tenure: 11 months or 2 years

Website: http://cisac.stanford.edu/docs/fellowships/science.php

Award Area: Engineering/Mathematics and Scientific/Medical Research

U.S. Environmental Protection Agency (EPA)

Award: National Risk Management Research Laboratory Postdoctoral Program

Summary: Research into ways of preventing and reducing risks from pollution that threaten human health and the environment.

Amount: Up to $82,031 per year

Tenure: Up to 3 years

Contact Info:

U.S. Environmental Protection Agency
Human Resources Management Division
Attn: Postdoctoral Positions, MS-275
26 West Martin Luther King Drive
Cincinnati, OH 45268

Website: www.epa.gov/ORD/NRMRL/postdocfy04.htm

Award Area: Engineering/Mathematics and Scientific/Medical Research

United Negro College Fund—Merck

Award: UNCF—Merck Postdoctoral Science Research Fellowships

Summary: Objective is to increase the pool of well-qualified African-American research scientists in the biomedical sciences and related scientific disciplines.

Amount: Up to $55,000

Tenure: 12–24 months

Contact Info:

UNCF—Merck Science Initiative

United Negro College Fund

8260 Willow Oaks Corporate Drive

PO Box 10444

Fairfax, VA 22031-4511

Website: www.uncf.org/merck/programs/post.htm

Award Area: Scientific/Medical Research

United Negro College Fund—Pfizer Biomedical Research Initiative

Award: UNCF—Pfizer Biomedical Research Initiative Postdoctoral Fellowships

Summary: Support the career development of under-represented minority post-graduates in the biomedical research fields.

Amount: Up to $44,500

Tenure: 12–24 months

Contact Info:

UNCF—Pfizer Biomedical Research Initiative

United Negro College Fund

8260 Willow Oaks Corporate Drive, Suite 110

Fairfax, VA 22031-4511

Website: www.uncf.org/pfizer/textpage.htm

Award Area: Scientific/Medical Research

United States Department of Agriculture (USDA), Agricultural Research Service (ARS)

Award: Postdoctoral Research Associate Positions

Summary: Scope varies by position.

Amount: $45,239–$54,221

Tenure: Up to 2 years

Contact Info:

USDA / ARS Human Resources Division

5601 Sunnyside Avenue

Beltsville, MD 20705

Website: www.afm.ars.usda.gov/divisions/hrd/hrdhomepage/
vacancy/04050.htm

Award Area: Engineering/Mathematics and Scientific/Medical Research

United States Department of Energy (DOE), Brookhaven National Laboratory

Award: Postdoctoral Research Associateships—Biology Department

Summary: Research associateships in the biology department are intended for developing computational aspects of high-throughput structure determination by X ray crystallography as part of the human proteome project at the laboratory.

Amount: Unspecified

Tenure: Unspecified

Contact Info:

Brookhaven National Laboratory

Human Resources Division, Building 185

PO Box 5000

Upton, NY 11973-5000

Website: www.bnl.gov/HR/jobs/#biology

Award Area: Scientific/Medical Research

United States Holocaust Memorial Museum Center for Advanced Holocaust Studies

Award: Visiting Scholars Fellowships Program

Summary: Fields of inquiry include, but are not limited, to: Historiography and documentation of the Holocaust, ethics and the Holocaust, comparative genocide studies, the impact of the Holocaust on contemporary society and culture, ideas of refuge and rescue, propaganda and mass media as they relate to genocide.

Amount: Up to $3,000 per month

Tenure: 1 semester–1 academic year

Contact Info:

Visiting Scholars Program

Center for Advanced Holocaust Studies

United States Holocaust Memorial Museum

100 Raoul Wallenberg Place, Southwest

Washington, DC 20024-2126

Website: www.ushmm.org/

Award Area: Humanities and Social Sciences

University Corporation for Atmospheric Research (UCAR)

Award: Visiting Science Program—NOAA Climate and Global Change Postdoctoral Fellowships

Summary: The objective is to train researchers who will be able to provide predictors and assessments of global climate change on seasonal to centennial time scales.

Amount: Unspecified

Tenure: Unspecified

Contact Info:

UCAR / Visiting Scientist Program

Visiting Scientist Programs

PO Box 3000

FL-4, Suite 2200

Boulder, CO 80307-3000

Website: www.vsp.ucar.edu

Award Area: Scientific/Medical Research

University of British Columbia (UBC) Faculty of Graduate Studies

Award: Killam Postdoctoral Fellowships

Summary: These awards are available for most fields of research to pursue postdoctoral research at the University of British Columbia. Applicants are selected based on high academic achievement, personal qualities and demonstrated aptitudes.

Amount: $44,000 per year

Tenure: 2 years

Contact Info:

Chair, Killam Postdoctoral Fellowship

University of British Columbia

Vancouver, BC V6T 1Z1

Canada

Website: www.grad.ubc.ca/awards/index.asp?menu=015,000,000,000

Award Area: All disciplines

University of California—Berkeley

Award: S.V. Ciriacy—Wantrup Postdoctoral Fellowships in Natural Resource Studies

Summary: Applications are open, but not limited, to scholars working in the areas of Agricultural and Natural Resource Economics, Business, Energy Studies, Environmental Engineering, Environmental Sciences, Forestry, Geography, Law, Natural Resource Management, Public Health, and Public Policy.

Amount: $41,940 per year

Tenure: 1–2 years

Contact Info:

Office of the Vice Chancellor for Research

119 California Hall

University of California

Berkeley, CA 94720-1500

Website: http://research.chance.berkeley.edu/ciriacy/index.htm

Award Area: All disciplines

University of California—Lawrence Livermore National Laboratory

Award: Lawrence Fellowship

Summary: Fellowships are awarded to candidates with exceptional talent, credentials, scientific track record, and potential for significant achievements.

Amount: $7,583 per month

Tenure: 3 years

Contact Info:

All contact and application must be made through website.

Website: http://universitygateway.llnl.gov/postdoc/lawrence/

Award Area: Engineering/Mathematics and Scientific/Medical Research

University of California—Los Angeles (UCLA) Department of Psychiatry and Biobehavioral Sciences

Award: Psychobiology Postdoctoral Fellowship

Summary: Research projects may involve basic laboratory studies as well as clinical studies of patients with psychiatric and medical syndromes. Departmental laboratory facilities are available for human and animal studies in psychopharmacology, psychoneuroimmunology, behavioral genetics, clinical neurophysiology, brain imaging, neurochemistry, cellular neurophysiology, and neuropsychology. In addition, specialty clinical programs in alcoholism and the addictions, aging, mood disorders, schizophrenia, and other illnesses provide ample opportunity for clinical research and collaboration.

Amount: Variable

Tenure: Unspecified

Contact Info:

Postdoctoral Research Training Program

UCLA Department of Psychiatry and Biobehavioral Sciences

760 Westwood Boulevard, Room 37-426

Los Angeles, CA 90024

Website: www.npi.ucla.edu/psychobiodescrip.html

Award Area: Social Sciences and Scientific/Medical Research

.ఽ

University of California—Los Angeles (UCLA) Institute of American Cultures

Award: Postdoctoral and Visiting Scholar Fellowship Program in Ethnic Studies

Summary: Research on African Americans, Chicanos/-as, Asian Americans, and American Indians.

Amount: $30,000–$35,000

Tenure: 9 months

Contact Info:

Institute of American Cultures

1237 Murphy Hall

Box 951419

University of California–Los Angeles

Los Angeles, CA 90095-1419

Website: www.gdnet.ucla.edu/iacweb/iachome.htm

Award Area: Social Sciences

University of California—San Francisco (UCSF) School of Medicine, Institute for Health Policy Studies

Award: Postdoctoral Fellowship in Health Services and Health Policy Research

Summary: Multidisciplinary training program that provides advanced training and education to individuals with doctoral degrees, social scientists, and other health professionals who plan careers or want to broaden their knowledge in the fields of health services and health policy research.

Amount: Up to $44,412

Tenure: 1 year

Contact Info:

Institute for Health Policy Studies

University of California—San Francisco

3333 California Street, Suite 265

San Francisco, CA 94143-0936

Website: http://ihps.ucsf.edu/servlet/HomeServlet

Award Area: Social Sciences

University of Chicago Population Research Center

Award: Fellowships in Population Studies and the Economics and Demography of Aging

Summary: Fellowships in Population Studies and the Economics and Demography of Aging.

Amount: Variable

Tenure: Unspecified

Contact Info:

Population Research Center

NORC & The University of Chicago

1155 East 60th Street

Chicago, IL 60637

Website: www.src.uchicago.edu/prc/index.php

Award Area: Social Sciences

University of Chicago Society of Fellows

Award: Harper and Schmidt Fellows

Summary: The Fellows are members of the College Faculty whose primary responsibility is to teach in the general education (Core) program.

Amount: Unspecified

Tenure: Unspecified

Contact Info:

The University of Chicago Society of Fellows Search

5845 South Ellis

Chicago, IL 60637

Website: http://fellows.uchicago.edu/

Award Area: Humanities and Social Sciences

University of Houston—Institute for Space Systems Operations

Award: Postdoctoral Aerospace Fellowship Program

Summary: Fellowships in a variety of space system-related fields.

Amount: Unspecified

Tenure: Unspecified

Contact Info:

UH—Aerospace Postdoctoral Fellowship Program

Institute for Space Systems Operations

617 Science & Research 1, Mail Code 5005

University of Houston

Houston, TX 77204

Website: www.isso.uh.edu

Award Area: Engineering/Mathematics

University of Illinois—Urbana-Champaign, Beckman Institute

Award: Beckman Institute Fellows Program

Summary: A program of postdoctoral fellowships in the behavioral and biological sciences, chemistry, engineering, and physics.

Amount: $51,000 per year

Tenure: Up to 3 years

Contact Info:

Beckman Institute for Advanced Science and Technology

University of Illinois—Urbana-Champaign

405 North Mathews Avenue

Urbana, IL 61801

Website: www.beckman.uiuc.edu/outreach/fellowshome.html#2

Award Area: Engineering/Mathematics/Scientific/Medical Research, and Social Sciences

University of Pennsylvania

Award: Penn Humanities Forum Andrew W. Mellon Postdoctoral Fellowships in the Humanities

Summary: Teaching-research fellowships for candidates whose proposals are interdisciplinary, who have not previously used the resources of the University of Pennsylvania, and who would particularly benefit from and contribute to its intellectual life.

Amount: $42,000

Tenure: 1 year

Contact Info:

Director, Penn Humanities Forum

University of Pennsylvania

3619 Locust Walk

Philadelphia, PA 19104-6213

Website: http://humanities.sas.upenn.edu/mellon_description.htm

Award Area: Humanities

University of Southern California (USC)

Award: Mellon Postdoctoral Fellowships in the Humanities

Summary: Teaching-research fellowships in Art History, Classics, Comparative Literature, East Asian Languages and Cultures, English, French and Italian, German, History, Linguistics, Philosophy, Religion, Slavic Languages and Literatures, and Spanish and Portuguese.

Amount: $40,000

Tenure: 1 academic year

Contact Info:

Dean of Faculty

College of Letters, Arts, and Sciences

University of Southern California

Bovard Administration Building, Room 304

Los Angeles, CA 90089-4012

Website: www.usc.edu/schools/college/faculty/mellon.html

Award Area: Humanities and Social Sciences

Valparaiso University

Award: Lilly Fellows Program in the Humanities and the Arts

Summary: For young scholars to renew and deepen their sense of devotion within a Christian community of learning; includes teaching responsibilities.

Amount: $41,000 per year

Tenure: 2 years

Contact Info:

Lilly Fellows Program

Linwood House, 1401 Linwood Avenue

Valparaiso University

Valparaiso, IN 46383

Website: www.lillyfellows.org

Award Area: Humanities

W.F. Albright Institute of Archaeological Research, Jerusalem

Award: National Endowment for the Humanities Fellowship

Summary: Open to postdoctoral scholars in humanities.

Amount: Up to $40,000

Tenure: 4–12 months

Contact Info:

Department of Art and Art History

Providence College

Providence, RI 02918

Website: www.wfalbright.org/

Award Area: Humanities

Williams College

Award: Andrew W. Mellon Postdoctoral Fellowship

Summary: Fellowship offerings vary from one year to another; see website for details. In general, fellowships are in fields that will enrich the curricular offerings at Williams.

Amount: $35,000 per year

Tenure: 2 years

Contact Info:

Associate Dean of the Faculty

Williams College

PO Box 141

Williamstown, MA 01267

Website: www.williams.edu/admin/deanfac/fellowships.php

Award Area: Humanities and Social Sciences

Winterthur Museum, Garden & Library

Award: National Endowment for the Humanities Fellowships

Summary: Fellowships available to support research at the Winterthur Museum, Garden, and Library in the following fields: African-American history, anthropology, archaeology, architectural history, decorative arts, folklore, historic preservation, history of technology, urban studies, etc.

Amount: Up to $40,000

Tenure: 4–12 months

Contact Info:

Office of Academic Programs

Winterthur Museum and Country Estate

Winterthur, DE 19735

Website: www.winterthur.org/research/fellowship.asp?sub=fellowships_avail

Award Area: Humanities and Social Sciences

Women's Studies in Religion Program at Harvard University School of Divinity

Award: Research Associate and Visiting Lecturer

Summary: Open to doctorates in the fields of religion and to those with primary competence in other humanities, social science, and public policy fields who have serious interest in religion.

Amount: $40,000

Tenure: 1 academic year

Contact Info:

Women's Studies in Religion Program

Harvard Divinity School

45 Francis Avenue

Cambridge, MA 02138

Website: www.hds.harvard.edu/wsrp/

Award Area: Humanities and Social Sciences

Woodrow Wilson National Fellowship Foundation

Award: Academic Postdoctoral Fellowships in the Humanities

Summary: Fellowship provides time and resources for research, dissertation pre-publication revisions; broadens pedagogical experiences and abilities.

Amount: $30,000+ per year

Tenure: 2 years

Contact Info:

The Woodrow Wilson National Fellowship Foundation

PO Box 5281

Princeton, NJ 08543-5281

Website: www.woodrow.org/academic_postdocs/Info/info.html

Award Area: Humanities

Woods Hole Oceanographic Institution, NOAA

Award: Postdoctoral Scholarship Program

Summary: Study and research in the fields of chemistry, engineering, geology, geophysics, mathematics, meteorology, physics, biology, and oceanography.

Amount: $51,000 per year

Tenure: 18 months

Contact Info:

The Postdoctoral Fellowship Committee Clark 223, MS 31

Woods Hole Oceanographic Institution

360 Woods Hole Road

Woods Hole, MA 02543-1541

Website: www.whoi.edu/education/postdoctoral/scholarship.html

Award Area: Engineering/Mathematics/Scientific/Medical Research

Academic Job Portfolio

AN EXAMPLE OF AN ACADEMIC JOB ANNOUNCEMENT

> *The University of St. Elsewhere, a research-intensive institution, solicits applications for a tenure-track faculty position at the rank of assistant professor. A doctorate or equivalent is required of applicants, and postdoctoral research experience is preferred. The position carries responsibility that includes teaching graduate- and undergraduate-level courses in immunology and microbiology. Faculty members at St. Elsewhere are expected to obtain external research funding for research that involves both undergraduate and graduate students. Applications must include a curriculum vitae, graduate transcript, and three letters of references to Dr. Larry Robots, Chair of the Department of Biological Sciences, The University of St. Elsewhere, Midland/Odessa, TX 69696*

INTERPRETING THE JOB ANNOUNCEMENT

research-intensive institution: This is a Carnegie Classification definition (a widely used taxonomy of higher education in the U.S., developed by the Carnegie Commission on Higher Education). Research-intensive institutions do not produce as much research or as many PhDs as research-extensive schools, so less may be expected of you in the lab because you'll be spending more time in class. (Expectations may vary according to the department, however). If the job announcement doesn't indicate the type of institution, find out.

Visit the Carnegie Foundation's website (CarnegieFoundation.org) for more complete Carnegie Classification definitions.

tenure-track: This is what you're looking for if you want a "permanent" academic position. This means that in about six years, they'll evaluate you for a lifetime position. If you have met all expectations of your department, dean, and provost, the department is not being disbanded, and the institution is solvent, you will receive tenure. If not, you'll have a year to find another job in another place. Sometimes, this six-year process is broken up into two three-year contracts. This gives the department a chance to fire someone who doesn't have much of a chance of getting tenure.

assistant professor: An entry-level faculty position. This does not mean that some advanced faculty members somewhere else won't apply, but it does mean that the institution is not likely to cough up more than the salary for a beginner.

earned doctorate or equivalent of applicants: Doctorates in biomedical fields (including public health), physicians, and veterinarians are all eligible, but the degree has to be in hand.

is required: Whenever this appears, you'd better have it—or you're wasting your time.

postdoctoral experience: This could mean a typical academic research postdoc or a job in a related (e.g., biotech) industry.

is preferred: Not required, but you have to make a case that your experience and productivity make a postdoc superfluous.

teaching undergraduate and graduate courses in immunology and microbiology: This is open to interpretation because "microbiology" is a vague term covering courses in everything from viruses to worms. It might be a good idea to call the chair of the search committee to find out what courses really need to be covered. While you are on the phone, you can also ask how many courses and labs the faculty teach per semester at St. Elsewhere.

external research funding: Expectations are wonderful, but how real are they? You can get an idea by looking at the publication and funding record of existing faculty. Look at their biographies in the departmental profile or do an author search at the library. Any publication will list support. Nevertheless, if you don't have funding during your six-year internship as an assistant professor, it will be an easy excuse to let you go.

graduate transcript: The search committee just wants to know that you really attended your doctoral institution and took the courses that you claimed to have taken. GPA won't enter the picture unless it's particularly awful.

letters of reference: Job announcements will either direct you to have your references send a letter directly to the hiring institution, or (as in this example) the hiring institution will first make a cut and send out requests of their own.

An Example of a Cover Letter

Remember, you want to demonstrate that your credentials fit the job description and that you have even more to offer. In this case, your strengths lie in your research publications and your training in immunology. Your weakness is a poor background in the common sub-fields of microbiology, especially bacteriology. It doesn't hurt that you are doing your postdoc at the Yale Medical School, but there's no need to rub St. Elsewhere's noses in it. (You might toot your horn louder if you were applying to another Ivy League school.)

31 October 2004

Professor Larry Robots, Chair
Department of Biological Sciences
University of St. Elsewhere
Midland-Odessa, TX 69696

Dear Professor Robots:

I am applying for the faculty position in immunology and microbiology at the University of St. Elsewhere. My dissertation research identified the host plasma proteins on the surface of a blood-borne pathogen, and my postdoctoral research concerns the identification of microbial molecules that negatively affect the mammalian host immune system. My work has resulted in five presentations at professional meetings and seven publications. My postdoctoral research was supported by university and NIH fellowships. Once I get a faculty position, I want to continue my work with the immunological dysfunctions caused by African trypanosomiasis. Since these pathogens are considered one of the primary reasons why tropical Africa remains undeveloped, I suspect that the National Institute of Allergy and Infectious Disease, the Burroughs-Welcome Fund, and the World Health Organization will be interested in funding my research. I also want to study other aspects of the immune system, and I can see possible collaborations with many of the researchers at St. Elsewhere (e.g. Professor Snook's work on tumors; Professor Blind's work on insect hemolymph).

Since my research involves both infectious agents and the immune system, I've kept current in both fields. I have memberships in both the American Society of Microbiology and the American Association of Immunologists. More importantly, this means that my lectures in microbiology and immunology will be up to date. Considering the courses that I have taken and research experience that I have gained, I can teach upper-level general microbiology, immunology, and parasitology courses and labs to undergraduate biology majors and advanced immunology, infectious disease, and immunochemistry courses to graduate students. I suspect that the undergraduate courses will be popular with premedical students and the immunochemistry course of interest to any scientist who needs a powerful and discriminating tool for his or her research. The advanced immunology and infectious agent courses will be designed to interest students conducting research in cell development, tumor biology, or the host-parasite relationship.

Sincerely,

Peter Diffley

AN EXAMPLE OF A CV

The information in a CV usually remains the same regardless of the position you apply to, but its arrangement depends upon whether you're applying to a teaching institution or a research university.

PETER DIFFLEY

Work Address

Department of Epidemiology and Public Health
Yale Medical School
330 Cedar Street
New Haven, CT 55555

Diffley.1@yale.edu
Tele: 333-555-1212

Education

Tulane University	BS	Biology	1988–1992
University of Montana	MA	Zoology	1996–1998
University of Massachusetts	PhD	Zoology	1998–2002

Master thesis: Studies of Laboratory Subcutaneous Infection of *Naegleria fowleri.*

Advisor: F. Bernal

PhD dissertation: Immunologic Analysis of Host Plasma Proteins Bound to Bloodstream Forms of African Pathogenic Trypanosomes.

Advisor: B. M. Berg.

Postdoctoral Experience

James Hudson Brown Postdoctoral Fellow, 2002–2003, Deartment of Pathology, Yale Medical School.

Sponsor: Byron H. Waxman

NIH Postdoctoral Fellow, 2003–present, Department of Epidemiology and Public Health, Yale Medical School.

Sponsor: Anil Jayaward.

Teaching Experience

Teaching Assistant, University of Montana and the University of Massachusetts, 1996–2002. Labs taught: *Mammalian Physiology, Human Physiology, Cellular and Molecular Biology, Evolution, Introductory Biology, Parasitology.*

Laboratory Instructor, Yale University School of Medicine, 1978–1980. Lab taught: *Medical Parasitology.*

Military Training

Officer, U.S. Navy. 1992–1996. Operations Officer, USS Bold MSO 424; Chief Staff Officer, Mine Division 114; ADCOP training officer, Pensacola Junior College.

Honors and Appointments

NROTC scholarship	1988–1992
Scabbard and Blade Honor Society	1992
Phi Sigma Honor Society	1998

Dept. nominee for university teaching award	2000
President, Dept. graduate student organization	2001
Sigma Xi Honor Society	2002

Professional Societies

American Society of Parasitologists	1993
International Society of Protozoologists	1998
A.A.A.S.	1998
American Society for Microbiology	2000
American Association of Immunologists	2003

Presentations

1. Diffley, P., and B. M. Berg. The presence of rat plasma components on *Trypanosoma congolense*. 51st annual meeting of the American Society of Parasitologists, San Antonio: 2000.

2. Diffley, P., and B. M. Berg. Identification of host albumin and IgG on the surface of *Trypanosoma congolense*. Fifth International Congress of Protozoology, New York City: 2001.

3. Diffley, P. Host plasma-parasite interactions in rats infected with *Trypanosoma rhodesiense*. Fourth International Congress of Parasitology, Washington, DC: 2002.

4. Diffley, P. Complement consumption caused by pathogenic African trypanosomes. 53rd annual American Society of Parasitology meeting. Athens, GA: 2002.

5. Diffley, P. Binding of host plasma proteins on parasites. Invited to participate in a symposium on parasite evasion strategies at the annual American Society of Tropical Medicine and Hygiene meeting, New Orleans, LA: 2003.

Articles in Refereed Journals

1. Diffley, P., M. R. Skeels, and F. Bernal. Delayed type hypersensitivity in guinea pigs infected subcutaneously with *Naegleria fowleri*. *Z. Parasitenk.* 49:133–137, 2000.

2. Diffley, P., B. M. Berg, and F. A. Mohn. An improved method of cryopreservation of *Trypanosoma congolense* in liquid nitrogen. *J. Parasitol.* 62: 136–137, 2000.

3. Diffley, P., and B. M. Berg. Fluorescent antibody analysis of host plasma components on bloodstream forms of African pathogenic trypanosomes. I. Host specificity and time of accretion in *Trypanosomacongolense*. *J. Parasitol.* 63: 599–607, 2001.

4. Diffley, P. and B. M. Berg. Immunologic analysis of host plasma proteins on bloodstream forms of African pathogenic trypanosomes. II. Identification and quantitation of surface found albumin, nonspecific IgG, and complement of *Trypanosoma congolense*. *J. Parasitol.* 64: 674–681, 2002.

5. Diffley, P. A comparative immunologic analysis of host plasma proteins bound to the bloodstream forms of *Trypanosoma brucei* subspecies. *Infect. and Immun.* 21: 605–612, 2002.

6. Diffley, P., J. E. Strick, C. L. Pat, and B. H. Waxman. Identification and quantification of variant specific antigen in the plasma of rodents infected with *Trypanosoma brucei brucei*. *J. Parasitol.* 66: 532–537, 2004

7. Diffley, P. and A. N. Jayward. Comparative analysis of procedures for isolating variant antigen from trypanosomal homogenates and from infected plasma. *Infect. and Immun.* In press.

8. Diffley, P. and A. N. Jayward. Blood clearance, organ preference, and lymphocyte binding of variant antigen from *Trypanosoma brucei brucei*. In prep.

Current research interests

Acute African trypanosomiasis causes immunological dysfunctions that may ultimately prove to be lethal to the mammalian host. The surface coat of *Trypanosoma brucei* constitutes 10 percent of the soluble proteins of the parasite and is shed in microgram quantities into the blood of its experimentally infected rodent host. I am currently conducting experiments to determine if the shed trypanosomal surface coat causes nonspecific immunosuppression and/or polyclonal B-cell activation, two dysfunctions associated with the disease.

Teaching competence

My training and research experience enable me to teach immunological methods and immunity to infectious diseases to graduate students. The former course will be important for researchers using antibodies in qualitative and quantitative assays. The latter course is important for students in immunology, parasitology, medical microbiology, and virology. For advanced undergraduates, I can offer the classes and laboratories for three courses: immunology, medical microbiology, and parasitology. For biology majors, I can teach cell biology or human physiology. For non-science majors, I can develop a course on common human diseases.

References:

    Master's advisor: Professor Franklin Bernal

                                       Department of Biology

                                       Southern Methodist University

                                     Dallas, TX 75275

    Doctoral advisor: Professor B. M. Berg

                                       Department of Biological Sciences

                                     University of Massachusetts

                                     Amherst, MA 01002

    Postdoctoral sponsor: Professor Byron H. Waxman

                                       Department of Pathology

                                     Yale School of Medicine

                                     New Haven, CT 55555

APPENDIX D

Non-Academic Job Portfolio

EXAMPLE OF A NON-ACADEMIC JOB ANNOUNCEMENT

*Immunox Incorporated has an opening for a **research scientist** to join a team that is developing **vaccines** against various pathogens of **veterinary** importance. **Requirements** for the position include an **earned doctorate, DVM, or equivalent degree**, significant research in **immunity to infectious diseases**, and skills that include microbial cell culture and identification and biochemical isolation of protective antigens. **Demonstrated communication skills** both orally and in writing are preferred. Applications should include a **resume**, graduate transcript(s), and **contact information** for three references. The **deadline** for applications is May 15, 2007.*

INTERPRETING THE JOB ANNOUNCEMENT

While academe is looking for someone to develop his or her own self-sustaining and productive research projects, the private sector often hires its staff around a business plan to achieve a specific—that is, marketable—goal.

The R&D staff knows what skills they need. Your cover letter and resume need to convince them that you fit the bill. Bring to the table all of your research (even the stuff that didn't end up in the dissertation or in a publication), courses and teaching laboratories, part-time and summer jobs, and life experiences pertaining to the job description.

research scientist: You'd better like the challenge of research, because you'll be doing it all day. Your postdoc experience should tell you what the job will be like.

vaccines against pathogens of veterinary importance: This is the research team's mission. If you would rather do something else, don't apply.

required: You absolutely need the advanced degree. Any postdoc experience is a bonus you should exploit.

earned doctorate, DVM, or equivalent degree: Your biggest competitors will be those who earned their doctorates in an Agricultural or Veterinary School. DVMs will have more experience with veterinary diseases, but they probably will not have as much research training as you do.

cell culture/biochemistry: You'll be the part of the team that develops the vaccines. The R&D staff didn't mention a particular pathogen in the announcement. Maybe they don't want to tip off the competition about a specific target; maybe they are looking at several different diseases. Research "Immunox" and give the chair of the search committee a call. If you can't discover specifically what the team is working on, your resume and letter should describe all your experience with microbes and their cultivation. Your list of biochemical techniques should concentrate on protein isolation and characterization, since most antigens are proteins.

demonstrated communication skills: Even if these skills aren't mentioned in the job announcement, list them in your resume and discuss their relevance to the job in your letter. Your teaching experience and dissertation writing are important assets. Presentations and publications provide additional evidence of your ability to communicate in a professional manner.

preferred: If you don't have this asset, it won't be a deal-breaker. But if you do have the asset, bring it up.

resume: The staff isn't interested in what you taught, presented, or published. They just want a list of your pertinent credentials.

contact information: The staff doesn't want letters of recommendation. They will probably call your dissertation advisor or postdoctoral sponsor for their opinions—so be sure to warn them.

deadline: Academics seemingly take forever to make up their minds about filling a faculty slot. The private sector generally wants someone yesterday. You better have all the credentials (including the degree in hand) at the deadline, and you'd better be ready to move within a month or two.

An Example of a Non-Academic Cover Letter

15 March 2005

Search Committee
Immunox Incorporated
PO Box 666
Bar Harbor, ME 56699

Dear search committee members;

I am applying for the research scientist position that involves vaccine development against pathogens of veterinary importance. My master's thesis research involved the cell immune response to mouse and guinea pig infections with cell cultures of *Naegleria fowleri*, the etiologic agent for primary amoebic meningoencephalitis. Working with Professors Franklin Bernal and Carl Larson and a fellow graduate student, I developed an antigen preparation that provoked a delayed-type hypersensitivity reaction in guinea pigs that had survived a subcutaneous injection of the pathogen (1). For my dissertation, I used various serologic methods (e.g., fluorescent antibodies, immunoelectrophoresis) to identify host plasma proteins on the surface and in homogentates of *Trypanosoma brucei* and *T. congolense*, two pathogens that keep livestock out of tropical Africa (2–4). In the course of this research, I learned how to cryopreserve bloodsteam forms of the parasite and culture the insect form. I also learned how to inject, monitor infections, immunize and bleed mice, rats, and rabbits. In a comparative analysis of alternate complement pathway fixation, I even learned how to draw blood from cattle.

My graduate coursework was focused on understanding the host-parasite relationship. In addition to the several immunology and medical microbiology courses and labs, I took biochemistry (two semesters), biostatistics, histology, cell biology, vertebrate physiology, etc.

Upon graduation, I was awarded a postdoctoral fellowship to work with Dr. Byron Waxman's group at Yale Medical School. My current research involves the identification of molecules from African trypanosomes that cause immunity and immunological dysfunction in their mammalian hosts. I have learned how to purify the surface coat glycoprotein using ion-exchange chromatography and lectin- and antibody-affinity columns (5) and measure the amount that is shed into the blood during infection (6). I am currently conducting a study to determine the optimal amount of the glycoprotein that stimulates immunity and the amount that blocks a protective immune response.

In summary, I have the skills necessary to join your vaccine team at Immunox. I have considerable experience in immunological, biochemical, and microbial methods. My research has always involved pathogens because I never have to explain why my work is important. I have operated as a team member, especially during my military service and master's training, and I have demonstrated communication skill and productivity with eight journal articles and four presentations at professional meetings. I discovered at the university that teaching was fun but tends to look backward to the known. Research, on the other hand, is exciting for me because it is always looking forward to the unknown. Immunox Inc., with its focused mission and new facilities, is just the environment that I am looking for to start my career in research.

Sincerely

Peter Diffley, PhD

LITERATURE CITED

1. Diffley, P., M. R. Skeels, and F. Bernal. 2000. Delayed type hypersensitivity in guinea pigs infected subcutaneously with *Naegleria fowleri. Z. Parasitenk.* 49: 133–137.

2. Diffley, P., and B. M. Berg. 2001. Fluorescent antibody analysis of host plasma components on bloodstream forms of African pathogenic trypanosomes. I. Host specificity and time of accretion in *Trypanosomacongolense. J. Parasitol.* 63: 599–607.

3. Diffley, P., and B. M. Berg. 2002. Immunologic analysis of host plasma proteins on bloodstream forms of African pathogenic trypanosomes. II. Identification and quantitation of surface found albumin, nonspecific IgG, and complement of *Trypanosoma congolense. J. Parasitol.* 64: 674–681.

4. Diffley, P. 2002. A comparative immunologic analysis of host plasma proteins bound to the bloodstream forms of *Trypanosoma brucei subspecies. Infect. and Immun.* 21: 605–612.

5. Diffley, P., and A. N. Jayward. Comparative analysis of procedures for isolating variant antigen from trypanosomal homogenates and from infected plasma. *Infect. and Immun.* In press.

6. Diffley, P., and A. N. Jayward. Blood clearance, organ preference, and lymphocyte binding of variant antigen from *Trypanosoma brucei brucei.* In prep.

PETER DIFFLEY

LABORATORY OF EPIDEMIOLOGY AND PUBLIC HEALTH,

YALE SCHOOL OF MEDICINE,

330 CEDAR STREET, NEW HAVEN, CT 55555

PHONE 333-555-1212 • E-MAIL DIFFLEY@YALE.COM

EXPERIENCE

Postdoctoral Fellow. 2002–present.

- Immunological techniques: isolation and histological examination of lymphoid organs; white blood cell identification, isolation, and short-term culture; mitogen and plaque-forming cell assays.
- Animal procedures: intravenous injections and collection of rodent blood via cardiac puncture.
- Biochemical techniques: ion exchange, antibody-affinity, and lectin-affinity column chromatographic isolation of the trypansomal surface coat, radio-iodination of proteins.

Doctoral Student. 1998–2002.

- Immunological techniques: gel diffusion, immunoelectrophoresis, rocket IEP, complement fixation, fluorescent antibody microscopy.
- Animal procedures: intraperitoneal injections, cardiac blood collection.
- Microbial procedures: monitoring of infectin, ion-exchange collection of trypanosomes, homogenization, cryopreservation, fixation for microscopic examination; cultivation in semi-defined, axenic medium.
- Biochemical techniques: alum precipitation and fluorescent tagging of Immunoglobulin.

Master's Student. 1996–1998.
- Immunological techniques: measurements of cutaneous delayed hypersensitivity reactions.
- Animal procedures: intra-cranial and nasal injections of mice; subcutaneous injections of guinea pigs; necropsy, collection of tissues, paraffin embedding, H&E stain and sectioning, histological examination of tissues for amoebae or evidence of delayed hypersensitivity.
- Microbial procedures: in vitro growth of N. fowleri in axenic and green monkey kidney cell cultures, collection and preparation of an antigen preparations.

Officer, U.S. Navy. 1992–1996.
- ADCOP Training Officer: directing 200 senior petty officers at Pensacola Junior College.
- Chief Staff Officer, MINEDIV 113: second in command of over 100 enlisted men in five detachments stationed in Saudia Arabia.
- Operations Officer, USS Bold, MSO 424: in charge of a twenty-man division and responsible for ship's communication, sonar, radar, and navigation.

EDUCATION

University of Massachusetts	1974–1978	PhD	Zoology
University of Montana	1972–1974	MS	Zoology
Tulane University	1964–1968	BS	Biology

REFERENCES

Postdoctoral Sponsor: Dr. Byron H. Waksman
Department of Pathology
Yale School of Medicine
330 Cedar Street
New Haven, CT 55555

PhD Advisor: Professor B.M. Berg
Department of Zoology
University of Massachusetts
Morrill Science Building
Amherst, MA 01002

MA Advisor: Professor Franklin Bernal
Department of Biology
Southern Methodist University
Dallas, TX 75275

DECODING DEGREES

With the multitude of advanced degrees out there, the bridge between abbreviation and full name can be tough to decipher, so here's a little help when parsing them.

DA . . . . Doctor of Arts

DAS . . . . Doctor of Applied Science

DArch . . . . Doctor of Architecture

DBA . . . . Doctor of Business Administration

JCD . . . . Doctor of Canon Law

DChem . . . . Doctor of Chemistry

DC or DCM . . . . Doctor of Chiropractic

DCL . . . . Doctor of Comparative/Civil Law

DCJ . . . . Doctor of Criminal Justice

DCrim . . . . Doctor of Criminology

DDS . . . . Doctor of Dental Science

DrDES . . . . Doctor of Design

EdD . . . . Doctor of Education

DEng . . . . Doctor of Engineering

DESc or ScDE . . . . Doctor of Engineering Science

DED . . . . Doctor of Environmental Design

DEnv . . . . Doctor of Environment

DFA . . . . Doctor of Fine Arts

DF . . . . Doctor of Forestry

DGS . . . . Doctor of Geological Science

DHS . . . . Doctor of Health and Safety

DHL . . . . Doctor of Hebrew Literature/Letters

DHS . . . . Doctor of Hebrew Studies

DIT . . . . Doctor of Industrial Technology

SJD . . . . Doctor of Juridical Science

JSD . . . . Doctor of Juristic Science

DLS . . . . Doctor of Library Science

DMD . . . . Doctor of Medical Dentistry

MD . . . . Doctor of Medicine

DMin or DM . . . . Doctor of Ministry

DM . . . . Doctor of Music

DME . . . . Doctor of Musical Education

DMM . . . . Doctor of Music Ministry

DML . . . . Doctor of Modern Languages

DMSc . . . . .Doctor of Medical Science

DMA . . . . .Doctor of Musical Arts

DNSc . . . . .Doctor of Nursing Science

OD . . . . .Doctor of Optometry

DO . . . . .Doctor of Ostepathy or Osteopathic Medicine

PharmD . . . . .Doctor of Pharmacy

DPE . . . . .Doctor of Physical Education

DP or PodD . . . . .Doctor of Podiatry

DPS . . . . .Doctor of Professional Studies

DPA . . . . .Doctor of Public Administration

DPH . . . . .Doctor of Public Health

DRec or DR . . . . .Doctor of Recreation

RhD . . . . .Doctor of Rehabilitation

DRE . . . . .Doctor of Religious Education

DSM . . . . .Doctor of Sacred Music

STD . . . . .Doctor of Sacred Theology

DSc or ScD . . . . .Doctor of Science

DScH . . . . .Doctor of Science and Hygiene

DScD . . . . .Doctor of Science in Dentistry

DScVM . . . . .Doctor of Science in Veterinary Medicine

LScD . . . . .Doctor of the Science of Law

DSSc . . . . .Doctor of Social Science

DSW . . . . .Doctor of Social Work

ThD . . . . .Doctor of Theology

DVM . . . . .Doctor of Veterinary Medicine

JD . . . . .Juris Doctor

MAcc . . . . .Master of Accountancy

MAA . . . . .Master of Applied Anthropology

MArch . . . . .Master of Architecture

MA . . . . .Master of Arts

MAief . . . . .Master of Arts in International Economics and
Finance

MAR . . . . .Master of Arts in Religion

MAT . . . . .Master of Arts in Teaching

MBA . . . . .Master of Business Administration

MBOL . . . . .Master of Business and Organizational Leadership

MCP	Master of City Planning
MCRP	Master of City and Regional Planning
MCJ	Master of Criminal Justice
MDiv	Master of Divinity
MEd	Master of Education
MEng	Master of Engineering
MFA	Master of Fine Arts
MFS	Master of Forensic Sciences
MHA	Master of Health Administration
MHS	Master of Health Science
MHL	Master of Hebrew Letters
MID	Master of Industrial Design
MLA	Master of Landscape Architecture
LLM	Master of Laws
MLA	Master of Liberal Arts
MLS	Master of Library Science
MLIS	Master of Library and Information Science
MM or MMus	Master of Music
MOT	Master of Occupational Therapy
MPhil	Master of Philosophy
MPS	Master of Professional Studies
MPM	Master of Project Management
MPA	Master of Public Administration
MPH	Master of Public Health
MPP	Master of Public Policy
STM	Master of Sacred Theology
MS	Master of Science
MSFS	Master of Science in Foreign Service
MSN	Master of Science in Nursing
MSW	Master of Social Work
ThM	Master of Theology
MUP	Master of Urban Planning
MURP	Master of Urban and Regional Planning
DPM	Podiatric Medicine

References

Chapter II — How to Find the Best Program for You

How to Get In

Clark, R.E., and J. Palattella. Eds. *The Real Guide to Grad School*. LinguaFranca Books, 1997.

Doughty, H.R. *Guide to American Graduate Schools*. 8th ed. Viking Penguin Books, 1997.

Maher, B. Ed. *Research-Doctorate Programs in the United States*. National Academy Press, 1995.

Maier, Christopher and the Staff of The Princeton Review. *Complete Book of Graduate Programs in the Arts and Sciences. 2005 Edition*. The Princeton Review, 2004.

Chapter III — Paying For It

Diffley, P., and J. Russo. *Paying for Graduate School Without Going Broke*. 2nd ed. The Princeton Review, 2005.

From Chapter IV — What to Expect When You Get There

Other References on Life in Graduate School

Kidwell, C.S., and C.A. Flagg. *Graduate School and You*. 5th ed. CGS Press, 2004.

Lazarus, B.B., L.M. Ritter, and S.A. Ambrose. *The Woman's Guide to Navigating the PhD in Engineering and Science*. IEEE Press, 2000.

Lovitts, B. *Leaving the Ivory Tower: The Causes and Consequences of Departure from Doctoral Study*. Rowman and Littlefield Publishing, 2001.

Merki, M., and D. Merki. *Jumping through the Hoops: A Survival Guide to Graduate School*. Great Activities Publishing, 1995.

References for Teaching

One source of inspiration is *The Chronicle of Higher Education* (www.chronicle.com), which always has timely pieces. For instance:

- Bain, K. 2004. "What Makes Great Teachers Great?" *CHE* of 9 April. B7–9.

- Brem, R. 2004. "Excuses, Excuses: Students' Sad, Endless Stories." *CHE* of 13 Feb. B15–16.

- Lewis, A.C. 2004. "Game, Set, Teach." *CHE* of 7 May. B5.

- Oppenheimer, M. 2004. "In Praise of Passionate, Opinionated Teaching." *CHE* of 21 May. B7–9.

Davidson, C.I., and S.A. Ambrose. *The New Professor's Handbook: A Guide to Teaching in Engineering and Science*. Anker Publications, 1994.

Lambert, L.M., S.L. Tice, and P.H. Featherstone. *University Teaching: A Guide for Graduate Students*. Syracuse University Press. Syracuse, NY, 1996.

Lewis, K.G. Ed. *The TA Experience: Preparing for Multiple Roles*. New Forum Press. Stillwater, OK, 1993.

McGlynn, A.P. *Successful Beginnings for College Teaching: Engaging Your Students from the First Day*. Atwood Publishing, Madison, WI, 2001.

McKeachie, W.J. Ed. *Teaching Tips: Strategies, Research, and Theory for College and University Teachers*. 11th ed. Houghton Mifflin Co. 2001.

Ramsden, P. *Learning to Teach in Higher Education*. Routledge Press, 1992.

CHAPTER V — PREPARING FOR THE JOB MARKET

Two great books concentrate on academic and non-academic jobs:

Heiberger, M.M., and J.M. Vick. *The Academic Job Search Handbook.* 3rd ed. University of Pennsylvania Press, 2001.

Newhouse, M. *Outside the Ivory Tower: A Guide for Academics Considering Alternative Careers.* Office of Career Services. Harvard University Press, 1993.

SELECT BIBLIOGRAPHY

Bain, K. 2004. "What Makes Great Teachers Great?" *CHE* of 9 April. B7–9.

Brem, R. 2004. "Excuses, Excuses: Students' Sad, Endless Stories." *CHE* of 13 Feb. B15–16.

Clark, R.E., and J. Palattella. Eds. *The Real Guide to Grad School.* LinguaFranca Books, 1997.

Davidson, C.I., and S.A. Ambrose. *The New Professor's Handbook: A Guide to Teaching in Engineering and Science.* Anker Publications, 1994.

Diffley, P., and J. Russo. *Paying for Graduate School Without Going Broke.* 2nd ed. The Princeton Review, 2005.

Doughty, H.R. *Guide to American Graduate Schools.* 8th ed. Viking Penguin Books, 1997.

Heiberger, M.M., and J.M. Vick. *The Academic Job Search Handbook.* 3rd Ed. University of Pennsylvania Press, 2001.

Lambert, L.M., S.L. Tice, and P.H. Featherstone. *University Teaching: A Guide for Graduate Students.* Syracuse University Press. Syracuse, NY, 1996.

Lewis, A.C. 2004. "Game, Set, Teach." *CHE* of 7 May. B5.

Lewis, K.G. Ed. *The TA Experience: Preparing for Multiple Roles.* New Forum Press. Stillwater, OK, 1993.

Maher, B. Ed. *Research-Doctorate Programs in the United States.* National Academy Press, 1995.

Maier, Christopher and the Staff of The Princeton Review. *Complete Book of Graduate Programs in the Arts and Sciences.* 2005 Edition. The Princeton Review, 2004.

McGlynn, A.P. *Successful Beginnings for College Teaching: Engaging Your Students from the First Day.* Atwood Publishing, Madison, WI, 2001.

McKeachie, W.J. Ed. *Teaching Tips: Strategies, Research, and Theory for College and University Teachers.* 11th ed. Houghton Mifflin Co, 2001.

Merki, M., and D. Merki. *Jumping through the Hoops: A Survival Guide to Graduate School.* Great Activities Publishing, 1995.

Newhouse, M. *Outside the Ivory Tower: A Guide for Academics Considering Alternative Careers.* Office of Career Services, Harvard University Press, 1993.

Oppenheimer, M. 2004. "In Praise of Passionate, Opinionated Teaching." *CHE* of 21 May. B7–9.

Ramsden, P. *Learning to Teach in Higher Education*. Routledge Press, 1992.

ABOUT THE AUTHOR

Peter Diffley received his BS in biology at Tulane University, an MA at the University of Montana, and his PhD at the University of Massachusetts. After six years of graduate school, he was awarded an NIH postdoctoral fellowship to do research at the Yale Medical School. He then spent three years as an assistant professor at Texas Tech and six years at the University of Notre Dame. As a faculty member in the Department of Biological Sciences, he served on the graduate admissions committee, on many dissertation committees, and in several faculty search committees. In 1990, Dr. Diffley became an associate dean in the Graduate School at Notre Dame. He oversaw university tuition scholarships, fellowships, and assistantships and helped students in their search and application for outside fellowship support. In 2006, Dr. Diffley became the first dean of the graduate school at University of Hartford. He is past chair and treasurer of the Association of Graduate Schools in Catholic Colleges and Universities and past chair of the Midwest Association of Graduate Schools.

Lower your monthly student loan payments by
up to 51%

Call The Graduate Loan Center to find out how

Federal student loan consolidation is a free, government-backed program created to save you money. Call now and you can:

- **Lower your monthly payments by up to 51%**
- **Make just one payment each month**
- **Choose your own repayment plan**

Call right now and you can lock in the lowest fixed interest rates in history.

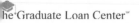
he Graduate Loan Center™

Call 1-866-581-4GLC
(581-4452

The Graduate Loan Center^{SM}

MANAGE STUDENT LOAN DEBT LIKE A PRO

The day finally came. It was the moment you had been waiting for. The past four years melded into one huge blur of quirky professors and impossible exams. All of the seemingly endless headaches and the occasional heartaches that you experienced throughout your college career became part of an expansive collage of scrapbook memories. The day you thought would never come not only arrived, but now it's a distant memory.

Now that graduation has passed, it is time for you to face the "real" world and do things that you thought could never be accomplished. Many exciting journeys lay ahead such as getting your first job and moving away from home. However, combined with these exciting journeys, there are some pretty big obstacles like buying a home and paying off your student loans.

Many people find it exceptionally difficult, if not impossible, to pay their college tuition without taking out loans. Fortunately, the United States Federal Government recognized this problem several years ago and developed a program that helps ease the pain of repaying student loan debt.

In 1965, the Federal Government passed *The Higher Education Act*. This legislation was passed to strengthen the educational resources of our colleges and universities. It provides financial assistance to students who are enrolled in postsecondary and higher education programs; thereby encouraging more students to pursue their college dreams.

Average college tuition increases have outpaced the growth in personal and family income over the past two decades. For this reason, the need for private and federal aid has increased dramatically. As school has become more expensive to attend, students and parents have been required to increase the amount they need to borrow to finance their education. Consequently, the loan amount that students and parents have to pay on a monthly basis has also increased.

In order to ease the financial burden on student and parent borrowers, Congress passed the *Consolidation Loan Program* under the *Higher Education Act in 1986*. Through this program, student loan borrowers are able to benefit by combining all of their existing variable rate federal loans into one new loan, locking in a low fixed interest rate for the life of the loan and extending the term in which they need to repay the loan. By consolidating, in some cases, borrowers can lower their monthly payments by up to 51%.

The Federal Consolidation Loan Program

The Federal Consolidation Loan Program is a unique program offered by the Federal Government that provides student loan borrowers with the following benefits:

- Borrowers can lower monthly loan payments up to 51%.

- Borrowers have the ability to lock in a low fixed interest rate for the life of the loan.

- All existing federal loans are combined into one new loan, requiring you to make only one payment per month.

- All existing deferment options are maintained and there are no prepayment penalties. (Deferment is the postponement of payment on student loans. While in deferment, all subsidized loans will accrue zero interest).

- There are several types of payment plans to choose from. In some cases you can take up to 30 years to repay and you can change the plan annually without any penalties.

- Additional borrower benefits may be offered by the lender to reduce the interest rate even more substantially

- Borrowers can apply with no application fees or credit checks required.

The eligibility guidelines for this program are very simple. In order to be eligible for a consolidation loan:

- The borrower's loans must be in their repayment (including deferment and forbearance) or grace period.

- The borrower must not be in default on their loans.

- The borrower must have at least $10,000 in total outstanding loans. This minimum balance may vary, depending on the lender

Qualifying Loans Under the Federal Consolidation Loan Program:

Several types of student loans are eligible for consolidation, including:

- Federal Family Education Loan Program (FFELP)
  - o Federal Subsidized and Unsubsidized Stafford Loans
  - o Federal PLUS Loans
  - o Federal Consolidation Loans
- Direct Loan Program
  - o Direct Subsidized and Unsubsidized Stafford Loans
  - o Direct PLUS loans
  - o Direct Consolidation Loans
- Perkins Loan Program
  - o Federal Perkins Loans
- Health Profession Student Loans (HPSL)
- Federal Education Assistance Loans (HEAL)
- Federal Nursing Student Loans (NSL)

The Six Month Grace Period = Opportunity for Big Savings

Most borrowers know that they do not have to start paying off student loans until six months after graduation. This six month period is called the 'Grace Period'. Recent graduates are awarded time to start planning for their future before they are required to make payments on their student loan debt.

Contrary to popular belief, the grace period is actually the best time to begin repaying student loans. During the grace period, student loan interest rates are actually over half of a percent lower than when the borrower is required to make payments six months later.

If student loans are consolidated while they are in their grace period, a borrower may be able to enjoy up to 51% additional savings each month on their loan payments. Depending on the total amount due on the borrower's loans, this savings could translate to hundreds of extra dollars in the borrower's pocket each month..

Student Loan Interest Rates

Not all student loan borrowers have - or lock-in - the same interest rate when they take advantage of the Federal Family Education Loan (FFEL) Consolidation Program. This is not due to the borrower's personal credit or the lender selected, but rather, it's due to rules mandated by the government. A borrower's interest rate is determined by several factors. For each of the following Stafford loan scenarios, we are at very low interest rates.

- Originated after 07/98 in grace period or any type of deferment—4.70%

- Originated before 07/98 in grace period or any type of deferment—5.50%

- Originated after 07/98 in repayment or forbearance—5.30%

- Originated before 07/98 in repayment or forbearance—6.10%

FFELP Consolidation is a federal program. The actual interest rate is determined by a set of rules defined by the U.S. Department of Education. The interest rate is determined by taking the weighted average of all of the loans being consolidated and rounding up to the nearest 1/8th of a point. This new interest rate is fixed, rather than variable, and locked-in for the life of the loan. For this reason, the maximum increase of 1/8th of a point, or 0.1249%, is minimal. And, this is the only cost associated with consolidation.

As of July 1, 2004, interest rates on Federal Stafford Loans, the most common type of education loan, have dropped to nearly their lowest point in years. The interest rate is 4.70% in school, grace or deferment status and 5.30% for loans in repayment. Parent PLUS loans have a rate of 6.10%. Rates are adjusted on July 1 of each year based on the final auction of the 91-Day T-Bill for loans disbursed after 7/1/98. The PLUS loan interest rate is equal to the weekly average of the one-year constant maturity Treasury yield for the last calendar week ending on or before June 26 of each year.

Many mailings and advertisements from consolidation lenders promote the lowest possible interest rates and favorable borrower benefits. It is standard practice for companies to offer a 0.25% interest rate reduction for making automatic payments from a checking account. Many lenders also offer a 1% interest rate reduction once a certain number of on-time payments have been received. The actual interest rate is mandated by the federal government and is the same for all companies.

Repayment Options

The Federal Consolidation Loan Program allows borrowers to get the best payoff terms without imposing penalties for early re-payment. All Stafford loans are initially based on a ten-year payoff plan and the borrower is able to opt for a non-payment status such as deferment or forbearance when experiencing a cash flow problem. Many borrowers want lower monthly payments and may choose to have the payoff term on their loans extended. Switching to a longer-term payoff plan provides an immediate increase in short-term cash flow. Since there is no pre-payment penalty in the program, a borrower can make aggressive payments toward the principal at any time.

Most lenders do not require a borrower to accept the extended terms associated with repayment plans. At the borrower's request, the servicer of his/her consolidation can adjust the payment plan to a ten-year payoff schedule. Borrowers are initially set up on the following terms based upon the balance of their Consolidation Loan:

Total Loan Balances	Maximum Repayment Period
$10,000 to $19,999	15 years
$20,000 to $39,999	20 years
$40,000 to $59,999	25 years
$60,000 or more	30 years

A borrower may choose among four types of repayment plans:

- **Level Repayment**
  The level repayment plan, which is by far the most common method selected, provides for a fixed monthly payment throughout the life of your loan..Many borrowers choose this plan because they like the security and simplicity of a fixed monthly payment. But, more important, the level repayment plan usually is the least expensive in terms of total interest charges. The latter plans cost more because they slow down the repayment of the principal.

- **Graduated Repayment**

  The Graduated Repayment Plan offers more affordable payments throughout the early years of repayment and increases gradually over the remaining period of the loan.. The payments increase no more than 4% every couple of years. The loan is repaid in the same timeframe as the Level Repayment program, but the total interest costs are slightly higher. The purpose of this payment plan is to provide the borrower with more disposable income immediately upon beginning repayment.

- **Extended Repayment**

  This plan allows the borrower to repay their Federal Consolidation Loans over a 25-year period under a level or graduated repayment schedule. In order to qualify for this plan, the oldest Federal Stafford (subsidized and unsubsidized), Federal PLUS and/or Federal Consolidation Loan must have been disbursed on or after October 7, 1998. In addition, the combined outstanding balance on all eligible loans must be between $30,000 and $40,000.

- **Income-sensitive repayment**

  The income-sensitive plan is targeted to those borrowers who have con-siderable financial difficulty. Under this plan, monthly payments rise and fall on an annual basis and are tied to the borrower's income. This is the most flexible plan, but it also could prove to be the most expensive in the long run. It's also important to note that the borrower must reap-ply for the plan annually.

Thirty years is the maximum length for a loan unless a borrower takes out another federal loan. For those who qualify, a new federal loan allows a borrower to consolidate again with new payment terms. While extending the repayment term may increase the overall amount of interest paid over the life of the loan, those who have higher interest debt often find the longer payoff schedule to be acceptable.

In addition to the choice of plans, the borrower can switch from one repay-ment plan to another once a year. There's no additional cost or penalty, but not everyone qualifies for this service.

Making the Right Decision

Now that all of the benefits of the Federal Consolidation Loan Program have been explained in their entirety, it is up to you, the borrower, to make the final decision. Find the company that offers the best explanation of terms, or find the one with the best incentives. Remember, the actual interest rate is the same everywhere. The decision simply becomes a matter of personal choice. So what are you waiting for? Consolidate your student loans today and save money tomorrow!

The Graduate Loan Center, based in Chicago, Illinois, helps borrowers manage paying for the high cost of education by offering the Federal Consolidation Loan Program and Private Loan Programs. The Graduate Loan Center works with some of the nation's leading financial institutions, which combined have consolidated well over $1 Billion in student loans. Call today to speak with one of our specially trained Financial Aid Advisors.

More expert advice from
The Princeton Review

Increase your chances of getting into the graduate school of your choice with The Princeton Review. We can help you get higher test scores, make the most informed choices, and make the most of your experience once you get there. We can also help you make the career move that will let you use your skills and education to their best advantage.

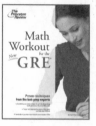

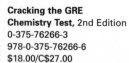